Mastering Adobe Illustrator

Mastering Adobe Illustrator®

David A. Holzgang

SYBEX®

San Francisco ■ Paris ■ Düsseldorf ■ London

Cover design by Thomas Ingalls & Associates
Cover photography by Casey Cartwright
Book design by Amparo del Rio
[Screen reproductions produced by XenoCopy]

Library of Congress Card Number: 88-61247
ISBN 0-89588-463-1
Manufactured in the United States of America
10 9 8 7 6 5 4 3 2 1

Acknowledgments

Production of a book involves many people besides the author. For this book, in particular, I am indebted to the support, aid, and encouragement of a small army of patient and dedicated professionals, who have contributed mightily to the finished product you hold right now.

As so many books have, this book started with the help of Bill Gladstone of Waterside Productions, who took my rough proposal and sold the idea. Barbara Gordon at Sybex encouraged me in my format and helped refine the contents and approach in the book. David Kolodney reviewed the first draft and provided his usual pointed and valuable advice. Jim Compton and Chuck Ackerman also helped with advice on direction and content.

My editor, Marilyn Smith, has exhibited the patience of a saint (or a mother) in handling the innumerable delays, questions, and crises that attend working with prerelease software and confused authors. She further helped organize and define the necessarily numerous figures and inserts. Finally, like all good editors, she also clarified both the prose and the format; this book is a better and more useful guide because of her efforts.

The other Sybex personel who contributed to this book are Jeff Giese, technical reviewer; Bob Myren and Jocelyn Reynolds, word processors; Cheryl Vega, typesetter; Maria Mart, proofreader; Amparo del Rio, book design and production; and Ted Laux, indexer.

I also had generous help from Yvonne Perry at Adobe Systems, who first introduced Illustrator to me many months ago, and helped me in every way. I would also like to thank John Kunze at Adobe for his help and courtesy. In addition, I must thank Keith Ohlf, who provided invaluable advice from his unique talents as both artist and technician; without his help, I would probably never have discovered many of the advanced tricks and effects that make Illustrator so rewarding.

On the personal side, I would like to thank Shirley for her chicken soup, and Chani for sitting on my lap.

Table of Contents

Table of Contents

Table of Contents

Introduction

The Adobe Illustrator program represents a new and exciting way of creating complex drawings that include both graphics and text. It provides fast, powerful methods for handling text and graphics, but these features have not developed in a vacuum. They are a natural outgrowth of the continuing development of the microcomputer as a tool for processing words and graphics. These facilities have now made it possible to create documents such as brochures, newsletters, books, and magazines with the kind of sophisticated typography, graphics, and layout that used to be available only by using much more costly and complex equipment and techniques.

FROM WORD PROCESSING TO GRAPHICS PROCESSING

Up to now, computer handling and processing of graphics has been limited. There has been a lack of graphics capabilities comparable to the facilities available for text and numbers; a lack of an ability to put the equivalent of word-processing power into the hands of artists and enable them to cut, paste, revise, and reshape graphic images quickly and easily.

Graphics Processing Requirements

Ideally, the graphic designer and artist should be able to work with images from external sources, such as photographs or other artwork, or create new images directly on the computer. These images should be easy to revise without redrawing them from scratch. It should be easy to make multiple copies, or use portions of one image combined with another. In short, the essential advantages that word processing offers for text should be available for graphics.

In addition, although a picture may be worth a thousand words, usually even the best graphic requires at least a few words to make its point. This means that software to produce and manipulate graphics should also have the capacity to integrate text and image to form a single graphic unit. Again, ideally, the text portion should have at least the same output quality as would be produced by sophisticated word-processing or page-composition software. Finally, the artist should be able to output the complete graphic unit by itself or insert it into a page-composition program for further manipulation and output.

We can denote all of these reasonable desires as a requirement for "graphics processing." But such processing presents many frustrating problems for the software designer and program developer. These problems are rooted in the disparate variety of output devices that must be supported to provide graphics processing and the integration of such graphics with text output.

Output Device Disparities

The vast majority of the devices that are available to output graphics fall into the broad, general class of raster-output devices. These devices form all characters and images out of a series of dots that are activated in some way. These "dots"—which may, in fact, be square or oval—each represent one picture element, or *pixel.* The number of pixels per unit area is a measure of the ability of a device to render images in greater or less detail, and is called the *resolution* of the device.

Each of these devices has distinctive characteristics that make graphics processing quite difficult. To begin with, different groups of devices have widely varying resolutions, ranging from 50 to 100 dots per inch on screen output devices to more than 2000 dots per inch for high-quality typesetting machines. In addition, most devices have individual command structures to drive the device and to create graphic output. Finally, each device has individual addressing and movement parameters for producing output.

One common method of producing images on raster-output devices is to "paint" the image onto the device by setting each pixel individually and explicitly on or off. An image produced by such a process is called *bit-mapped.* This technique avoids many of the problems associated with different command and addressing structures for individual devices, but still leaves the problems of variation in resolution; it also introduces some additional problems of its own.

LIMITATIONS OF BIT-MAPPED GRAPHICS

The differences in device resolution cause a problem because a bit-mapped image that is tailored to a low-resolution device will have too little information for a device of higher resolution, and a high-resolution bit-mapped image will have too much information for a low-resolution device. In addition, a bit-mapped image cannot be separated into component parts, which can then be handled separately. For example, you cannot have a bit-mapped page and then add a line of text and reformat the page, as you could in a word-processing environment, any more than you can take letters painted on a picture and edit them. You can erase and replace them; you can add new ones; but you can't change a misspelled name without repainting.

In summary, bit-mapped graphics are limited by the resolution of the device they were created on, and they must be handled as complete and unchanging units. Thus, bit-mapped graphics cannot provide true graphics-processing capabilities.

POSTSCRIPT—A COMMON LANGUAGE

Adobe Systems created a page-description language, PostScript, which elegantly solves the problem of output device differences, and designed Illustrator to take advantage of it. The PostScript language provides a way to describe both text and graphic output independently of any specific device limitations and yet allows the output to take full advantage of the capabilities of each different device. In addition, PostScript provides graphics-processing capabilities of the kind described above: it allows a graphic element to be cut, pasted, altered, or moved in a wide variety of ways. Illustrator provides a flexible and "friendly" way to generate PostScript programs without knowing how to use PostScript itself, in fact without even being aware of its presence.

Illustrator provides all the desirable qualities outlined above in a form and format that is much more accessible than PostScript itself. There is no need for you, as the user, to worry about how PostScript translates your work. On the other hand, you can access and modify the PostScript code if you want even more flexibility. However, you are likely to find the extensive capabilities provided by Illustrator more than adequate for a full range of sophisticated graphics work. All in all, Illustrator is a remarkable and powerful product that you will find fascinating to use.

BOOK GOALS

At the broadest level, the goal of this book is to help you understand and use Illustrator. Specifically, it has two objectives:

- To teach you to use the Illustrator tools. You should be able to choose and use tools for most ordinary work without reference to any additional materials. You should also understand the basic processes of creation and modification of artwork, whether beginning with a template or starting from a blank Illustrator desktop.
- To teach you techniques that produce results. This means that you should develop a working knowledge of the processes that generate the effects that are essential to making graphic images: shadowing, contouring, and so on.

Each objective supports and involves the other. And the book does not distinguish each objective but, like any good text, tries to combine both in each exercise or lesson. In this way, you will learn the Illustrator operations individually and the process of combining those operations into Illustrator procedures in a unified way.

BOOK ASSUMPTIONS

Because this book could not possibly cover all the procedures involved in working with your computer and printer, I have made some assumptions about its readers. To begin with, I assume that you are willing to work through the examples. Illustrator really is like any other toolkit in that ease and proficiency come from practice. So you should do the exercises and examples, perhaps even more than once. I would encourage you to try alternative approaches, and print out your variations to see how you are progressing. One of the most interesting things about Illustrator, in my experience, has been how much pure fun it is to play with. You can generate an amazing variety of graphics just by trying options and tools. Please enjoy this experience; it will make the whole process more satisfying for you.

One thing that is not covered here is general computer concepts. Although I try to define all the terms that are intrinsic or even related to using Illustrator, there are certainly a number of concepts that apply to computers generally and Macintosh operations that I do not discuss specifically. I'm not going to tell you how to turn on the computer or the printer, nor how to start up your programs (other than Illustrator, that is).

In addition, there is very little information about printer operations or other output devices. The entire issue of output processing is particularly complex for Illustrator. Because Illustrator can drive a wide range of output devices, it is impossible to give much consistently applicable advice regarding output problems that may crop up. If you have trouble, look first at the operations manual (or manuals) that came with the computer, then try the device manual for your specific output device, and finally try this book and the Illustrator *User's Manual.*

VERSIONS OF ILLUSTRATOR

Two versions of Illustrator have been released: version 1.1 was released in 1987, and the upgraded version, called Illustrator 88, was released in May 1988. Illustrator 88 is used for the exercises and examples in this book.

Most of the features and tools available in Illustrator 88 are also available in Illustrator 1.1, so readers who have the earlier version can do almost all the exercises. In some cases, you may have to use slightly different techniques or access a different menu to accomplish the same results. Where possible, I noted the version 1.1 methods for your use. However, there are some features in Illustrator 88—most notably the new blend, autotrace, and freehand tools—that are not available in Illustrator 1.1.

Adobe Systems has offered all registered users of Illustrator 1.1 an upgrade to Illustrator 88 for an additional charge of $100. Given the new tools and powerful new techniques available with the new release, I think this is a great opportunity. If you have any doubts, you can review the new tools in this book and see how valuable they might be in your own environment.

BOOK STRUCTURE

The book's structure is designed to present the various Illustrator operations in a natural way. There are ample exercises and examples to help you apply the concepts presented in a practical setting.

Both the exercises and examples are to some extent cumulative. The techniques and tools that are covered earlier in the book are not usually presented with much explanation when you use them again. Also, there are several images that are worked with repeatedly and enhanced or modified to demonstrate certain techniques. This approach allows you to concentrate on the new and unfamiliar rather than spend too much time redoing work that you already know. If you come across a technique that you're not sure about, try looking back in the chapter, or use the index, to find a previous reference that contains the full explanation.

DEVICE USE

The work in the book is based solely on Illustrator. No other software was used to prepare the output pages. All the output images were produced on a standard Apple LaserWriter, which is the most common PostScript output device. The exercises were also tested using a QMS PostScript-equipped laser printer to ensure that they worked on more than one device.

But there are a wide variety of output devices that support PostScript, and more are announced every week it seems. I cannot guarantee that all the various output devices available will produce the same results. In particular, a typesetting system may produce some changes in the output. All the exercises should run, however, on any PostScript device, and should produce output that is similar to the output shown in the figures.

Fast Track Chapter 1

7 **To start Illustrator,**
double-click on the program icon or click on the icon once and choose Open from the File menu (or press ⌘O).

10 **To use a tool**
from the Illustrator toolbox (the bar on the left side of the screen), click on it and move the cursor onto the desktop (the Illustrator screen).

11 **To begin creating original artwork**
(without a template), select New from the File menu, and then click on None on the template selection screen.

12 **To display the rulers**
along the bottom and right edges of the desktop, select Show Rulers from the View menu (or press ⌘R).

15 **For quick access to the hand tool**
(for moving around the desktop), press and hold down the space bar.

16 **To constrain a line**
to be exactly horizontal, vertical, or at a multiple of 45 degrees, hold down the Shift key while you create the line.

17 **To quickly undo an error,**
immediately after the mistake, pull down the Edit menu and click on the first selection, which will be to undo the last action (e.g., Undo Pen), or press ⌘Z.

17 **To delete everything**
you've done since you started a figure, press the Backspace or Delete key twice.

18 **To see various views**
of the Illustrator artwork (e.g., reduced, artwork only, or a preview), use the options on the View menu.

Fast Track

20 **To select a portion**
of a figure for modification, click on that part with the selection tool and then make your changes.

21 **To set the stroke and fill**
for figures (how figures are outlined and filled in), use the Paint option on the Style menu (or press ⌘I) to access the Paint dialog screen.

25 **To draw any kind of ellipse**
(including circles), use the circle tool.

26 **To constrain the circle tool**
to draw only a circle, hold down the Shift key as you draw the shape.

27 **To reorder the overlay**
of figures, use the Bring To Front (or press ⌘=) and Send To Back (or press ⌘–) options on the Edit menu.

29 **To save artwork,**
use the Save option on the File menu (or press ⌘S).

31 **To choose page setup options**
for printing, select Page Setup from the File menu.

31 **To print artwork,**
select Print from the File menu (or press ⌘P).

Chapter 1

YOUR FIRST STEPS

In this chapter, we'll cover the basic information that you need to begin working with Illustrator, and then you'll create and print out a simple logo design.

WHAT IS ILLUSTRATOR?

Illustrator is an artist's tool that can be used to create complex drawings with both graphics and text. However, as you will see in this book, the program is as appropriate for making simple forms and logos as it is for creating detailed artwork. Illustrator provides tools to manipulate images for *graphics processing* in much the same way that electronic word processing allows you to manipulate text.

Illustrator can generate output of the highest quality on a wide variety of output devices, from dot-matrix printers, through laser printers, to the highest resolution typesetting machines. In each case, Illustrator will adapt its output to the output device and generate the same image shown on the computer screen. It does this by producing output in the PostScript language. Illustrator's use of PostScript allows users to produce images that would be impossible to generate with earlier graphics-processing technologies.

Illustrator provides "tools" for electronically "drawing" an image onto the computer screen. This image may consist of straight and curved lines, with closed shapes that are clear, white, black, or any shade of gray. If you have a color monitor, you can display images in any color. Illustrator, with its associated utility Adobe Separator, can also generate color output.

Images may be magnified, reduced, and moved around on the drawing surface. Illustrator also provides methods for transforming graphic images into new shapes and forms in a number of unusual ways. Thus, Illustrator not only aids the user by facilitating the more routine and repetitive aspects of artwork, but also promotes creativity by allowing the artist to develop new and exciting images.

TERMINOLOGY

In this book, I will be using words like *draw* and *trace* to describe the creation and manipulation of graphics on your computer. These terms seem to translate quite naturally from their usual context of pencil and paper to the computer environment of mouse, cursor, and screen image. As you click and drag the mouse (operations I assume you are familiar with), you draw on the screen.

The specific Illustrator terms used throughout this book are template, artwork, tools, and menus. In order to work with the program, it is essential that you understand how each of these items relates to Illustrator and to one another.

The terms *template* and *artwork* denote the two different types of images used by Illustrator. A template is a bit-mapped image that is simply a guide for your Illustrator drawing; it cannot be manipulated or changed by Illustrator itself. Templates are typically created by a graphics program such as MacPaint; however, they can originate in a variety of ways (as discussed in Chapter 2).

Artwork is the result of using Illustrator tools to create an Illustrator graphic. It can be generated by tracing a template, modifying existing artwork, or drawing from scratch. In this context, *tracing* a template means using the various Illustrator tools to create an artwork outline that overlays and matches the template image to whatever degree of precision you want. Because Illustrator created the artwork, these graphics can be changed, moved, and otherwise manipulated within the program. The artwork is the Illustrator graphic image, or *drawing*; it is what you will work on, modify and, ultimately, use for output.

Illustrator provides two ways to use its facilities: tools and menus. The *tools* represent a set of processes that are used to create, display, and manipulate Illustrator artwork. The *menus* are a series of choices that govern the source, destination, or modes of operation within the Illustrator program.

SAFETY FIRST

Before you begin using the program, you should make a working copy of your Illustrator program disk. I'm sure that you've heard this over and over regarding every piece of software that you have ever used; yet some people still fail to copy their programs. The first, and most obvious, reason to make a copy is to provide backup. However, you might overlook this step if that were the only reason because Illustrator comes with a backup program disk. The second reason is to maintain the original version of the system in the identical state that you received it—not just the Illustrator program, but the entire system. If you never write on your original disk, you can always go back to exactly what you had when you first purchased the system. If a problem arises while you are working with your copy, you can run the original version to determine whether it existed in the system as shipped from the manufacturer or whether it was somehow introduced later.

You may find that on first starting your working copy of the program, you get a copy-protection screen, which looks like Figure 1.1. If this happens, insert the original Illustrator program disk in place of the ejected working copy. After verification, the program will ask you to reinsert the working disk, and you can proceed. However, you can avoid this annoyance by returning your signed registration card to Adobe Systems. You will receive (along with some other goodies) a new copy of the program disk that is not copy-protected.

Another safety point, which you have also heard incessantly, is to make backup copies as you work. For real safety, you should do two things. First, you should regularly save your work onto a permanent storage device, such as a disk, to ensure that you don't lose a substantial amount of time and effort. Some people advocate saving at a standard interval, such as every quarter or half hour. I prefer to save the work when I have finished a major section. That means I may save the work very often or not at all, depending on what I'm doing and how fast I'm working. The timing is up to you; just remember to save your work now and then as you proceed.

A third safety measure is to make complete backup copies on another disk of all your work on some regular schedule. This schedule depends on how much you work with the program. For example, an artist using Illustrator for several hours daily should probably make (or update) backup disks daily, but someone who only uses it a few hours a

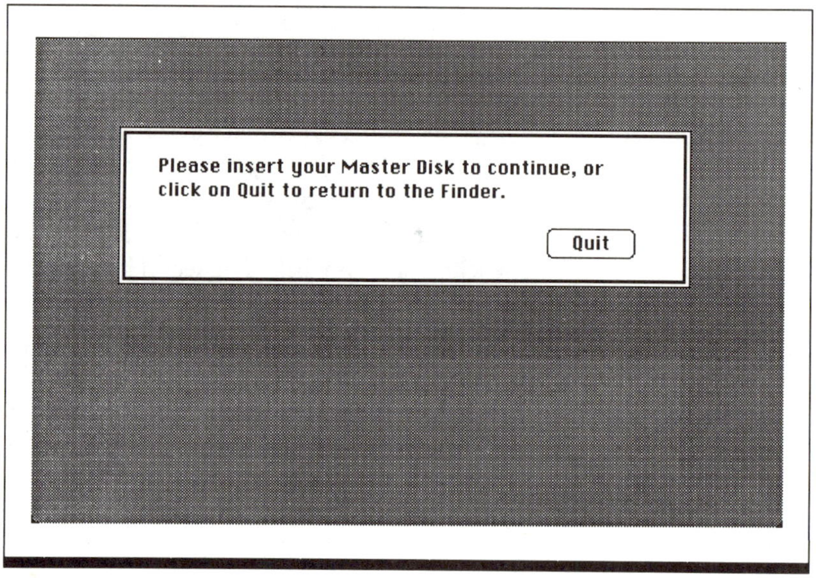

Figure 1.1: *The copy-protection screen*

week might make copies less frequently. The essential point is to remember to make the backup copies regularly enough to protect your work in case you lose or damage the originals.

THE KEYBOARD AND THE MOUSE

Like all Macintosh programs, many Illustrator functions can be accessed through both the mouse and the keyboard. Although I myself am partial to the keyboard, this book concentrates on the mouse operations because they are the easiest and most universal method of access for the Macintosh. Furthermore, all Illustrator operations can be carried out using the mouse, but only some of them can be done with the keyboard. In cases where the keyboard functions are significantly easier and faster, we will use them.

If you have trouble with the mouse, try using the keyboard access route. The keys to use for initial operations are listed in Table 1.1, and a summary of the various keyboard accesses appears on the inside cover.

TOOLS	KEYS
Hand tool	Space bar (press and hold)
Selection tool	Command (⌘) key (press and hold)
MENUS	
File menu New Open Save Quit	 ⌘N ⌘O ⌘S ⌘Q
Edit menu Undo/Redo	 ⌘Z
View menu Actual Size Show/Hide Rulers	 ⌘H ⌘R
Style menu Paint	 ⌘I

Table 1.1: *Keyboard Access for Initial Operations*

STARTING THE PROGRAM

Adobe Illustrator 88™

You can start the Illustrator program either by double-clicking on the program icon or by clicking on the icon once and choosing Open from the File menu on the desktop. You will first see a logo screen with some copyright and authorship information, and then you will see a selection screen displaying seven (or six with version 1.1) standard Macintosh pull-down menu choices across the top of the screen).

At this point, there are only four menu options available. Show Clipboard is the only active choice on the Window menu (or the Edit menu in version 1.1). The File menu has three active options: New, Open, and Quit. Choose the New option, and you will see a template selection screen, as shown in Figure 1.2. If you were going to start a new piece of artwork using a template, you would now choose that template. In this case, however, click on None. You see a blank Illustrator desktop, as shown in Figure 1.3.

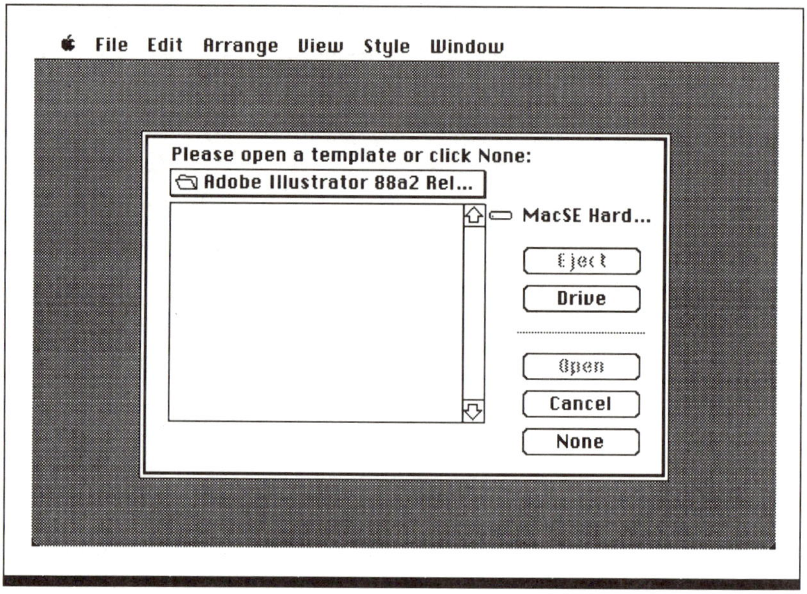

Figure 1.2: *Template selection screen*

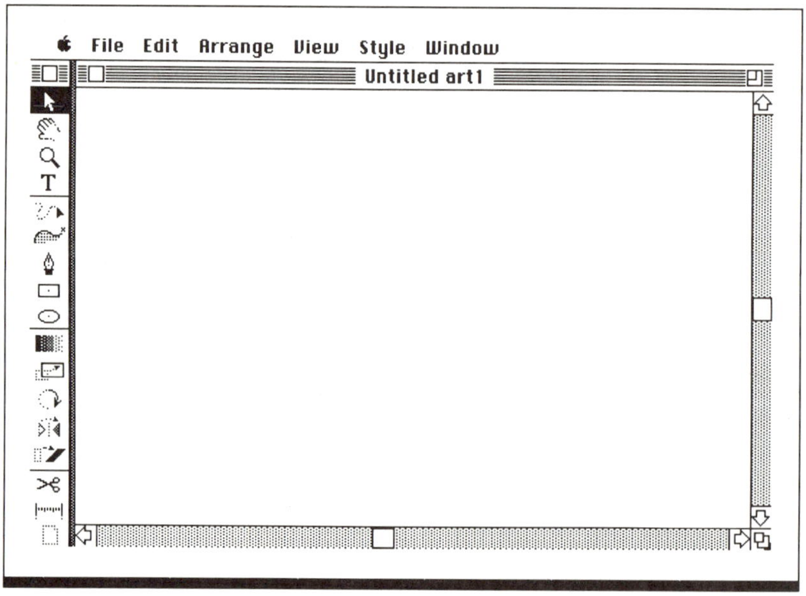

Figure 1.3: *Blank Illustrator desktop*

Layout of the Illustrator Desktop

The layout of this screen is quite similar to the screens of other Macintosh applications. The top line is the *menu bar*, which shows seven options: the standard Apple menu (denoted by the Apple icon on the far left of the menu bar), followed by the File, Edit, Arrange, View, Style, and Window menu choices. (We will review each of these, and their associated commands, in detail throughout the book.)

Just below the menu bar is the *title bar*, which contains the title of the artwork, template, or both (if you are using both). For a new document, as we have here, the title bar shows *Untitled art1*, which will be changed when you save the document. In addition, this bar has the standard Macintosh *close box* on the left and the *zoom box* on the right.

There are also standard Macintosh *scroll bars* on the right and at the bottom of the screen, and a *size box* at the bottom-right intersection of the two scroll bars. If you are not familiar with these standard Macintosh bars and their use, see your Macintosh documentation. In all cases, these functions work exactly the same way in Illustrator as they do in other Macintosh system applications.

Illustrator Tools

The left bar, on the other hand, is distinctively Illustrator. This shows the selection of Illustrator tools available for your work. This bar is called the Illustrator *toolbox*, or the *toolbox window*. At the top of the bar is a close box that governs the bar itself; if you click on this, the toolbox display disappears from the screen. This allows you to see more of the document that you're working on, but limits your selection of tools to those that can be accessed from the keyboard.

Here are the tool icons displayed and the names of the tools that they represent:

 Selection tool

 Hand tool

 Zoom tool

 Type tool

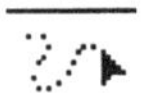 Freehand tool

 Autotrace tool

 Pen tool

- Square tool
- Circle tool
- Blend tool
- Scale tool
- Rotate tool
- Reflect tool
- Shear tool
- Scissors tool
- Distance tool
- Page tool

You select a tool by positioning the arrowhead (which is automatically displayed when you enter the toolbox area) on the tool that you want and clicking the mouse. The selected tool is highlighted by reverse video.

You should not make too much of the similarity between tools used in other applications (such as MacPaint and MacDraw) and those used in Illustrator; even where the icon and the function are the same, the actual use will probably be somewhat different.

GENERATING ORIGINAL ARTWORK

As an introduction to using Illustrator, we will design, construct, and print an Illustrator document. This artwork will be a simple logo for an imaginary company, Mountain Sports, Ltd.

We could start by using some graphic package, such as MacPaint or MacDraw, to design the logo as a template and then simply import the template into Illustrator as a beginning step. However, I would like to begin by showing you some things that can be done without using any template at all. In the next chapter, we'll cover the use of templates in detail.

SETTING UP THE ARTWORK

In this exercise, we will start with a blank Illustrator desktop and proceed to generate an original piece of artwork. This artwork is considered "original" because there is no template for the document; instead, you will lay out the design in detail and use Illustrator's rulers to establish the location of the design elements.

The logo design consists of a mountain range, represented by three overlapping triangles, under a summer sun, represented by a single circle. The layout and sizing of the various elements of the logo are given in Figure 1.4.

The elements of the logo are scaled in arbitrary units at this point; as you proceed, you will determine what those units will represent on the page. The two smaller triangles are both the same size: 6 units wide by 5 units high. The larger triangle in the center is 8 units by 8 units. The circle is centered at the point that is 14 units from the left edge of the logo and 9 units from the bottom edge, and it is 1.5 units in radius. This puts the center 1 unit above the top of the largest triangle and 1 unit past the end of the rightmost triangle. The important point to note here is that the element sizes are all in relative units.

Creating the Logo Border

As a preliminary, I suggest that you create a new folder on your working disk to hold the artwork and templates associated with the exercises in this book. If you decide to do this, you should create the folder now so that it will be available when you save your work.

If you have followed along so far, you should now have the blank Illustrator desktop (Figure 1.3) on your screen. If not, open Illustrator

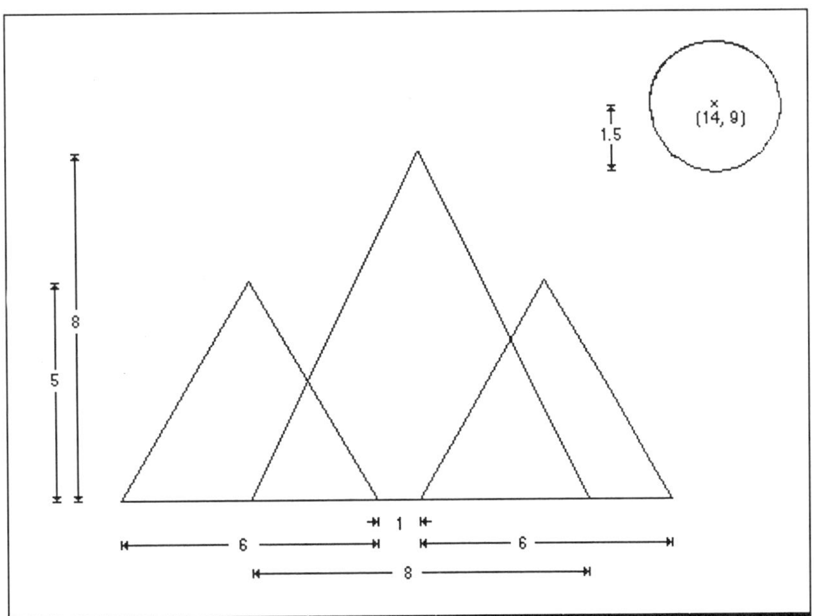

Figure 1.4: *Logo layout and size*

and, from the selection screen, pull down the File menu and select New. When you see the template selection screen, click None. Now follow these steps to create the logo border:

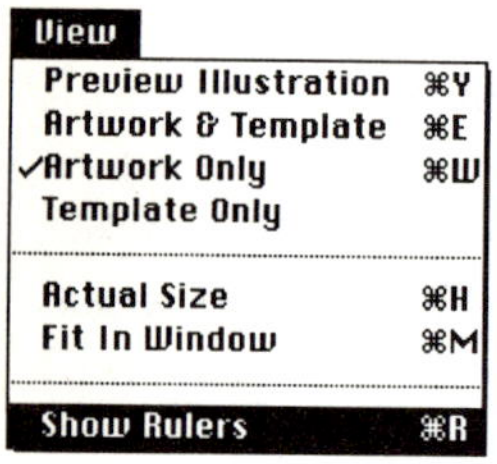

1. **From the Illustrator desktop, pull down the View menu and select Show Rulers. You will see two rulers along the bottom and right edges of the desktop, just inside the scroll bars, as shown in Figure 1.5.**

The dotted marker on each ruler corresponds to the position of the cursor (the selection arrow, in this case), which is in the upper-left corner of the screen. The marker on the bottom ruler appears between 10 and 11, and the one on the right ruler is on 40. The easiest way to discuss these rulers is to call the bottom one the x-coordinate and the right one the y-coordinate. This gives the cursor a position that we will call point (10.5, 40), taking the x-coordinate first.

These coordinates are not arbitrary numbers. The rulers measure actual size, and at this point, the units are picas (1 pica = 1/6 inch) and points (1 point = 1/72 inch). The rulers measure from the bottom-left corner of the output page, which is (0, 0) in the coordinate system.

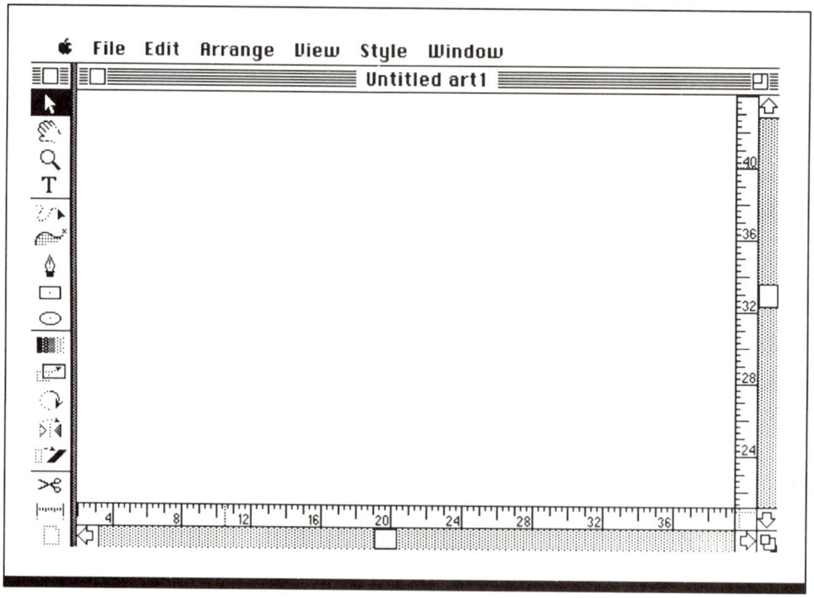

Figure 1.5: *Desktop with rulers*

Currently, the cursor is located 10.5 picas from the left edge of the paper and 40 picas from the bottom edge.

2. Select the hand tool by clicking on it in the toolbox.

You will see the cursor change to the hand icon. The hand tool is the one that you will normally use to move around the desktop. When you are holding down the mouse button, the hand tool works like your own hand to pull whatever is on the desktop in the direction that the hand moves. You need to hold down the mouse button to make the hand move; if you don't, you will just reposition the hand on the screen without moving anything on the desktop itself.

3. Place the hand tool in the upper-left corner of the screen, at about (10, 40), and click and drag it toward the bottom right of the screen (you will see the hand icon become the clock icon occasionally as Illustrator is busy moving and redrawing the desktop image). Continue dragging until point (0, 61) is in the upper-left corner of the screen. You will also see a point indicated by two crossed, dotted lines. This represents the top-left corner of the page. Your screen should now look like Figure 1.6.

Generally, this point is not the top-left corner of the physical output page, but rather the top-left corner of the printable area. Most printing devices require some margin around the page for paper handling and other functions and cannot print all the way to the edge of the page. The coordinates shown by Illustrator represent the actual printing area of the page, so you don't have to worry about device-dependent margins and nonprint areas on the page.

4. We will construct the drawing using the layout and coordinates detailed in Figure 1.7. Select the pen tool by placing the cursor on the pen icon and clicking once. When you move the cursor out onto the page, you will see that it is now shaped like a small x. Position it on point (2, 58) and click the mouse button. This generates a small, square, black box at the designated point, and changes the cursor to a +, to indicate that you have started a figure. At this point, your screen should look like Figure 1.8.

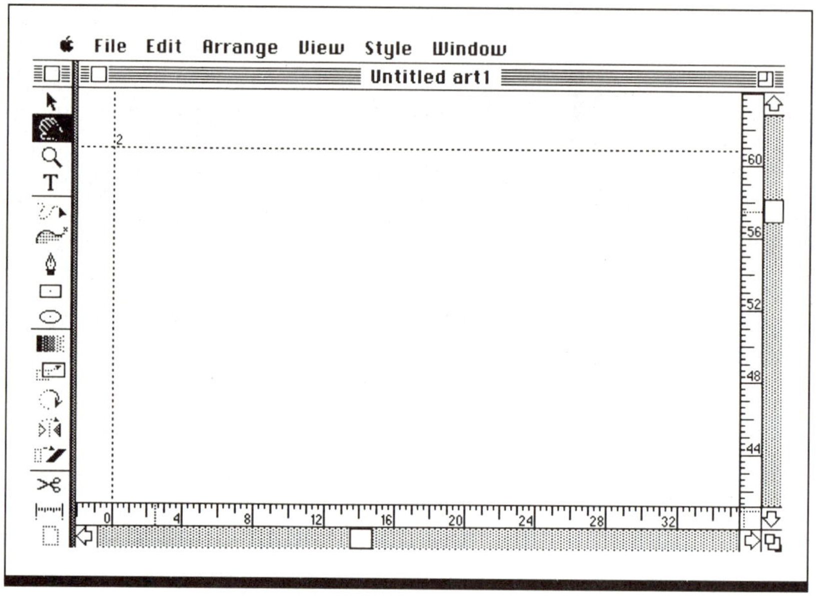

Figure 1.6: *Desktop at point (0, 61)*

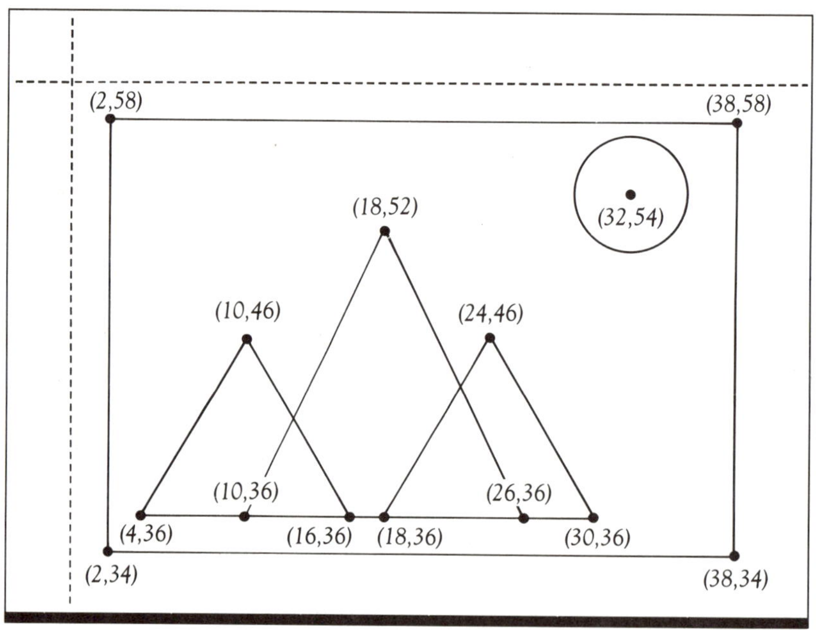

Figure 1.7: *Logo page layout and coordinates*

The printable area is approximately 8 inches, or 48 picas wide. We will enlarge the original design by making each unit equal to 2 picas, for a figure 31 picas wide and 21 picas high. For ease of computation, you can use 32 by 22, which gives an extra pica as a small border. A rectangular frame has been added around the whole figure, at a position 2 picas away from the border of the logo graphic itself, and the whole image is positioned in the upper-left corner of the page.

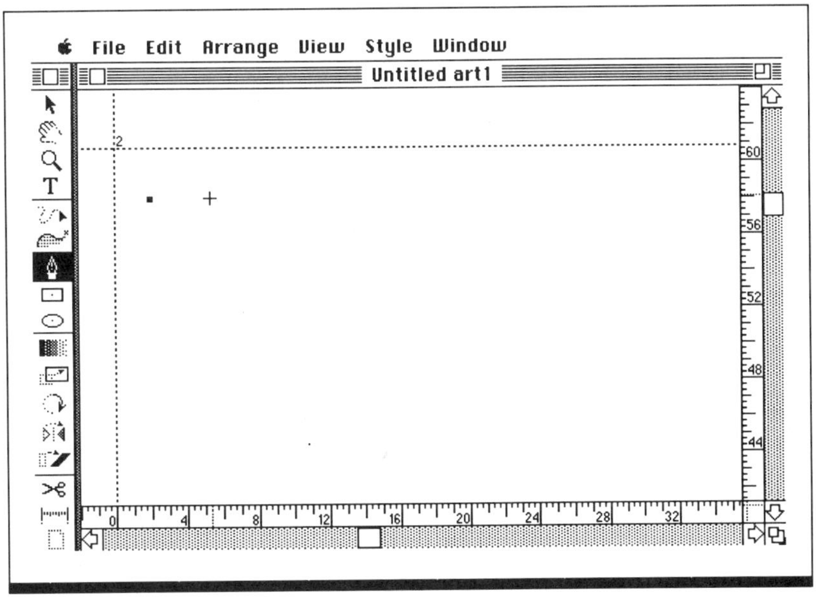

Figure 1.8: *Screen after beginning border*

Illustrator provides a significant amount of information regarding its present status by changes in the cursor form. You must pay careful attention to the form of the cursor and other changes to the desktop as you work with Illustrator. In this case, for example, whenever you have the pen tool selected and the cursor is a cross, you are continuing an existing figure. The next time that you position the cursor and click the mouse, Illustrator will generate a line (or possibly a curve, which we will discuss later) connecting the current point with the last point. The last point in the current figure is always denoted by a small, black box, as you see now at position (2, 58).

If you have a large screen display, you can see point (38,58). However, you should still practice scrolling with the hand tool.

5. Now we want to move the cursor (the +) to point (38, 58). In order to do this, we need to move the image to the left, since the point is off to the right of the screen. Press and hold down the space bar to access the hand tool and push the image to the left. Be sure to continue to hold down the space bar as you move; if you don't, the cursor will return to being a pen and you will generate a line instead of moving the image. When you have scrolled far enough to have point (38, 58) on the screen, stop scrolling by releasing the mouse button and the space bar. The cursor will change back into the + form.

We could have used the scroll bars on the screen to move the image; however, the scroll bars don't provide the same accuracy in positioning that the hand tool does.

6. **Position the cursor on point (38, 58), checking against the ruler marks on the side and bottom of the screen. Then press and hold down the Shift key and click the mouse button. A line connecting the first point to the current point appears. This line will form the top edge of the border.**

By holding down the Shift key, you forced the line to be exactly horizontal, so if your hand wiggled a little or you were off by a notch or two, the line will still come out correct. This is an example of a general technique, called *constraining*, which can be very useful. By holding down the Shift key when you create a line, you will force the resulting line to be either vertical, horizontal, or at a multiple of 45 degrees. We will use this technique for each of the border lines in this image.

Again, point (38,34) will be visible on a large screen.

7. **Move to point (38, 24). Once again, this point is off the current screen and you will have to use the hand tool (press and hold down the space bar) to move the image.**
8. **Press and hold down the Shift key and click the mouse button at point (38, 34) to generate the right edge of the border.**
9. **Move to point (2, 34), using the same method. Press the Shift key and click the mouse button to make the bottom of the border.**
10. **Scroll up until point (2, 58) is on the screen again. You can see the top line of the border extending off the screen to the right and the first point you started at is marked by a small open box.**
11. **Position the cursor on the open box, press the Shift key, and click the mouse button again to complete the border. The open box is replaced by a small, black box, and the cursor itself changes back into an x. At this point, the screen looks like Figure 1.9.**

The x is the same shape that the cursor started in, and its transformation shows that you have closed the figure. Illustrator assumes that the next point you click on will start a new figure, and therefore no line should connect this last point and the following one.

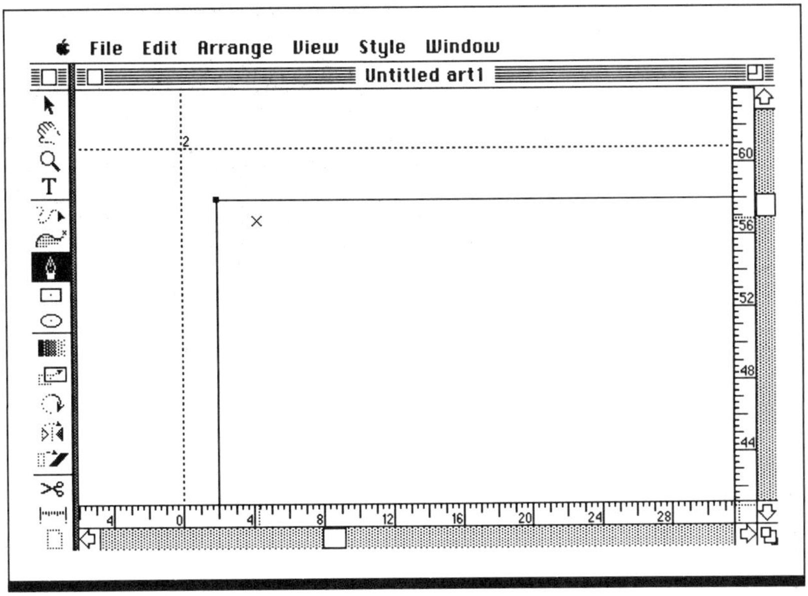

Figure 1.9: *Screen after completing border*

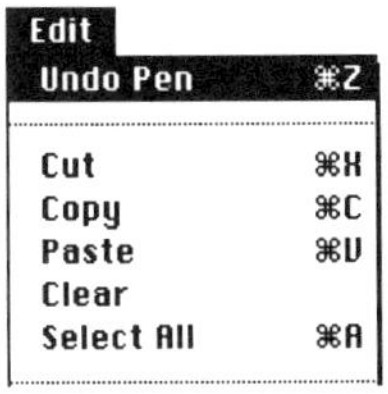

Error Correction

Suppose that while you were moving the hand tool to position the cursor, you didn't hold down the space bar, and you mistakenly drew a line (in step 5 above). If you made that mistake, or some other mistake, and got a line that you don't want, you can easily correct it. After the mistake, immediately move up to the menu bar and pull down the Edit menu. Click on the first selection on the Edit menu, Undo Pen. This removes the unwanted line and returns the cursor to the original state before you accidentally clicked the mouse. Generally, the first selection on the Edit menu will allow you to undo your last action. In fact, it works even when the last action was an Undo. For example, if you just used Undo Pen and pull down the Edit menu again, you'll see the option Redo Pen. The Undo (and Redo) option is available for most Illustrator operations.

Suppose, however, that you are completely unhappy with the figure so far or have accidently created two or more lines that you don't want. What can you do to return to the starting point? You can easily delete everything that you have done since you started the figure by pressing the Backspace or Delete key twice. This will remove all lines that you have drawn since you started a figure and return the cursor to an x, showing that you are ready to begin a new figure. Any completed figures remain in the drawing; it only clears the figure that you are currently working on (which is the *selected* object, as discussed later).

VIEWING THE BORDER

At this stage, it's a good idea to see something of how the drawing looks using the View menu options.

Enlarging the Display

First we'll view the entire drawing rather than just a piece of it.

1. **Pull down the View menu, which you already used to display the ruler bars.**

Notice that the menu shows the selection Hide Rulers, instead of Show Rulers, because the rulers are presently displayed. Also notice the symbol ⌘, followed by a letter, to the right of the selections. They show the keys to use for commands that can be executed from the keyboard. In all cases, the combination requires that you hold down the key that is marked with the ⌘ symbol while you press the letter key shown on the menu. In this book, the keyboard command combination is written as ⌘, followed by the letter.

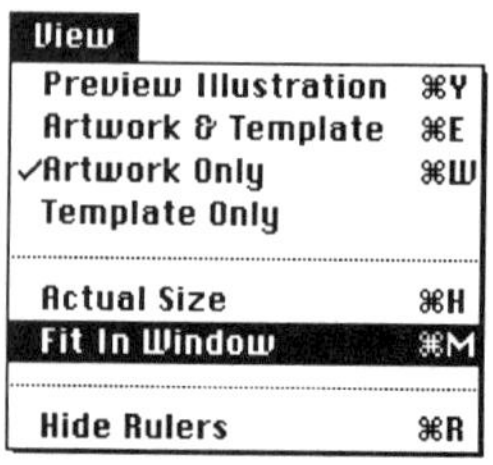

2. **To reduce the screen display to show the entire figure, use the Fit In Window option, in the middle of the menu, either by selecting it or by pressing ⌘M. This generates the display shown in Figure 1.10.**

This display shows the border lines that you have drawn, as well as the page area that Illustrator is working on. You might think of Illustrator working on a large space, like the top of a drafting table. The area is 14 by 14 inches, or 84 by 84 picas. This is larger than a piece of paper, and Illustrator automatically divides the space up into pages of output, shown by the dotted lines on the screen. The large area in the center, where your drawing is shown, is the main page of output, approximately 8 by 10 inches (48 by 60 picas). This is surrounded by eight other areas, all smaller than the main page because they don't require a full 8- by 10-inch page for output. However, each one will generate a separate page of output if there is anything on it to print. The net result would be several output pages, if necessary, with the drawing joined across the

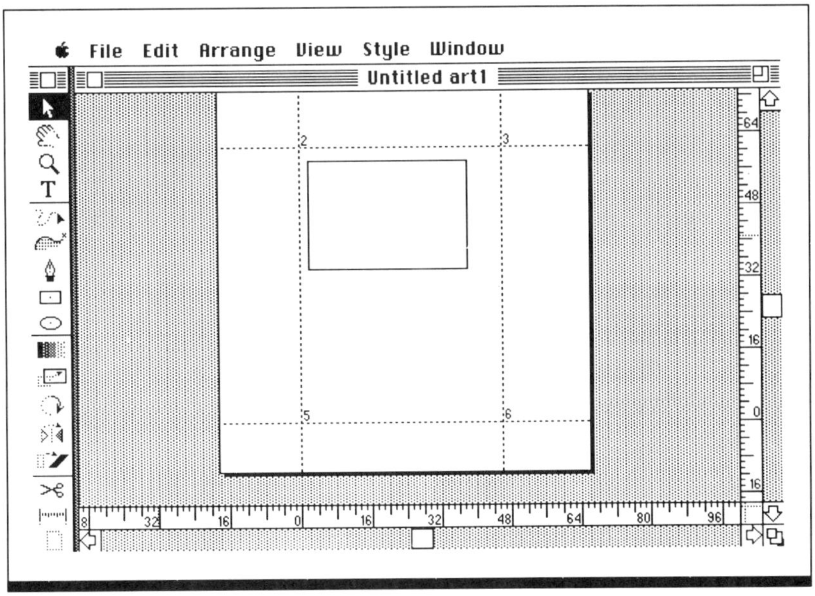

Figure 1.10: *Display after selecting Fit In Window*

pages at the dotted lines shown on the screen. This effect is known as *tiling* a drawing. The small numbers shown in the bottom-left corners of some of the pages represent the sequence of the page during the tiling operation (these numbers are not printed).

The border drawing is placed just below and to the right of the top-left corner of the main output page. Notice that the rulers have expanded with the view, so that the scale and divisions of the ruler are magnified to accommodate the size of the view. If you position the selection arrow on the bottom-right corner of the drawing, you will see that the index lines on the rulers show point (38, 34).

Viewing Options

Now let's explore the other viewing options.

1. Pull down the View menu again.

The first command block on the menu has the options Preview Illustration, Artwork & Template, Artwork Only, and Template Only. These are the commands that govern the display options for the Illustrator screen. The checkmark by Artwork & Template indicates that this is the option governing the current screen display. As its name implies, this selection displays both the current artwork and the current template (if both exist) on the screen simultaneously.

2. Select Artwork Only, and the display will remain the same.

This option displays the Illustrator artwork and excludes the template. Because we are not using a template, there is no difference between Artwork & Template and Artwork Only.

3. Select Template Only, and you will see a blank screen.

This option displays the template (none in this case), and excludes the artwork.

4. Pull down the View menu and select Preview Illustration.

The Preview Illustration option changes the screen to display the equivalent of the printed output that you will get from the figure. This is not precisely identical to the printed or film output because the screen is a much lower resolution device than the printer or typesetter. Nevertheless, within the limits of the resolution of the screen, this is an exact representation of the output that you will get on the printer or whatever output device you are using.

You may be surprised by the preview image, which is a black square filling the entire area bounded by the border lines. This happened because Illustrator's default options for closed figures is to fill them with black. The solution is to change those default options for this figure.

Changing the Style Options for the Border

We now want to change the options governing our border lines. Instead of filling in the figure, we want to outline, or *stroke* it. Be sure that you have the border lines selected (the corners are all boxes—either hollow, white boxes or boxes filled in with black). Illustrator automatically selects a figure when it is completed. If you have not done anything else in the meantime, the border lines will be selected. If they are not selected, click on the selection tool (the arrowhead), position the arrow on any one of the border lines, and click the mouse.

1. Select Artwork & Template from the View menu, and then pull down the Style menu.

As you see, there are four options on the Style menu: Paint, Type, Pattern, and Custom Color. The Type option governs the selection and display of text for figures, which we will cover in Chapter 3. The Pattern and Custom Color options define specific aspects of how you fill or stroke objects; they are beyond the scope of this book.

2. Select Paint, and you will see the dialog screen shown in Figure 1.11.

The highlighted options are available, and the ones currently marked are the defaults. The options that are not highlighted are not currently available (this format is consistent with the usual Macintosh practice). The Fill and Stroke sections along the top of the screen govern how figures are filled in or outlined or both.

3. Because we do not want the border lines filled in at all, click on the button next to None in the Fill box.

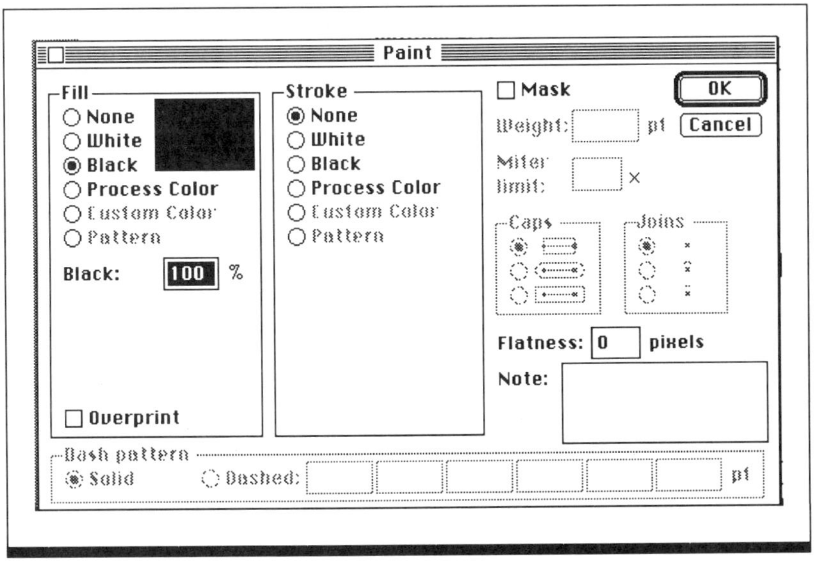

Figure 1.11: *Paint dialog screen*

4. **Move over to the Stroke box, and click on the button next to Black. Below the option list, you will see a box containing the default value of 100% Black (that's what we want, so leave it alone), and the other sections on the screen that are related to stroking figures become active.**
5. **Position the cursor behind the 1 that appeared in the Weight box and click. This generates a line cursor indicating where any values that you enter will go.**
6. **Press Backspace or Delete to erase the current value of 1, enter 2, and click on OK.**

We have changed the border lines from a closed, filled black box to an outlined box, where the lines that form the box have a width of 2 points. Illustrator uses points whenever measures finer than a pica are required.

If you would like to see the results of adjusting the border, pull down the View menu and select Preview Illustration again. You will now see an open box with fairly large and dark border lines.

Drawing the Mountains

If you are in preview mode, you must return to the Artwork Only view (through the View menu) to continue working with the figure. After you make this choice, you will see a Fit In Window view of the desktop. Before you proceed with the logo, pull down the View menu again and use the Actual Size option, either by selecting it or by pressing ⌘H from the keyboard. You will see the desktop return to the original dimensions that you started with, displaying only a portion of the border.

The First Triangle

We will begin by placing the leftmost triangle to form the first mountain.

1. **Move the screen until point (4, 36) is visible on the rulers and the bottom-left corner of the border is in the bottom-left corner of the screen. This should show a range on the bottom ruler from about 0 to 32, and a range on the righthand ruler from about 34 to 54.**
2. **Click on the pen tool again, if it isn't already selected.**
3. **Move to point (4, 36) and click for the first point of the mountain.**

4. **Move up to point (10, 46), and this time, click the mouse without pressing the Shift key.**

We will not use the Shift key to draw the mountains because we don't want to force the lines to be multiples of 45 degrees; we want these lines to go just where we put them. This means that you have to be precise in locating the coordinates, or your mountains will be lopsided.

5. **Move the cursor to point (16, 36) and click again. Remember, don't press Shift. Again, the line appears between the last point, at (10, 46), and the current point.**
6. **Return the cursor to (4, 36), which is marked by a small open box.**

This small open box indicates the presence of an anchor point, and is also one of the endpoints of an open figure. At present, there is no other endpoint because you are continuing a figure, which is shown by the + shape of the cursor. If you terminated the current figure at this point, by selecting another tool or forcing the start of a new figure (as discussed in the next chapter), the last point on the current figure—which, you will remember, is always shown as a small, black box—would become the final endpoint and would turn into another small open box.

7. **To finish the triangle, position the cursor on (4, 36) and click the mouse again.**

Notice that the cursor shape changes from a + to a small x to indicate that the next point will start a new figure and not be a continuation of the old figure, and that the endpoint marker has disappeared (the figure is now closed, and so there is no longer any real endpoint).

8. **With the figure still selected, pull down the Style menu and select Paint.**

Notice that the settings in the Paint dialog screen are still what you set for the borders earlier, not the previous default settings. Illustrator has remembered the settings from the previous figure in this drawing.

9. **Click on the button next to None in the Stroke box.**
10. **Click on the button next to Black in the Fill box.**

11. **Position the cursor between the first and second 0 of the default 100 that appears next to Black and click. The line cursor appears between the two figures.**
12. **Backspace twice and enter a 3, changing the value to 30. This means that the triangle will be set to 30% Black when it is printed.**
13. **Click on OK and return to the Illustrator desktop.**

The Middle Triangle

Now we want to add another mountain. You can work most easily if you proceed from left to right, so we'll create the large triangle next.

1. **Move the cursor to point (10, 36).**

This point is along the line that has already been drawn for the bottom of the first triangle and will overlap some of it.

2. **Click the mouse on this point.**

The usual effects appear at once: the cursor changes into a + and the initial point of the new figure is marked by a small, black box.

3. **Move to point (18, 52) and click the mouse to create the first side of the triangle.**
4. **Move to point (26, 36) and click to create the second side.**
5. **Move back to the start at (10, 36) and click to close the figure. When you are done, the large triangle is in place.**
6. **Pull down the Style menu and select Paint.**
7. **Change the 30% next to Black in the Fill box to 70%.**

This will make the triangle 70 percent black on the final output, which will be significantly darker than the other triangle, but still not all black.

8. **Click on OK and return to the Illustrator desktop.**

The Rightmost Triangle

Now we are ready to add the final triangle. We want this triangle to match the color and other attributes of the first triangle. There is a fast and easy way to do this, using the keyboard commands.

1. **Hold down the Command key (changing the cursor to an arrowhead to denote that the selection tool is in use), move the arrowhead to any point on the first triangle, and click. The triangle endpoints become boxes, showing that the triangle is selected.**
2. **Press ⌘I to bring up the Paint dialog screen.**

Notice that the options displayed are not those you just entered, but rather the ones for the selected triangle, which we want to duplicate.

3. **Press Return (or click on OK) to make the Paint options the current default for the next triangle.**

Illustrator automatically returns you to the desktop, with the pen tool still enabled.

4. **For the last triangle, start at point (18, 36) and click the mouse button for the first point of the triangle.**
5. **Move to (24, 46) and click to draw the first side.**
6. **Move to (30, 36) and click to draw the second side.**
7. **Close the figure by returning to its starting point.**

ADDING THE SUN

Our final figure to add to the logo design is the sun. This can be done easily using the Illustrator circle tool.

1. **Select the circle tool from the toolbox and move the cursor onto the desktop.**

Notice that the cursor has the + form for this tool, which will help you position the circle on the drawing.

2. **Move the cursor to point (32, 54), which we determined to be the center of the circle.**
3. **Press and hold down both the Shift key, which constrains the figure to a circle, and the Option key, which allows you to draw from the center. (I'll explain why these keypresses are necessary after we draw the sun.) Click and hold the mouse button (the cursor changes to an arrowhead without any tail),**

then move the cursor down and to the right (you must move the cursor diagonally when constructing a circle) until the dotted indices on the rulers are about on point (34, 52). You won't get to exactly that point; you may be slightly beyond 8 or slightly beyond 34—the actual point that you can reach will depend on the precise angle of the cursor movement.

The circle appears as you move the cursor. It extends outward from the center you defined to the point that you are moving, which defines the circumference of the circle.

4. **Release the mouse button and then release both the Option and Shift keys. Be sure to do it in that order; if you don't, the figure will change drastically in front of your eyes.**

If you do release the buttons in the wrong order, remember what we said earlier about corrections to a line. Just pull down the Edit menu, choose Undo Oval, and the error will disappear. Then go back and do the circle correctly. Notice that the menu option is related to the current operation, so you can undo whatever you just did.

5. **To set the style values for the sun figure, make sure that the circle is selected and pull down the Style menu.**

The figure should still be selected. In previous exercises, you could tell that a figure was selected because its corners were all little boxes, either open or all black. In this case, you should see five small, black boxes: four at opposite points of the circumference (matching where the x- and y-axes would intersect the circle) and one at the center. If you don't see these boxes, click on the selection tool, move the cursor onto any point of the circle, and click the mouse.

6. **Choose the Paint option from the menu, and you will see the familiar dialog screen for setting the Paint attributes.**
7. **Select None for Fill and 100% Black for Stroke. Set the line weight to 1 if it isn't already that by default, and click on OK.**

You needed to hold down the Shift key to constrain the circle tool because the so-called circle tool is really an ellipse tool. That is, when you select this tool, Illustrator will allow you to create any kind of ellipse, and a circle is a special case of an ellipse. So for our logo, you needed to tell Illustrator that you want to constrain the ellipse to be only a circle. We used the same constraint technique earlier to ensure that the border lines were horizontal or vertical.

You also needed to hold down the Option key at the same time. Illustrator expects that you will want to create a circle or ellipse from edge to edge, rather than from the center. This is clearly the most likely form of construction when you are working from a template, as you normally would be. The template will show you the outline of a circle, which will give you no clue as to where the precise center of the circle would be. In this case, however, you didn't have a template to work from, but you did have a center point. Pressing the Option key allows you to draw the circle from the center to the edge rather than from edge to edge.

Reordering the Mountain Overlay

There is still one point that we need to take care of on our logo. This is the issue of the order of the three mountains in the final output. The artwork now on the screen just shows the outlines of each of the mountains, but when they are filled in, one will overlay the other.

Perhaps the best way to see this is to quickly preview the drawing. Pull down the View menu and select Preview Illustration. Be sure that you have a reasonable amount of the logo, including most of the mountains, on the screen. Your screen will look something like Figure 1.12.

As you see, the mountains have been filled in the same sequence that you created them, from left to right, with the first one in the back. This is not quite what we want. Let's move the large center mountain behind the other two to put the two smaller mountains in the foreground.

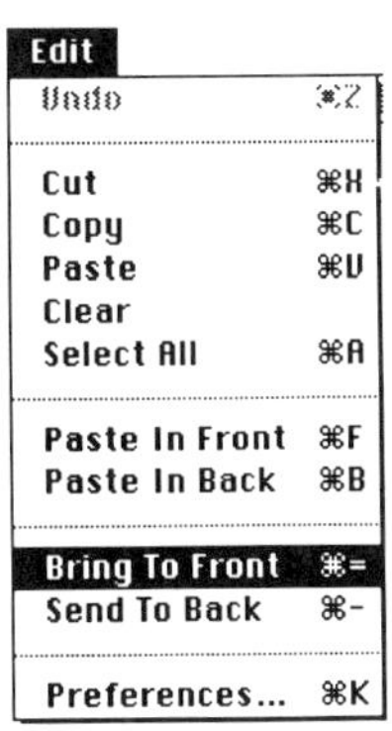

1. **To do this operation, you need to be in the Artwork & Template view. Return to that if you are still in preview mode.**
2. **Click on the selection tool and move the cursor to any point on the first (leftmost) mountain figure.**
3. **Hold down the Option key and click the mouse to select the entire first figure as a unit (this is shown by the appearance of black boxes at each of the corners).**
4. **Pull down the Edit menu and choose Bring To Front. (If you are working with version 1.1, see the section below.)**

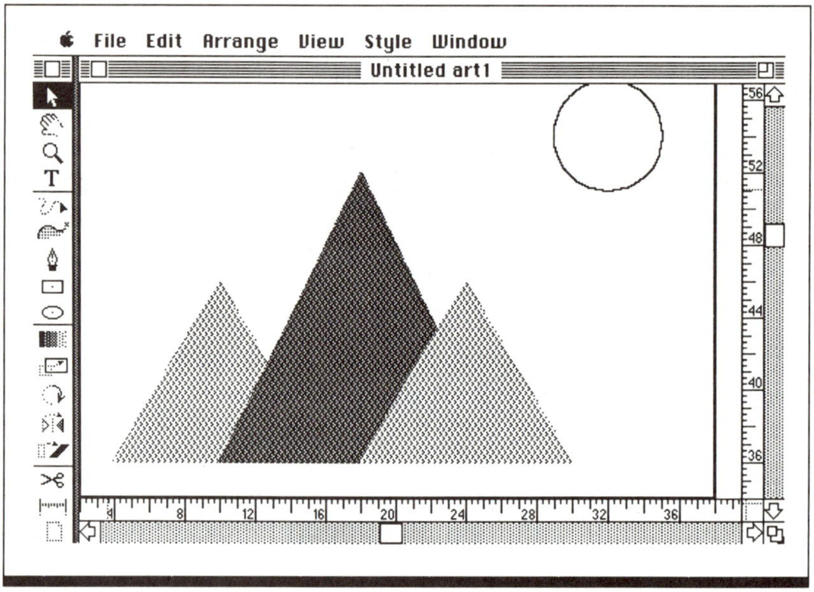

Figure 1.12: *First preview of the logo graphic*

You have changed the order of painting for the selected object (the first triangle) so that it will paint over all other objects that overlap it (in this case, only the second, larger triangle). This technique is efficient when you just want to change the order of the display of objects and don't need to move them on the desktop.

5. **Select Preview Illustration from the View menu, and you will see how the relative positions of the mountains have changed, as shown in Figure 1.13.**

Reordering Objects in Illustrator 1.1

Bring To Front, and the corresponding Send To Back, are new Edit menu options in Illustrator 88. If you have version 1.1, or you want to change the position of the object at the same time that you change the paint sequence, you would replace step 4 above with the following steps:

1. **Pull down the Edit menu and choose Cut. This moves the selected object (the first triangle) to the clipboard.**

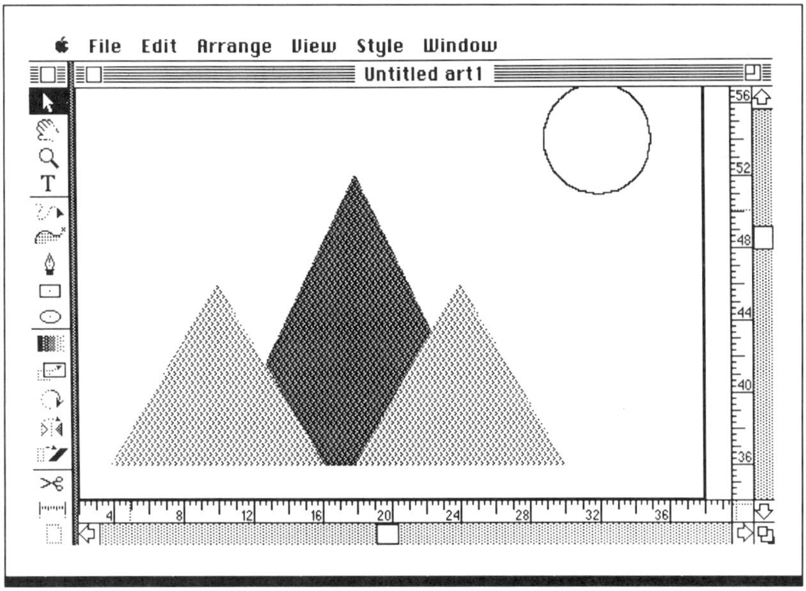

Figure 1.13: *Finished logo graphic*

2. Select Show Clipboard from the Edit menu (the Windows menu in version 88), and you will see a display that shows one artwork object, the triangle, on the clipboard.
3. Click on the close button to put away the clipboard.
4. Select Paste In Front from the Edit menu. This returns the object from the clipboard and puts it in front of the other figures on the artwork. (In this case, that will only affect the large mountain in the center.)

SAVING THE ARTWORK

Now we want to save the the artwork in its present form. Follow these steps:

1. Pull down the File menu and choose Save. You will see a dialog box that looks like Figure 1.14.
2. Enter the name *Logo art* in the Save illustration as box.

Notice that the Save option on the right side of the dialog box becomes active as you type. This is a context-dependent option—because you cannot save anything that doesn't have a name, the option is only available after some name has been entered.

3. Click on Save.

The artwork will be saved under the name *Logo art* in the currently open folder on the currently open disk, and you will be returned to the Illustrator desktop. You may change the folder and disk settings in the usual Macintosh fashion if you want to save the artwork somewhere else (for example, in a separate folder that you've set up for the exercises in this book). The artwork is saved in PostScript format, as represented by a PostScript icon.

The name of the artwork document is also entirely arbitrary. For clarity, Abobe suggests that artwork documents always end with the word *art* and templates with the word *template* so that you can distinguish them in the listings that appear in the dialog boxes. In this book, I will follow the Adobe suggestion.

When you return to the saved artwork, you'll notice that there is one change: the name that you just gave the document now appears in the title bar. If you choose Save again from the File menu, this is the name that will be used. Of course, you can always choose Save As from the File menu and give your artwork another name.

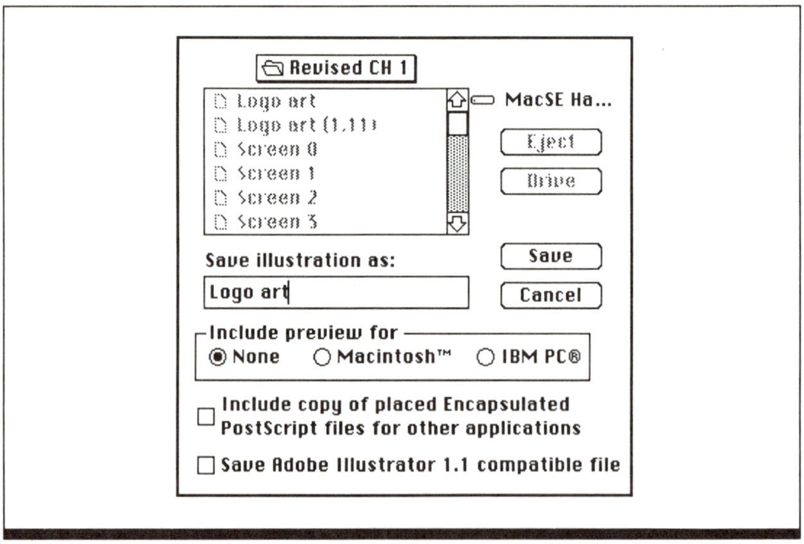

Figure 1.14: *Save dialog box*

PRINTING THE ARTWORK

Just as a reminder, I assume that your printer is already attached, chosen, and operating correctly. With that out of the way, there are still some preliminaries to printing your artwork.

1. **Pull down the File menu again and select Page Setup.**

This will display the Page Setup dialog box, which varies depending on your printer. In this book, I am working with the Apple LaserWriter, which produces the dialog box shown in Figure 1.15.

2. **Click on OK to choose all the default settings for your first printed output: US letter paper, portrait orientation, and 100% reduction.**
3. **Pull down the File menu and choose Print. This will also generate a dialog box, as shown in Figure 1.16.**
4. **Click on OK to proceed with printing.**

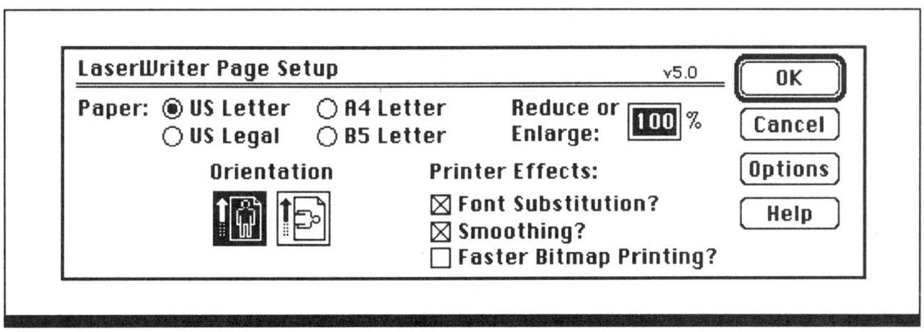

Figure 1.15: *Page Setup dialog box for an Apple LaserWriter*

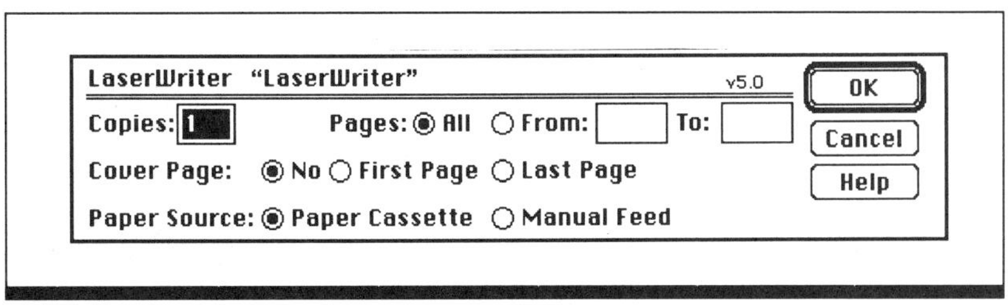

Figure 1.16: *Print dialog box*

The printing process generates several status messages as it proceeds. The final output looks like the screen preview that you saw earlier, as shown in Figure 1.17.

PRINTING OPTIONS

Let's look at some of the print options that are available to you. First pull down the View menu and select the Fit In Window option. This gives you the complete view of the Illustrator desktop, as we discussed earlier.

Page Setup Options

Pull down the File menu and select Page Setup again. Let's review the options displayed in this box. Options similar to those shown in Figure 1.17 would be displayed for other printers, such as the Apple LaserWriter Plus. The top line shows the version of LaserWriter software that is being used. This can be important because all users on an AppleTalk network must use the same version of software for compatibility.

There are four paper options displayed: US Letter ($8^{1}/_{2}$ inch by 11 inch), which is the default value; US Legal ($8^{1}/_{2}$ inch by 14 inch); A4 Letter (210 millimeter by 297 millimeter); and B5 Letter (176 millimeter by 250 millimeter). There are two possible orientations: portrait,

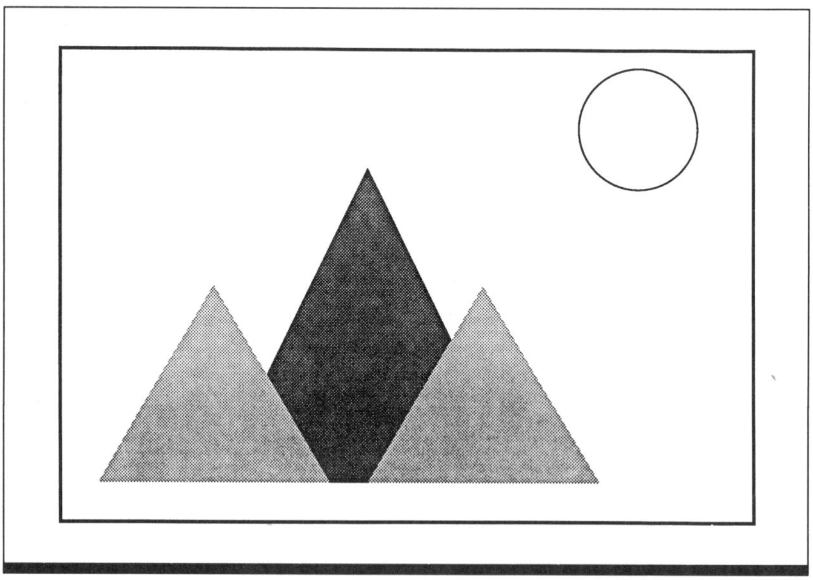

Figure 1.17: *Page output from Logo art*

which is the default and prints with the short side of the paper up, and landscape, which prints with the long edge of the page up. You can reduce or enlarge the artwork in percentages of the original size of the page, ranging from 25 to 400 percent. Finally, you should ignore the Printer Effects choices; the default values are correct for all Illustrator output.

To see the results of another Page Setup option, click on the landscape orientation and then click on OK. When you return to the drawing, you will notice that the orientation of the pages that tile the desktop has changed to conform to your new choice. You will also notice that the rulers have kept their orientation relative to the figure; they have not turned themselves on the side to follow the output pages. Therefore, point (0, 0) is still at the bottom-left corner of the primary output page, the x-coordinates now run across the width of the page, and the y-coordinates run up and down the page. Also, all the points we laid out earlier still maintain the same coordinates.

Return to the Page Setup dialog box again, set Reduce or Enlarge to 150%, and click on OK. This gives you a view of the desktop that looks like Figure 1.18.

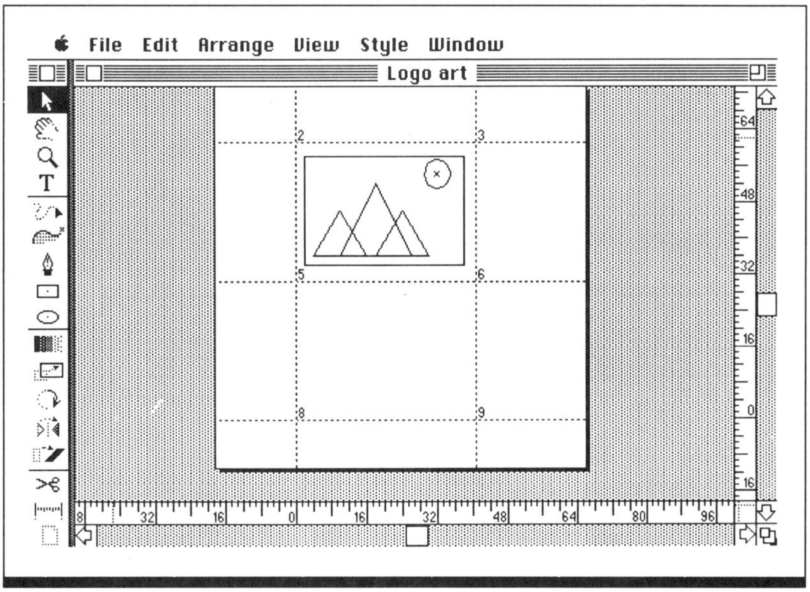

Figure 1.18: *Reoriented logo page*

Up until now, what you have seen on the screen is what you would get on your output—not only in shape and shading, but in size as well. For example, if you drew a 6-pica box, using the rulers, it would print as a 6-pica box, unless you change the page setup. When you modify the page setup, the 6-pica box will still be the same size on the screen (according to the rulers), but it won't print that size anymore. It will be larger or smaller, as you have specified in the Page Setup dialog box. To see the printed size, you must check the values in the Page Setup dialog box or view the entire desktop with Fit In Window.

Now the desktop is tiled with additional sheets to reflect the larger size of the drawing. As you can see, the artwork takes up almost an entire page of output. The rulers also change scale so that, once again, the coordinates of the figure remain constant. You might have supposed that only the figure would expand, and a point that had been (16, 24) would now be (24, 36), for example. That isn't how the scaling mechanism works. The divisions on the rulers have also been enlarged by 150 percent, so that one division on the ruler is 1.5 picas on the output page instead of only 1 pica. This is an important point to keep in mind. A change in the scale of the artwork works by stretching or shrinking the size of the rulers on the page, not by just enlarging or reducing the artwork.

Printer Options

To review the options in the Print dialog box, pull down the File menu again and select Print, or press ⌘P. This dialog box (Figure 1.16) also shows the version of the LaserWriter software that is being used. The options displayed are straightforward. They include a number of copies that you can set (the default is 1); an option to print all pages or from a certain page to a certain page; an option to print a cover sheet as the first sheet, the last sheet, or not at all (no cover sheet is the default); and the source of paper can be set to either cassette tray or manual feed (cassette tray is the default). You will very seldom need to change these defaults.

If you want to print the reoriented logo page, use the defaults and click on OK. Now when you save the logo, the scaling and orientation of the page will be stored with the file. This can be important because any change will affect the ruler size and orientation; you will want to remember when you have saved an artwork document with changes such as these because what you see on the screen will no longer be what you get as output.

This gives you some understanding of some of the choices that you can make to modify the output of an Illustrator document. You can reorient the artwork and shrink or expand it on the output page without making any direct change to the artwork itself.

Now that you've had some experience with the program and its tools, we'll proceed to create more complex artwork. In the next chapter, we'll use templates to produce images made up of curves and lines.

Fast Track Chapter 2

39 **Templates are bit-mapped images**
that you can display in Illustrator as drawing guides. You can use any MacPaint or MacDraw PICT file as a template.

40 **To associate a template with artwork,**
select the template from the template selection box displayed after you select New from the File menu. Templates associated with existing artwork are automatically displayed when you open the artwork.

42 **Illustrator curved-line segments**
are controlled by anchor points at the beginning and end and by direction points, which define the direction of the curve.

48 **To magnify an image**
around a point, click on that point with the zoom tool. To reduce an image around a point, click on the point with the zoom tool while holding down the Option key. Each click magnifies the image by twice the preceding size or reduces it by half.

52 **To trace curves,**
click on the point that you want to be an anchor point, and drag the direction point in the direction that you want the curve to go.

53 **To modify a direction or anchor point,**
select it with the selection tool, click, drag the point where you want it, and release the mouse button.

57 **To open existing artwork,**
select Open from the File menu, select the name of the artwork from the Open dialog box, and click on Open.

60 **To select an entire figure,**
move the selection tool anywhere on it, hold down the Option key, and click.

60 **To select specific points,**
either click on them in succession with the selection tool while holding down the Shift key or use the selection tool to draw a selection marquee around them.

Fast Track

63 **Guidelines for anchor and direction point placement**
include: start on a smooth curve, place anchor points on the sides of a bump, use the largest strides possible, and place the first direction point about one-third of the distance between the first and second anchor points.

68 **For quick access to the selection tool,**
press and hold down the Command key.

70 **To quickly magnify an image**
around the center of the screen, double-click on the zoom tool. To reduce the image, hold down the Option key while you double-click on the zoom tool.

73 **For quick access to the zoom tool,**
hold down the space bar and the Command key for magnification. For reduction, hold down the Option key as well as the space bar and Command key.

Chapter 2

Drawing Basics: Creating Lines and Curves

In this chapter, we will use templates to trace curved-line drawings. We'll begin with a brief discussion of the use of templates, including where to get them and how to associate them with your work. You'll also learn some important concepts to keep in mind when drawing any type of line with Illustrator. The exercises demonstrate the application of these concepts, as well as some shortcuts to producing your images.

USING TEMPLATES AS DRAWING GUIDES

A template is a bit-mapped image that is brought into Illustrator as a guide for production of artwork. (As you've seen, Illustrator artwork is the collection of line art and type that you generate on the screen using Illustrator tools.)

You can think of a template as an original projection or picture that you place under a piece of tracing paper in order to trace a drawing. In a similar way, the template lays under the Illustrator drawing area and shows through as a slightly-dimmed sketch.

Normally, you will use a template as a starting point for creating Illustrator artwork. It will probably be more natural for you to prepare drafts of graphic material in whatever manner you are accustomed to, and then use that image with Illustrator for final processing.

Sources of Templates

Templates must be in one of two basic formats, which can be generated from several sources. The formats are MacPaint files and MacDraw PICT files. You are probably familiar with both of these formats from your previous work on the Macintosh.

Most scanners allow you to choose from several formats for their output. Select the MacPaint format if you are going to use the output as a template in Illustrator.

You can create artwork in either the MacPaint or MacDraw program, save it in the appropriate format, and then use it with Illustrator as a template. You can also use a scanner that produces output in MacPaint format to create a template (which means that anything that can be scanned can generally be used as a starting point). Screen dumps (captured images of screens) and other types of graphic output, such as spreadsheet graphs, are also in MacPaint format, and so they can serve as template sources. In fact, most programs or applications that generate graphics and run on a Macintosh produce output in one of these two standard formats.

There is one additional source of template material that you should keep in mind. This is the large and varied selection of clip art disks that can be purchased or come with graphics programs. You may have noticed that the Adobe Tutorial disk that comes with your Illustrator documentation is a fine source of template material. On the other hand, you may have also discovered that the Collectors Edition disks that you received with the program do not contain templates for the elaborate images that they contain, only the Illustrator artwork.

ASSOCIATING TEMPLATES AND ARTWORK

Templates are associated with Illustrator artwork when you open the Illustrator application. As we discussed in the first chapter, you can begin work in Illustrator by selecting New from the File menu. For our first graphic design, we chose None from the template selection dialog box.

If you select a template to work with instead, that template will remain associated with the artwork you create. It will be included with the artwork display automatically when you next open the file.

If you select Open, you will see the Open dialog box, shown in Figure 2.1. From this box, you can either open existing artwork or open a template. If you open an existing artwork document, the template associated with it will automatically be included when the work is displayed on the desktop if the template is available. *Available* in this context means that the required template is in the same folder as the artwork, with the same name that it had when the association was originally made. If you open a template, you will get a fresh drawing surface, labeled *Untitled art1*, and the selected template. This method has the same effect as choosing New and then selecting the template, and it creates the same association of the template with the artwork.

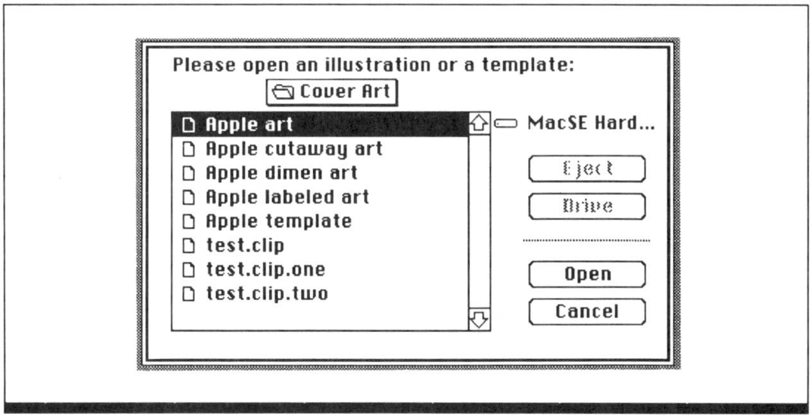

Figure 2.1: *The Open dialog box*

If the correct template is not available when you open an existing artwork document, Illustrator will present you with a dialog box similar to the template selection dialog box, which will allow you to associate a new template with the artwork. The only way to change the association of artwork with a template is to remove or rename the template, and then select a new template when you next open the artwork.

Distinguishing Templates and Artwork

Because of this persistent association of template and artwork, you need some way to distinguish one from the other while you are working in Illustrator. To some extent, you can tell the template from the artwork by its dimmed, or greyed-out, appearance; however, as you complete more of the artwork and match the template, it can become difficult to determine where the artwork leaves off and the template begins.

As you saw in the last chapter, the View menu provides three methods for viewing artwork and/or templates. The default option, Artwork & Template, displays both the artwork and the underlying template on the screen. This mode is the one that you will normally be working in because it allows you to see what you want to do by looking at the template and at the same time see what you have done by looking at the artwork.

If you select the Artwork Only option to remove the template, you can still work with and modify the artwork, just as in the default mode. You may want to use Artwork Only when you are working on complex graphics where the shading or other features of the template hinder your view of the exact placement or structure of the artwork.

The Template Only option is useful after you have accumulated a substantial amount of artwork which obscures the original lines of the template. You cannot modify the template in any way (the template is a bit-map of a graphic image and Illustrator does not provide any tools for handling bit-mapped images).

To edit or modify a template, you must use a graphic program, that is designed to alter bit-maps (such as MacPaint). Then you can use the modified template with Illustrator.

FORMING CURVED LINES

You may have noticed that Illustrator handles line creation differently than most other drawing programs. Typically, you "draw" a line by clicking and moving the mouse, and you can see the line as it is formed. When using the pen tool in Illustrator, you select two points, and then create a line joining them. You do not see the line until after you select the second point.

The freehand tool, which is new to Illustrator 88, can also be used to draw lines. However, the operations of the pen tool more clearly illustrate how the program forms line segments. In addition, the pen tool can create any type of line segment, while the freehand tool is more limited. For these reasons, we will continue to concentrate on the use of the pen tool in our current exercises and cover the freehand tool later in the book.

As you will see in the following exercises, curves are formed in a similar manner. Illustrator creates a curved-line segment based on the position of two end points, called *anchor points*, and two related control points, called *direction points*. Before we begin our curve-drawing examples, we'll discuss how Illustrator uses these points to generate lines.

CURVE CONCEPTS

Basically, all line segments in Illustrator are formed in the same way. Each has a beginning and an ending point, which are the anchor points, and each end of the segment has a controlling direction point. This is true for straight-line segments as well as curved-line segments; in the case of straight lines, the direction points are identical to the anchor points, so you don't see or use them. Figure 2.2 shows the anchor points and the direction points of four curved-line segments and a straight line.

All the lines are the same length; the only differences are in the placement of the direction points. The first two lines have direction points that move away from the anchor points at the same angle, but the second line's direction points are twice as far from the anchor points as those of the first line. As you can see, this results in more of a bow in the second line.

The third line has direction points that move away from the anchor points at twice the angle of the second line. Notice how the line curves

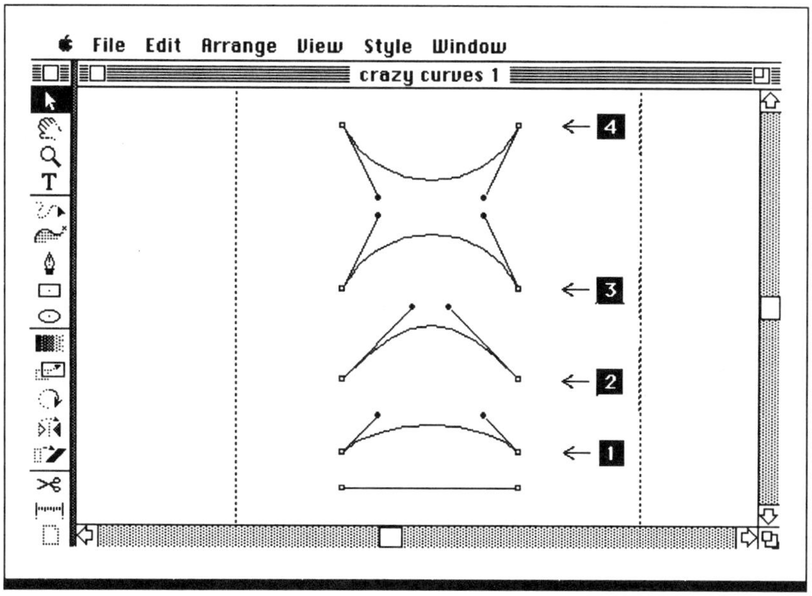

Figure 2.2: *Curved-line segments*

As you work with line segments, you should be sure that each segment starts fresh. That means that the pen cursor must be an x, not a +, when you start. Because these are not closed figures, Illustrator will not change automatically back to the x cursor when you finish a line. You must force a new line segment by clicking on the pen tool again before you start the new segment. Also, don't forget that you can always remove all of the current line by pressing the Delete or Backspace key twice.

more sharply toward the anchor points. Technically, the line segment that connects the two anchor points will always be tangent to the line from the anchor point to the direction point. Because the line from the anchor points to the direction points in the third line is steeper than in the second line, the line curves more sharply at the ends. In both cases, the line is smooth and rises to the same height (measured from a straight line connecting the two anchor points), but the third line curves more sharply initially and then flattens out, while the second line rises more gradually. This is entirely due to the placement of the direction points.

The fourth line curves in the opposite direction from the other lines because the direction points, which govern the direction of the curve as it moves away from the anchor point, are on the opposite side of the anchor points. The direction points are at the same angle and distance as in the third line, but in the opposite direction. You can see how the curve bends out to match. In all the lines, notice that there is a direct relationship between the bell to the curve and the distance that the direction points are from the anchor point.

Figure 2.3 presents four additional examples of the interaction of direction points and curves. Once again, these lines are all the same length and are shown with a straight line for comparison. This set of lines, however, has asymmetrical direction points to give you a sense of what you can do with these points. In the first line, the direction point on the right is twice the size and at twice the angle as the one on the left. The curve starts slowly on the left, and then curves further up and bends more steeply as it approaches the right anchor point. The height of the curve is still governed by the direction points, but where the curve moves smoothly with symmetrical points, it now adjusts its motion to match the imbalance between the asymmetrical points, as a kind of compromise between the two.

The second line shows the effect of different angles on each end of the curve. Again, the curve follows the same rules we observed earlier: the curved-line segment is always tangent to the line formed by the anchor point and the direction point at the anchor point. Like the first line, the curve forms a kind of compromise between the two angles, becoming flatter as it moves toward the right anchor point to match the flatness of the line between the direction point and the anchor point.

The third line shows how the curve changes when one direction point is pulling in the opposite way from the direction that the curve approaches the anchor point; that is, the two direction points are on opposite sides of the curve. Here, the left anchor point has a direction point that is at exactly the opposite angle of the right anchor point and

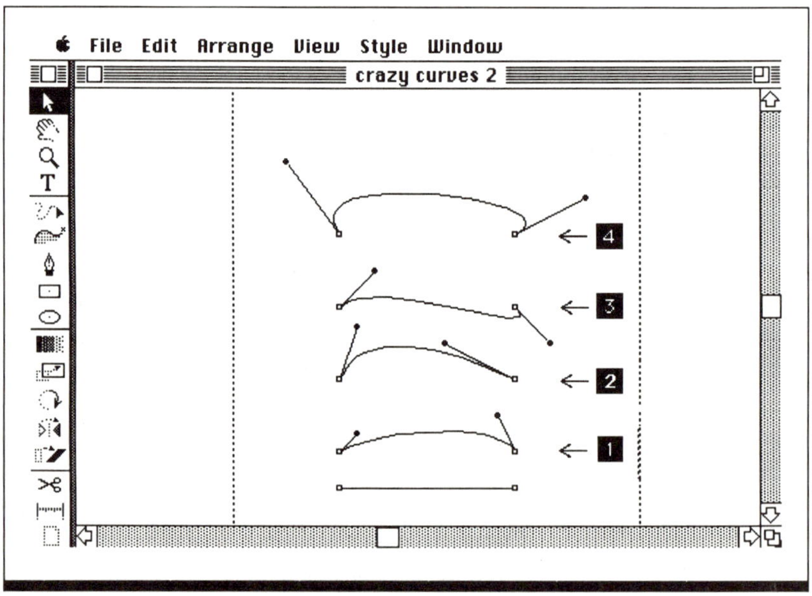

Figure 2.3: *More curved-line examples*

direction point. You can see how the curve starts out in a smooth way toward the second anchor point, but then curves past it and then sharply reverses direction. Because the curved-line segment must approach the anchor point on the same side as the direction point, it has to go past the anchor point and then turn back. This leaves a small S-bend in the curve near the left anchor point.

The fourth line shows the effect of having both direction points on the same side of the curve but headed away from the opposite anchor point. As you would expect, the curve starts to follow the direction point away from the anchor point, but then it starts very quickly to curve back toward the second anchor point and then passes over it to approach the anchor point from the correct angle—as defined by the tangent line. This gives a kind of egg shape to the final curve.

All these examples should give you some idea of the interaction of anchor points and direction points. You can open a new Illustrator file and experiment with the line segments shown in Figures 2.2 and 2.3. Try out various combinations of anchor and direction points to see the results, and note those that you think may provide interesting effects. As you explore, you will develop a sense of where the line segment is going to go when you place the anchor and direction points in a certain relationship.

CREATING CURVED-LINE ART WITH A TEMPLATE

As our first example in this chapter, we will take a simple template (a drawing of a light bulb) and convert it into Illustrator artwork. This light bulb template was prepared as a freehand drawing, using MacPaint. The output, as produced by MacPaint, is shown in Figure 2.4.

Copy this template, using whatever drawing software you have available. If you prefer, you can use a template of your own—one that consists of curved-line segments. Just follow the basic steps in the exercises, adapting the particular movements to your template's design.

The template is quite simple in concept, but even so, we are not going to do all of it at once. To begin with, you will just trace the outline of the bulb and the screw base. This will get you started in using several of the tools, as well as introduce you to the creation of curved lines.

Figure 2.4: *Light bulb template produced by MacPaint*

IMPORTING AND SIZING THE TEMPLATE

We'll begin by opening up the template in Illustrator.

1. **Start Illustrator by double-clicking on the Illustrator icon.**
2. **Select Open or New from the File menu and open your template. Either way, you will see a screen that looks like the one shown in Figure 2.5.**

Notice that the title in the bar shows two names separated by a colon, like this:

Untitled art1:Light Bulb template

This shows that the template used to open the file was named Light Bulb template and Illustrator has now associated it with the artwork that you are about to generate. Because that artwork does not yet exist, it has no name, and so Illustrator defaults to the name Untitled art1. After you name the artwork, it will appear in the title bar before the name of the template.

Also notice that the light bulb template has been positioned on the Illustrator page as a full-page image. If you selected Fit In Window from

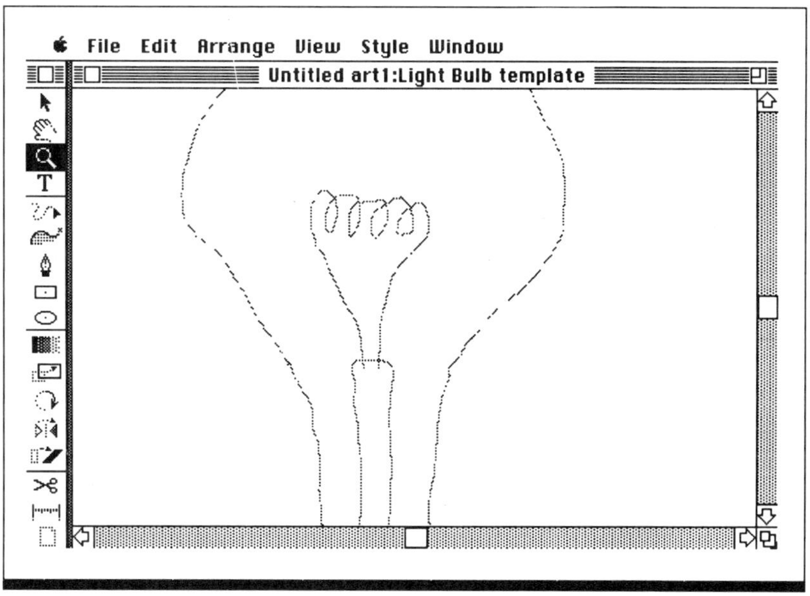

Figure 2.5: *First light bulb view*

the View menu, you would see that the light bulb image fills the page to the same degree that it does on the sample page output shown in Figure 2.4. When you start Illustrator, the window opens on the center of the page in the Actual Size view, so you see only a portion of the template.

At this point, you could use the hand tool to move the template down or up so that you can begin tracing it. This was the technique that we used in the last chapter to move around the screen. However, what we really need to do here is reduce the figure in order to work with it. Illustrator provides the zoom tool for both reducing and magnifying images. The zoom tool is represented by the magnifying glass icon in the toolbox.

3. Click on the magnifying glass icon in the toolbox to select the zoom tool and position the cursor just under the filament of the light bulb template.

The cursor now looks like a magnifying glass with a + in the middle. This indicates that the glass is in magnification mode, and when you click the mouse button, the image will be magnified to the next level of detail centered on the current cursor position. But we want to use the other function of this tool, and "zoom out" to reduce the image.

4. Hold down the Option key and click once. Your screen should look like Figure 2.6.

When you hold down the Option key, the magnifying glass has a – in it to indicate that the glass is in reduction mode, rather than magnification mode. If you want to, you can experiment with the zoom tool before proceeding. You will find that you can effectively move the image around on the drawing table by careful selection of the points for a zoom. You can always select Actual Size from the View menu (or use ⌘H from the keyboard) to get back to the same view you started with: actual size magnification and centered on the page. Before continuing with the light bulb, we'll discuss the uses of the zoom tool in a little more detail.

Reducing and Magnifying Images

Illustrator supports four levels of reduction and four levels of magnification from the initial actual size image. Each level is half (or twice) the preceding level, so that actual size, which is 100-percent magnification,

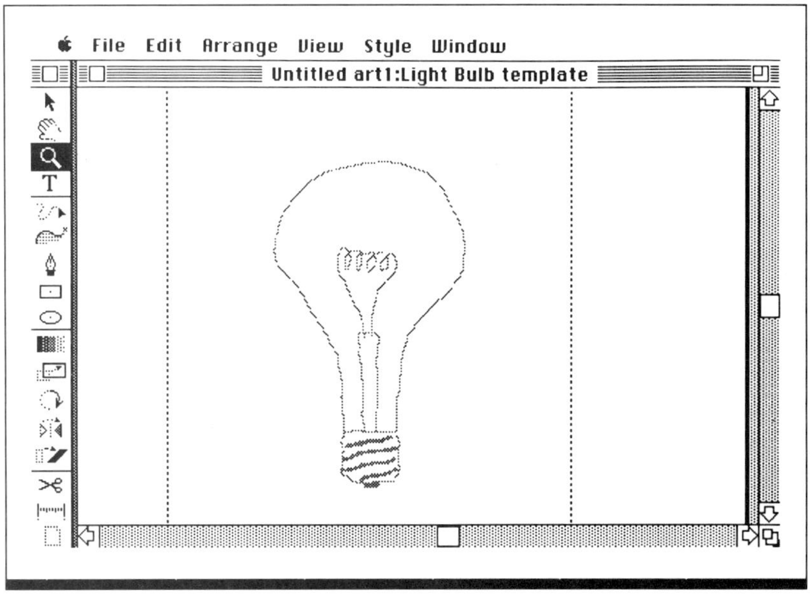

Figure 2.6: *Reduced view of light bulb*

is doubled to 200 percent or halved to 50 percent with the first click of the mouse and doubled again to 400 percent or halved again to 25 percent with the second click, and so on. With each application of the zoom tool, the rulers also change scale appropriately. The possible magnification values and associated ruler measures are listed in Table 2.1.

When you have reached the limit of magnification or reduction, the magnifying glass cursor is empty and no longer displays a + or −.

TRACING THE TEMPLATE

We'll cover the use of the autotrace tool (which is new to Illustrator 88) in Chapter 6.

Now that you have the reduced template on your screen, we're ready to begin. We'll start by tracing the template on the right side of the light bulb.

1. **Select the pen tool and move the cursor to the top of the light bulb template.**
2. **Click the mouse button and drag the cursor to the right.**

You will see the cursor turn into an arrowhead as long as you hold down the mouse button, and two points will extend from the center point

	RULER UNITS		
MAGNIFICATION	PICAS/POINTS	INCHES	CENTIMETERS
6.75%	64 picas	16 in.	10 cm
12.5%	32 picas	8 in.	10 cm
25%	16 picas	4 in.	5 cm
50%	8 picas	2 in.	5 cm
100%	4 picas	1 in.	1 cm
200%	2 picas	1/2 in.	1 cm
400%	1 pica	1/4 in.	0.5 cm
800%	6 points	1/8 in.	0.1 cm
1600%	3 points	1/16 in.	0.1 cm

Table 2.1: *Magnification and Ruler Values*

that you started from, as shown in Figure 2.7. The center point, which is a small square, is the anchor point. This is the same as the anchor points that mark the start and end of a line.

The two points at the end of the line extending out from the anchor point are direction points. These indicate the direction that the curve on each side will take from the anchor point. Illustrator assumes that the curve that you want to draw will be symmetric around the

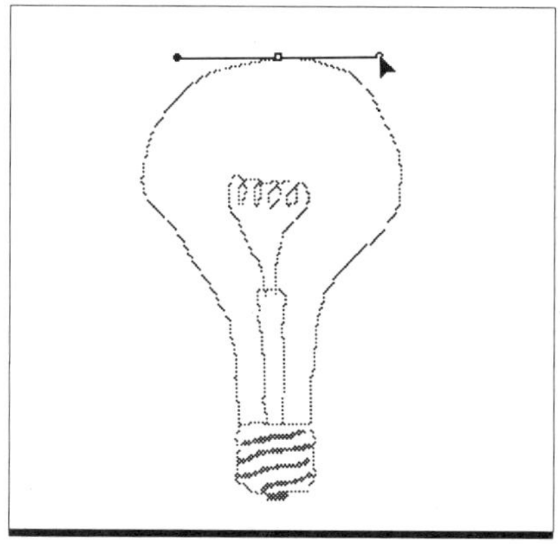

Step 2: *First anchor point*

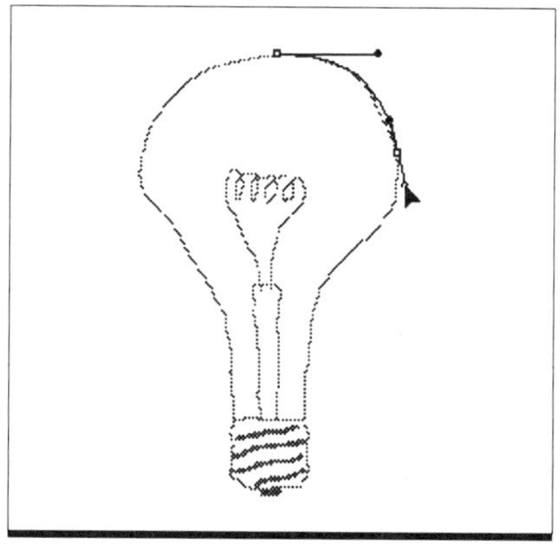

Step 5: *Second anchor point*

Step 6: *Third anchor point*

Figure 2.7: *Placing the first three anchor points*

anchor point, so both direction points move simultaneously in opposite directions. (Generally, this is a correct assumption; you will see later how you can change it.)

3. **Pull the direction point to the right about two-thirds of the way to the far right edge of the light bulb and release the mouse button.**

The cursor now changes from an x to a + form to show that you are continuing an existing line.

4. **Position the cursor about halfway around the globe of the light bulb and click and hold the mouse button.**

The cursor will become an arrowhead again, and you will see a curve spring up between the first anchor point and this new anchor point.

5. **Drag the direction point under the arrowhead cursor down a slight distance until the shape of the curve between the two anchor points matches the curve on the template, as shown in Figure 2.7.**

This is the basic technique for following curves. You click the mouse on the point that you want to be an anchor point and then drag the direction point in the direction that you want the curve to go. Later in the chapter, we will discuss some rules-of-thumb that you can use to estimate where to place anchor points and how far to drag direction points to get a good fit. Remember, if you make a mistake, you can undo the last segment of a line by selecting the Undo option from the Edit menu (or by using ⌘Z) or erase the entire current line by pressing the Delete or Backspace key twice.

6. **Move the cursor down to just above the point where the bulb shape curves down sharply toward the base of the light bulb and click and drag the direction point down toward the inside of the curve, as shown in Figure 2.7.**

This time you really can't get the curve to match the template very well. There is too much of a straight line between the two anchor points, especially up towards the top point—the second point that you placed. Because the curve on top of the second anchor point moves toward it at a different angle than it moves away from it, you can't match both sides of the curve. There is an easy way to correct this discrepancy.

7. **Move the cursor back to the direction point that extends from the second anchor point towards the third anchor point.**

You see that the anchor point is still a black ball, showing that it is selected for modification. As you may have guessed, you need to pull this direction point further down, without modifying the upper direction point, to change the curve to an asymmetrical shape and match the template.

8. **Press and hold down the Command key (the cursor changes to the selection arrow); then move the cursor to the direction point below the second anchor point.**
9. **Click and drag the direction point further down the template until the curve matches the template, as shown in Figure 2.8.**

You will notice that both the old and new lines remain visible in the artwork.

10. **Release the mouse button.**

The old line will disappear, and only the new one will remain. The result should look something like the modified curve shown in Figure 2.8, which clearly is a much better match to the template.

Notice that this modification only affected one side of the anchor point. That was because the top direction point is tied down; you can tell that it won't move because it doesn't appear as a solid black ball.

11. **Place another anchor point about the same distance down the stem of the light bulb as the third anchor point is above the point where the stem begins.**
12. **Click and drag to match the curve.**

This time, the curve is moving in the opposite direction than the earlier points, but the technique doesn't change.

13. **Place the next anchor point just at the junction of the base of the light bulb and the bulb itself (see Figure 2.8).**

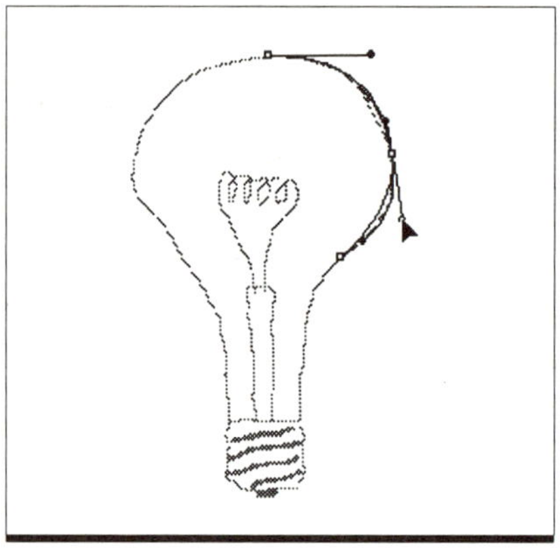

Step 9: *Modifying the second anchor point*

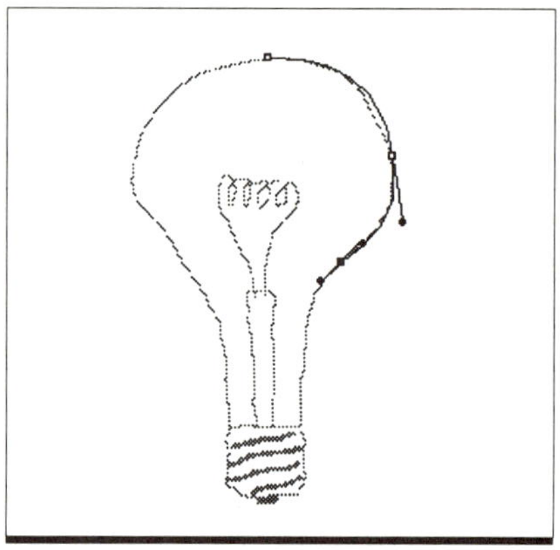

Step 10: *Curve after modification*

Step 13: *Anchor point at base and bulb junction*

Figure 2.8: *Modifying the curve*

14. Select the zoom tool, position the magnifying glass at the bottom of the light bulb template, and click twice.

This magnifies the image so that you can see the fine detail necessary to match the smaller curves that make up the screw base of the bulb, as shown in Figure 2.9. Notice that the template bits have become more pronounced, and that you still can see the last anchor point quite clearly, along with its direction points.

15. Begin placing anchor points to form the curves. Put one a short distance up the first screw ring, the next on the other side of the curve that marks the ring, the next near the bottom ring, and then one on the other side of the ring (see Figure 2.9).

16. Continue placing anchor points to trace the remainder of the base, as shown in Figure 2.9.

After you finish tracing the light bulb base, you need to reduce the figure to the size it was before.

17. Select and position the zoom tool on the light bulb base while holding down the Option key and click twice. You may also have to use the hand tool to return to the view that you started with.

18. Finish the light bulb, as shown in Figure 2.10. Close the figure by placing the last point on top of the first one (changing the cursor to an x again).

Now we need to set the painting parameters. As you saw in the last chapter, all figures default to being filled with black. Here we want a simple outline.

19. Pull down the Style menu and select Paint.

20. Set Fill to None and Stroke to 100% Black. Leave the line weight at 1 point.

If you selected Preview Illustration from the View menu now, you would see the light bulb outline, as shown in Figure 2.10.

21. Pull down the File menu, select Save, and name this drawing *Light Bulb art*.

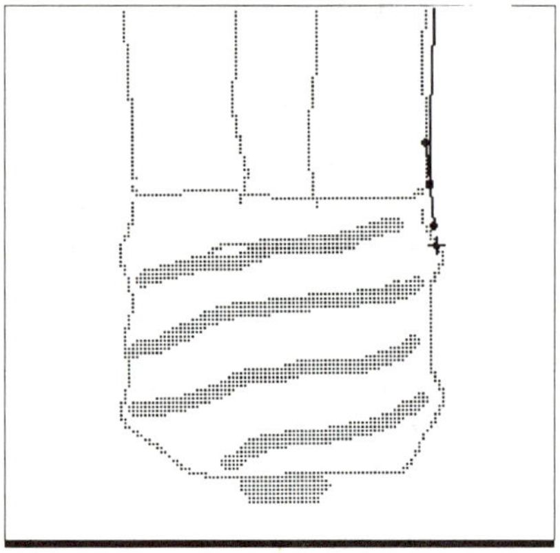

Step 14: *Light bulb base magnified*

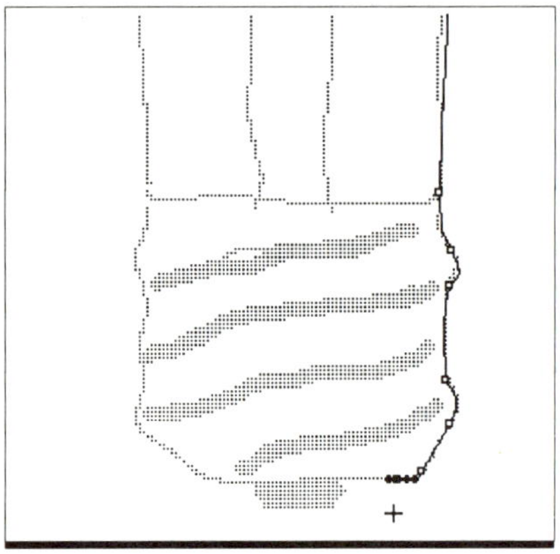

Step 15: *Beginning anchor points for base*

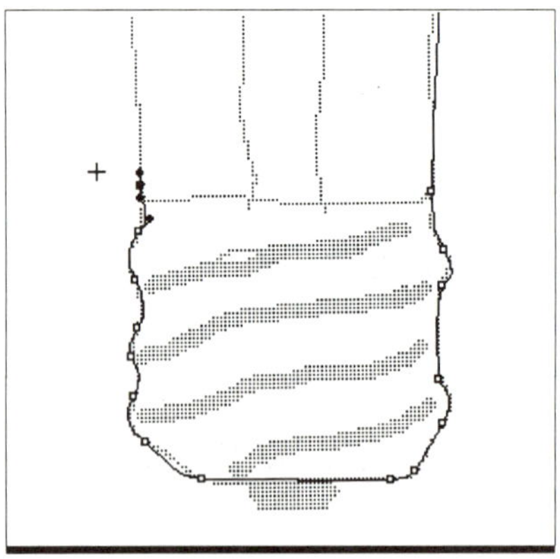

Step 16: *Light bulb base completed*

Figure 2.9: *Tracing the light bulb base*

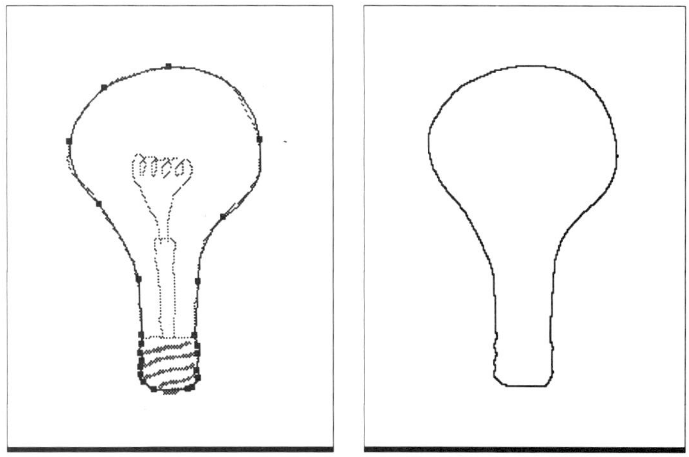

Step 18: *Finished light bulb outline* **Step 20:** *Preview of light bulb art*

Figure 2.10: *Completed light bulb outline and preview*

Now you have traced a complete, if basic, curved figure. You are familiar with how to place and maneuver anchor and direction points. You have seen how they look on the screen as artwork and how they affect the final image (displayed in preview mode). Next you'll see how to adjust the positioning of curved-line segments.

SELECTING AND CHANGING LINES

You can use the selection tool in a variety of ways to create and change line segments. We'll use this tool to make our light bulb more symmetrical.

1. **Select Open from the File menu, select Light Bulb art from the Open dialog box, and click on Open. Position the top of the light bulb in the center of the desktop.**

Rather than selecting Artwork Only from the View menu to see the best view of the selected line segments, leave the template in view so that you can see how the original artwork has been modified.

2. **Select the selection tool from the toolbox and click anywhere on the top-right side of the bulb.**

You will see all the anchor points on the figure displayed as small, open squares, as shown in Figure 2.11. The segment that you clicked on also shows the two defining direction points as black dots.

3. Drag the direction points to a new position to make the light bulb a little more symmetrical, as shown in Figure 2.11.

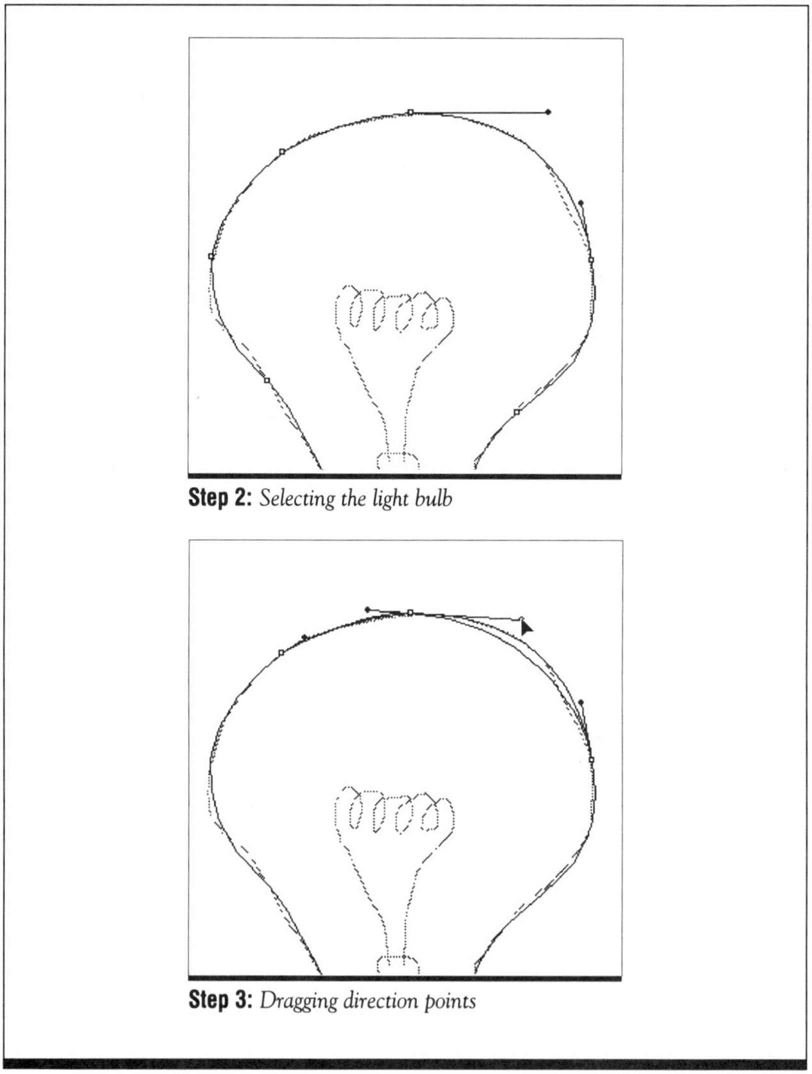

Step 2: *Selecting the light bulb*

Step 3: *Dragging direction points*

Figure 2.11: *Selecting and moving line segments (continues)*

As you saw before, Illustrator shows both the old and the new curve as you move the direction point. The old curve is only erased when you release the mouse button, leaving the direction point in the new position.

4. **Drag the anchor point on the right side of the bulb to a new location, as shown in Figure 2.11.**

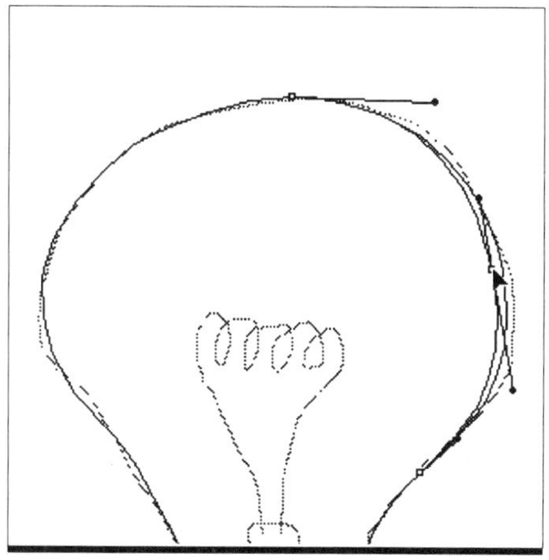

Step 4: *Dragging the anchor point*

Step 5: *Modified light bulb outline*

Figure 2.11: *Selecting and moving line segments (continued)*

This anchor point was the one that we adjusted earlier, where the direction points are not symmetrical. Notice that the direction point that governs the curve on the top of the anchor point is much closer to the anchor point than the one on the bottom of the curve. Both lie along a straight line, however, because the curve is defined as being tangent to that line at the anchor point. Later, in Chapter 4, you will see how to alter the direction points so that they don't have to lie on a straight line.

5. **Continue dragging selected anchor and direction points to modify the light bulb artwork so that it is more symmetrical, as shown in Figure 2.11.**

You may find it helpful to hide the template (since you are no longer following it) by choosing Artwork Only from the View menu.

6. **Save your modified artwork, either by selecting Save from the File menu or by using the ⌘S key combination.**

There is no dialog box this time because the file already has a name; the new version of the file simply replaces the old one.

Selecting Larger Areas

You've seen how to select and alter certain points on a drawing, but you will also want to select larger portions of drawings. If you want to select an entire figure, move the selection tool anywhere on the figure, hold down the Option key, and click. All the anchor points will appear as black squares, indicating that the entire figure is selected. No direction points will be visible; you cannot modify a single point when all points are selected. Figure 2.12 shows the entire light bulb artwork selected.

If you want to select more than one point, but not the entire figure, you can use one of two methods:

- Select any specific points by clicking on them with the selection tool in succession, while holding down the Shift key. This holds the previous selections and adds the newly selected point to the others. The points selected do not have to form a continuous segment; Illustrator will always show you exactly what is and is not selected by the coloring of the points. An example is shown in Figure 2.13.

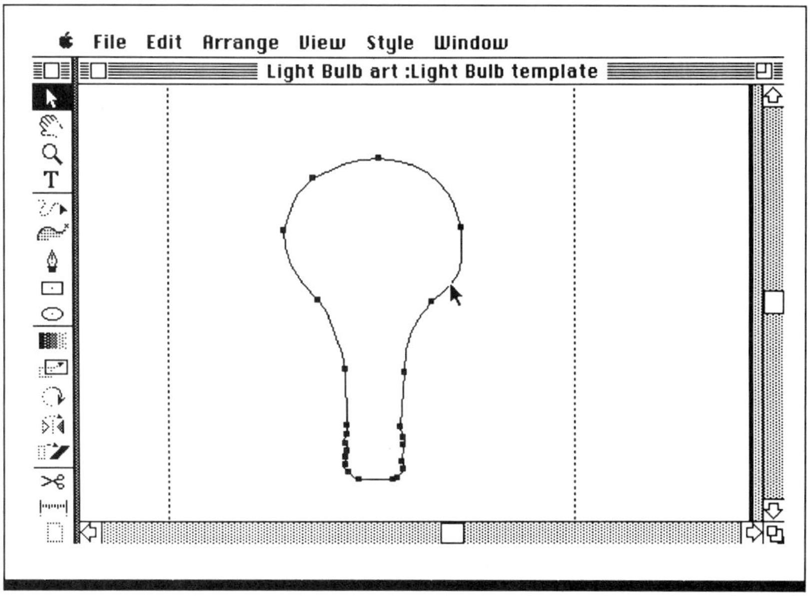

Figure 2.12: *Selection of entire artwork*

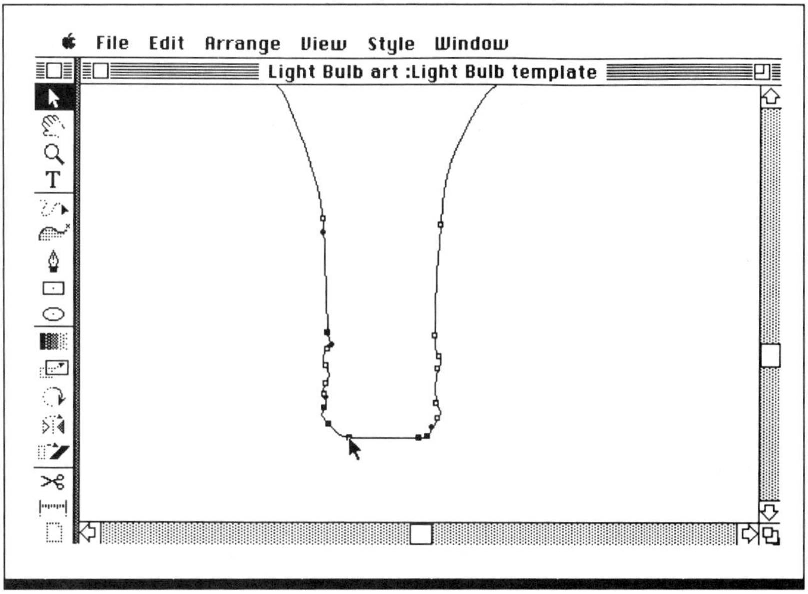

Figure 2.13: *Selection of several points*

- Use the selection tool to draw a selection marquee around a portion of the page, which can encompass a portion of a figure or figures, an entire figure, or multiple figures. All points within the box will be selected. Figure 2.14 shows a selection marquee and the selected points.

Remember that you can only modify the selected points. As we work along through more complex art, you will use the most suitable selection methods for the job at hand.

PRACTICING MATCHING CURVED LINES

In our next exercise, you will trace an outline drawing of an apple. This will help you practice matching curved lines to templates.

For this example, create the apple template shown in Figure 2.15 (another MacPaint format template). If you do not have a drawing program available, you can follow the placement of the anchor points to create the artwork without a template, matching the one shown in the figure as closely as possible.

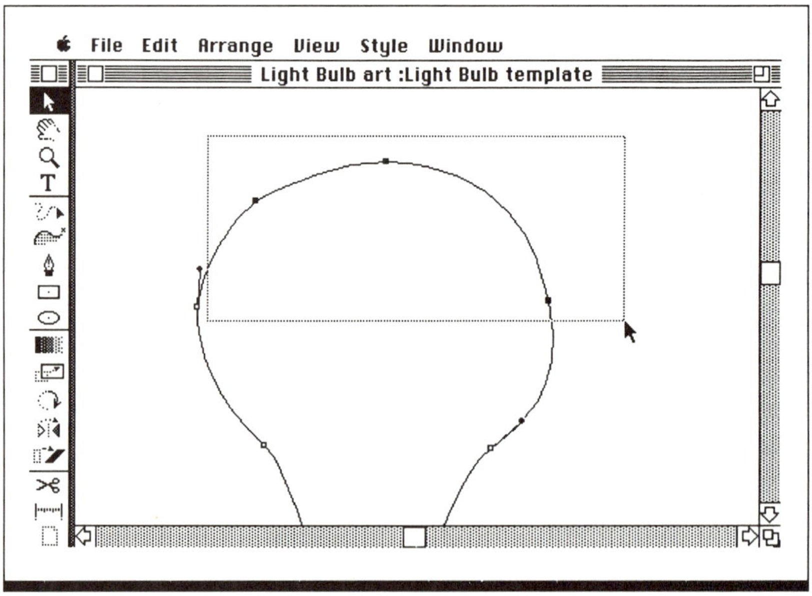

Figure 2.14: *Selection with a selection marquee*

GUIDELINES FOR TRACING CURVES

Before you begin tracing the template, we'll review some guidelines for anchor and direction point placement. Following these basic rules will make it easier for you to draw curves.

Start on a Smooth Curve

The best places to start tracing a template are those points that clearly will have an anchor point on them, no matter how you trace the image. Such points are usually the outside points of a smooth curve on the template, or sometimes at the top or bottom of a figure when the curve there is smooth. The important point to keep in mind is that the curve will move smoothly to and from the point you select.

If you place the first anchor point on a portion of the curve that is not smooth, you may find that you cannot make the artwork match the template when you return to that point to close the figure. This can be, to say the least, extremely frustrating; you have already traced the entire figure, only to discover at the end that you can't make it work. To avoid such annoying complications, always start on a smooth, even curve.

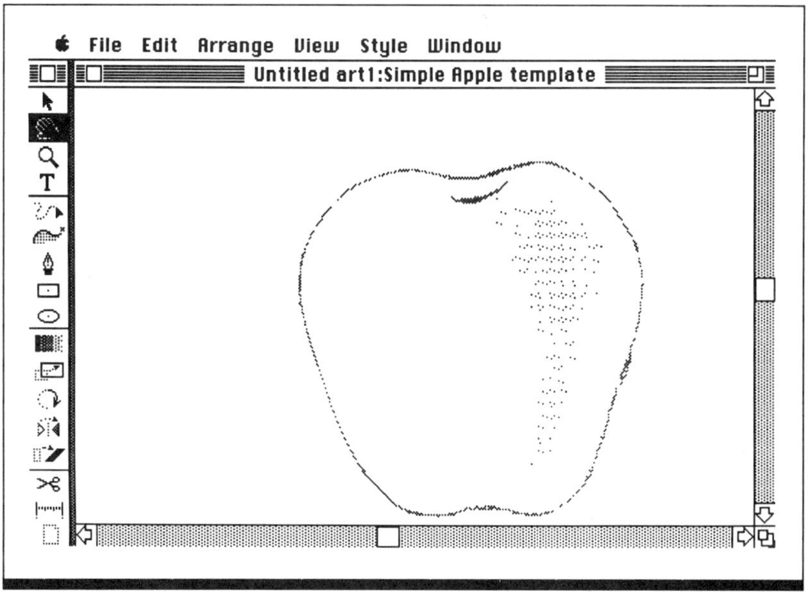

Figure 2.15: *Simple apple template*

The Bump Rule

Another rule that you should learn about placement of anchor points is to put them on either side of a "bump" rather than on the top or bottom. If you think of a curved line as a series of hills and valleys, this rule means that the anchor points should go on the sides of the hills, not on the peak, and not at the bottom of the valley.

If you look back at our earlier exercises, you will see why this rule works so well. Illustrator will always try to make a smooth curve going to and from an anchor point, and you can make the segment between the points curve as radically as you like. Placing the anchor points on the side of the hill gives you a lot more flexibility in matching the arc of the hill. Figure 2.16 illustrates this rule. The top line segment in the figure was created with anchor points placed on the sides of the bumps. The bottom line segment in the figure was created using anchor points at the tops and bottoms of the bumps.

The Stride Rule

You should trace a template using the largest strides possible that will still match the template. Another way to say this is that you should use

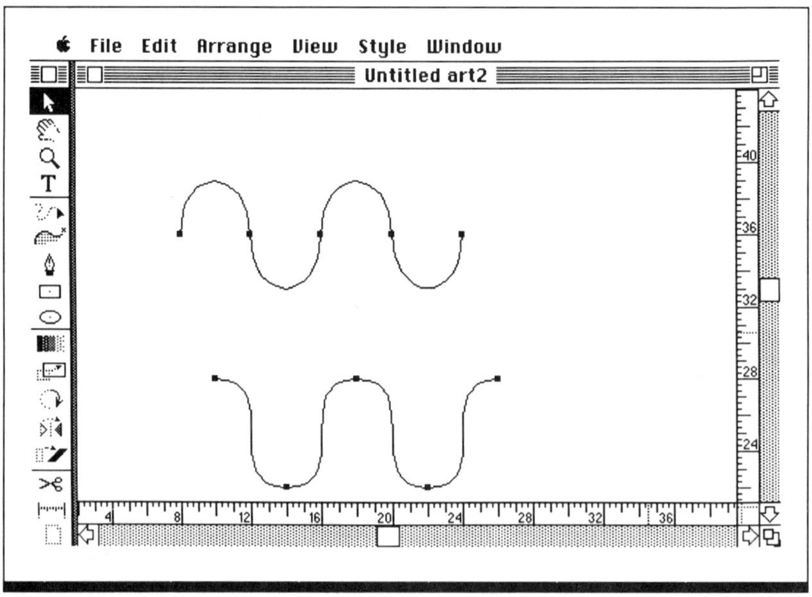

Figure 2.16: *Bump rule illustration*

the fewest number of line segments that will accurately render the template into artwork.

There are reasons of both efficiency and accuracy for following the stride rule. First of all, you will find it much easier to get a good match of a template when you use large segments. Smaller segments are harder to manipulate and more difficult to use to form a smooth curve. Since Illustrator does such a nice job of creating smooth curves, you really want to let it do as much of the curve matching as possible. Every anchor point constrains the curve to attach exactly to that point; therefore, the more anchor points you place, the more you are doing work that Illustrator could do for you. When there is a bump in the curve, you know that you have to guide the curve to match it by placing an anchor point; where there are no bumps, let Illustrator do the work.

Perhaps you can visualize this most easily by thinking of straight-line segments. For straight lines, corners are the equivalent of bumps for the curves. At every corner, you know you will have to place an anchor point because the line changes direction. But you also know that there isn't much point to placing anchor points between corners; since there is no change in direction, the line will run straight on without any additional constraint. The same process applies to curved-line segments. When there is a change in direction, at the beginning or end of a bump, you need to put in an anchor point; when there is no change, don't add an anchor point that you don't need.

Another reason for following the stride rule is program efficiency. Illustrator generates code to match the curve at each anchor point that you create. Each point represents information that has to be generated, transmitted, and interpreted within the output device to draw the line that you have specified. Less information required means less storage used, less transmission time, and faster output for your artwork.

The One-Third Rule

Besides these rules for placing anchor points, there is a good rule for creating direction points, known as the one-third rule. This rule says that you should make the line connecting the anchor point and the direction point about one-third of the total distance between the anchor point and the next anchor point. You will find this rule primarily useful for placing the first anchor point; after that, you will just position the direction points to match the template.

TRACING THE APPLE TEMPLATE

Now we are ready to draw some more curved lines.

1. **Place the anchor points for tracing the apple template, as shown in Figure 2.17.**

The placement of these anchor points follows the one-third, bump, and stride rules we just discussed. The point on the upper-right shoulder of the apple was chosen as the starting anchor point. Figure 2.18, which is the Artwork Only view of the apple, shows how the direction point extends about one-third of the distance of the first segment. If you look at the template, you will see that the direction of the line is tangent to the curve of the apple. However, the second and third anchor points illustrate very clearly how the one-third rule does not apply after you begin to trace. The curve takes such a slight bend here that the direction points are only a short distance from their respective anchor points, while the distance between the anchor points is much larger than the lines from the direction and anchor points.

There are clearly two bumps on both the top and bottom of the figure, and the slight but noticeable identation along the right side of the apple template forms another bump. It will require two points to determine each of these five bumps (one on each side, according to the bump rule), or a total of ten points. However, this is a closed figure, and two points will become one when you put the end of the last bump over the beginning of the first. Thus, you need nine points to define your artwork, and you should try to make the apple artwork consist of no more than nine strides, or segments (and no less—remember the bumps!).

2. **Pull down the Style menu and select Paint.**
3. **Set Fill to 50% Black, Stroke to 100% Black, and the line weight to .1.**
4. **Select Preview Illustration from the View menu. Your previewed artwork should look something like Figure 2.19.**

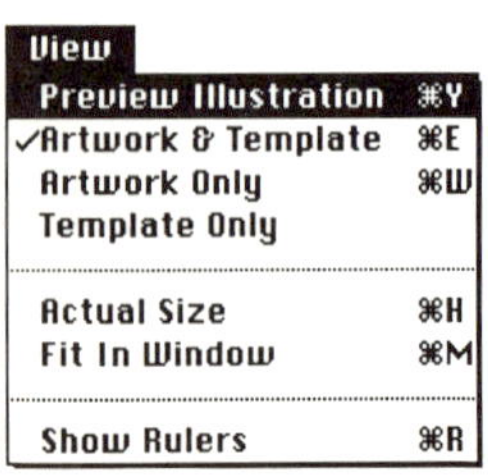

5. **Select Save from the File menu and save this artwork as Simple Apple art.**

We will use this apple template again in later chapters when we discuss techniques for adding complexity to existing artwork.

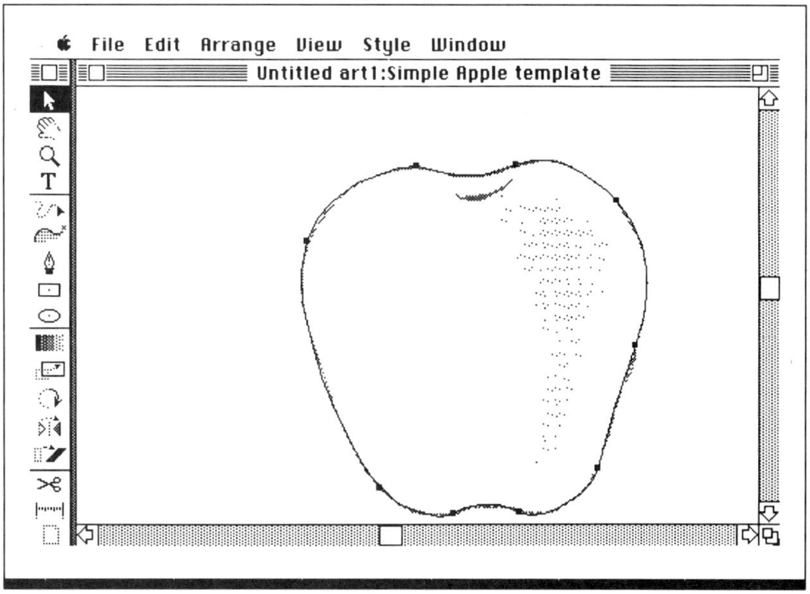

Figure 2.17: *Anchor points for apple template*

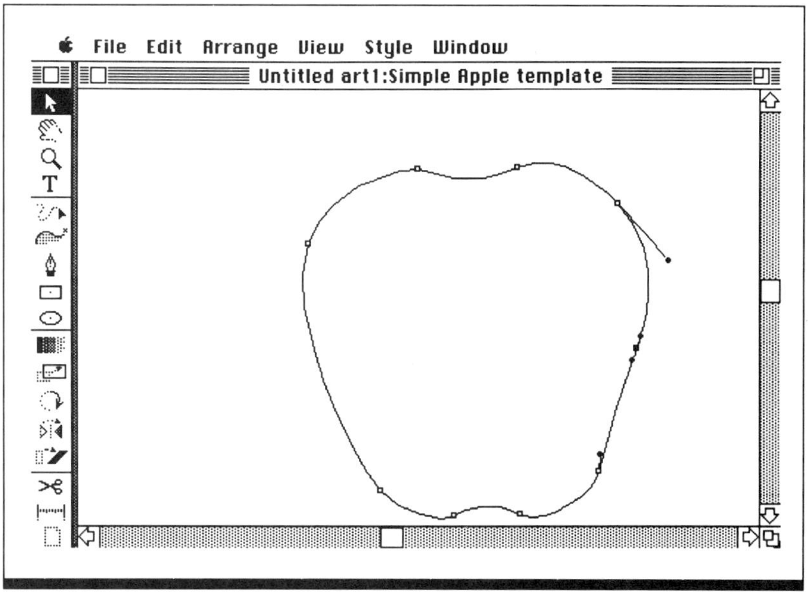

Figure 2.18: *Illustration of the one-third rule*

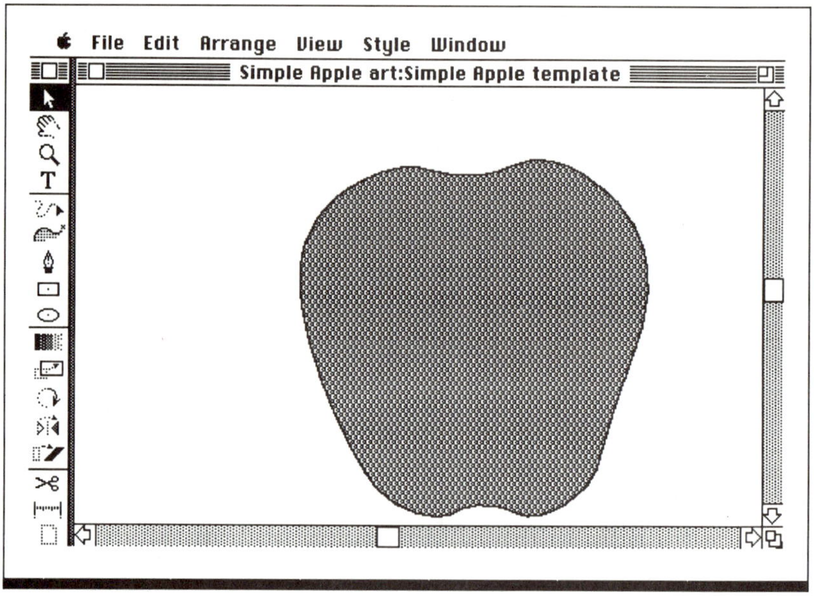

Figure 2.19: *Preview of apple artwork*

USING OPTIONS AND SHORTCUTS

This last section of the chapter covers a variety of ways to alter your artwork and discusses some shortcuts that you can take to make your work faster and easier. Table 2.2 summarizes these shortcuts.

You've already used the quick accesses to the zoom and hand tools. The one other tool that you will probably use frequently is the selection tool. As with the zoom and hand tools, Illustrator provides a quick method for accessing the selection tool. When you hold down the Command key, the cursor changes to the familiar arrow, indicating that the selection tool is in operation. In this mode, all the other optional key combinations will work on the selected area (while you keep the Command key depressed in addition to the other keys).

Along with being more convenient for correcting a curve you are drawing with the pen tool, this method of selection can prevent errors and extra work. For example, if you clicked on another tool when trying to choose the selection tool from the toolbox, or if you accidentally selected the wrong portion of the figure, Illustrator would assume that you are finished with the current segment (as indicated by the x form of the cursor). In this case, you would have to make some special effort to

FUNCTION	ACCESS
To access the hand tool	Press and hold down the space bar
To access the selection tool (arrow)	Press and hold down the Command (⌘) key
To access the zoom tool to zoom in	Press and hold down the space bar and the Command key
To access the zoom tool to zoom out	Press and hold down the space bar, Command key, and Option key tool icon
To zoom in on the center of the screen	Double-click on the zoom tool icon
To zoom out on the center of the screen	Double-click on the zoom tool icon while holding down the Option key
To select all points on a given figure	Press the Option key while selecting any part of the figure

Table 2.2: *Shortcuts to Accessing Tools and Features*

regenerate and connect the old part of the curve with the new. However, these types of errors are much less likely when you are using the optional selection cursor because you don't have to move and click the mouse so much.

Refining the Light Bulb Art

As a beginning, let's add some additional features to the light bulb you drew earlier in the chapter. Open the Light Bulb art document, and you will see the screen shown in Figure 2.20.

If you saved it correctly, you should also have the template associated with the artwork loaded automatically with it. If the template isn't loaded, locate it and associate it with the artwork as described earlier in the chapter. (Note that this is the modified version of the artwork, so it no longer conforms very closely to the template.)

Adding the Filament

Now we will add the filament in the center of the template to the original artwork. This is really two quite distinct objects: the filament and the rod, and it will be best to draw each of them separately and then combine them. Overlaying is a quite common and useful Illustrator

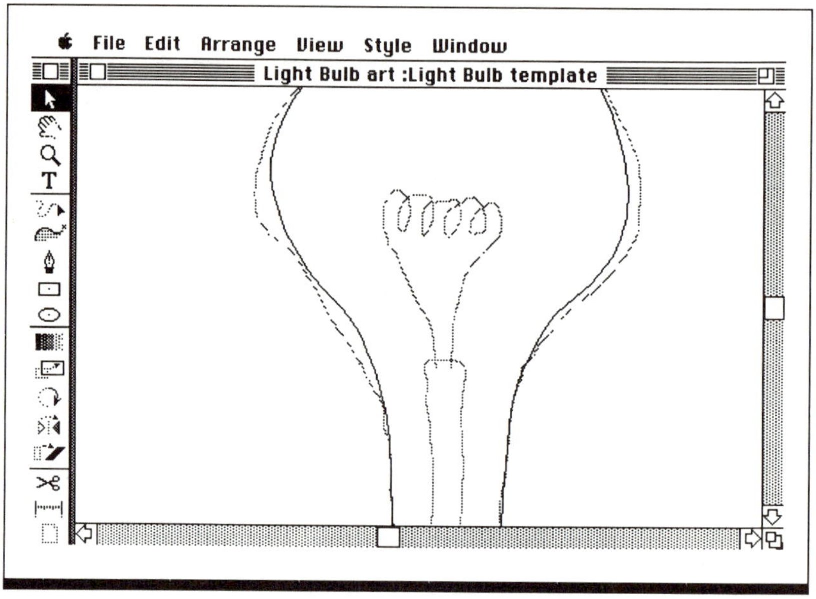

Figure 2.20: *Saved light bulb art*

technique. We will begin the work by drawing the actual filament in the center of the screen. This image is still rather small for the fine work that you want to do, so you need to zoom in on it. You could, of course, select the zoom tool from the toolbox, position it over the filament, and click—exactly as you have done several times before. However, there is a faster way.

1. **Double-click on the zoom tool, and Illustrator will magnify the image around the center of the screen, as shown in Figure 2.21. If the filament is not quite centered, use the hand tool to move the image until it appears as shown in the figure.**

This is one of the typical shortcuts that you can use to speed up your handling of images in Illustrator. If you had wanted to reduce the image instead of magnifying it, you could double-click on the zoom tool while holding down the Option key.

The filament is not a closed figure, unlike the previous portions of the artwork. As you can see, it begins and ends in the top of the rod.

2. **Select the pen tool and begin by placing three anchor points at the left side of the filament, at the top of the rod: one at the**

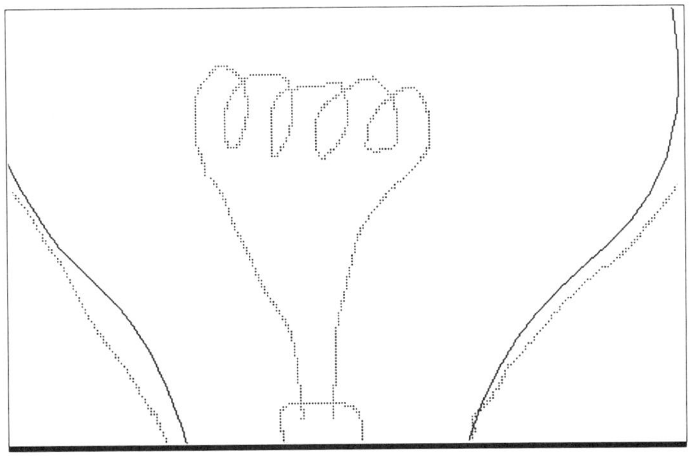

Step 1: *Magnifying the filament*

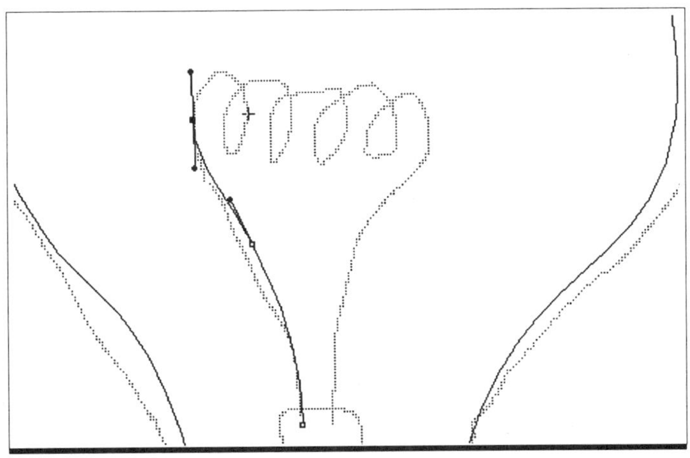

Step 2: *First four anchor points*

Figure 2.21: *Adding the filament (continues)*

start of the filament, one around the first curve (about halfway up the side), and a third at the edge of the spiral band, as shown in Figure 2.21.

Remember to use the bump and the one-third rules to help you place and adjust the first anchor points. Figure 2.21 also shows the positioning of the cursor for the fourth anchor point.

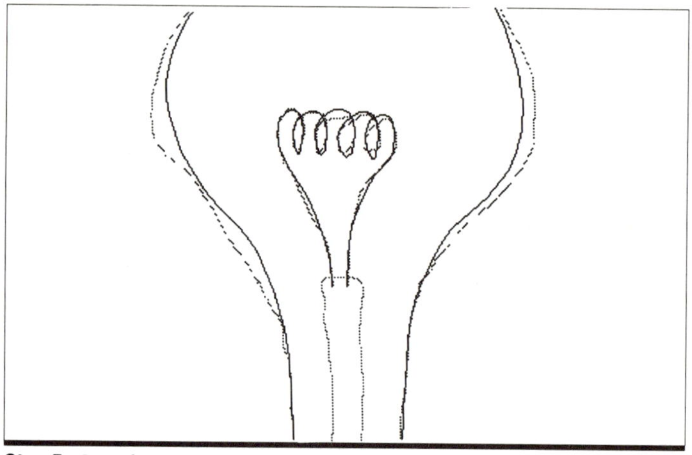

Step 5: *Completed filament*

Figure 2.21: *Adding the filament (continued)*

The spiral curve that forms the center of the filament is remarkably similar to the wave form that you saw in Figure 2.16 as an illustration of the bump rule. In this case the bumps overlap, but the principle for placement of the anchor points is the same.

3. **Complete the spiral curve. (You don't have to match the template; just use your own judgment to create a pleasing image.)**

Notice that Illustrator in pen mode is much easier to control than typical drawing programs (or in freehand mode) because you don't have to keep your hand steady while drawing the loops.

4. **Finish the rest of the filament by adding a point along the right side to bring the wire down, and then add the last point at the bottom right, opposite the starting anchor point, on top of the rod. If necessary, use the hand tool to adjust the image so that you can complete the figure correctly.**

You may find that, as you pull the direction point down from the final anchor point, you begin to go off the screen. This results in very rapid scrolling of the image in the direction that you're pulling, and you may lose sight of the anchor point. Don't be concerned. Just release the mouse button and change to the selection tool; then move the direction point back up toward the anchor point where you want it.

5. Double-click on the zoom tool while holding down the Option key to get a wider view. Your screen should look something like the finished art shown in Figure 2.21.

To complete this part of the exercise, let's set up the proper style options for the filament. We want the filament to paint as a thin wire, and the default settings would produce a filled black figure.

6. Select the selection tool from the toolbox, move it to any portion of the filament artwork, hold down the Option key, and click.

As we discussed earlier, this is the method for selecting an entire figure. All the anchor points should appear as black squares.

7. Pull down the Style menu and select Paint.

8. Change Fill to None, Stroke to 100% Black, and the line weight to .5 (or try another line weight).

9. Pull down the View menu and choose Preview Illustration.

10. Save the finished artwork so that you have a backup point to return to.

It's always a good idea to periodically save your work, especially when you come to a natural break point.

You may wonder why the filament artwork would paint as solid black when the figure isn't closed; after all, the two end points, although close together, are quite distinct. Actually, Illustrator will try to close any figure if the Fill option in the Paint dialog screen is set to any value. It does this by drawing an implicit line joining the two endpoints of the figure to be filled.

Drawing the Rod

We will continue to use some Illustrator shortcuts (such as zooming in and out quickly) to complete the light bulb artwork by adding the glass rod that supports the filament wire. To begin, be sure that the template is visible on your screen. If not, select Artwork & Template from the View menu.

1. Select the pen tool from the toolbox and move the cursor over to the top of the rod template.

2. Hold down the space bar and the Command key.

You will see the cursor change to the familiar magnifying glass with the + in the middle, indicating that the zoom tool is now in operation.

3. **While holding down these two keys, click the mouse button to magnify the image around the point where the cursor is positioned. Your screen should look something like the image shown in Figure 2.22.**

You can also invoke the reverse operation, reduction, by simply holding down the Option key in addition to the Command key and space bar to use the zoom tool with the – in the middle.

This portion of the template raises some interesting questions. You remember the bump rule, but how should you apply it here? Is the top of the rod one bump or more? Remember the sample curves that you saw earlier (in Figures 2.2 and 2.3), which showed that the curve between two anchor points will be smooth, even when you can force it to be asymmetric. The top of the rod is not smooth, although it is symmetric. The curve to define this portion of the template has to bend quite a bit, then flatten out for a way, and then bend quite a bit again. This will never happen with just one curve; this is two bumps.

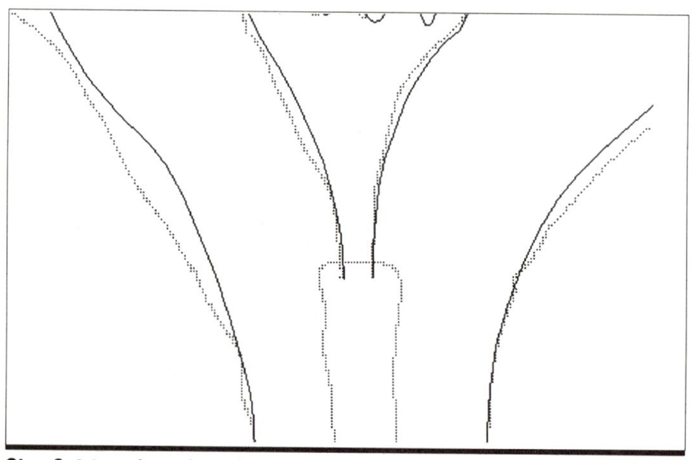

Step 3: *Magnifying the rod*

Figure 2.22: *Adding the rod (continues)*

4. Look at the top of the rod and estimate about half of the distance across the top. Move the pen cursor down the left side of the rod about that distance, or slightly less. Place your first anchor point there, and drag the direction point about even with the top of the rod.

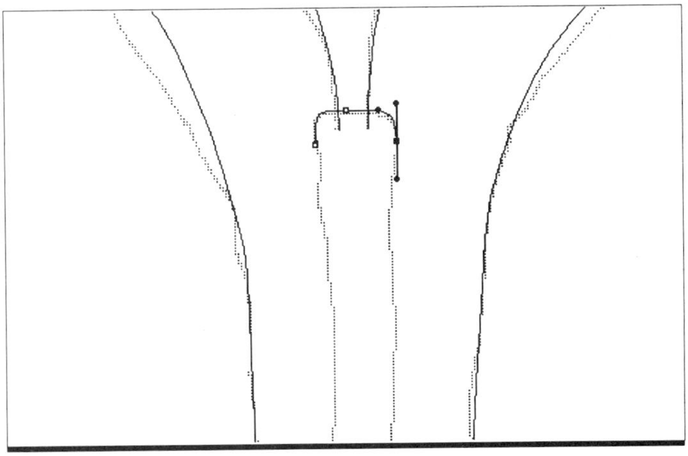

Step 6: *First three anchor points*

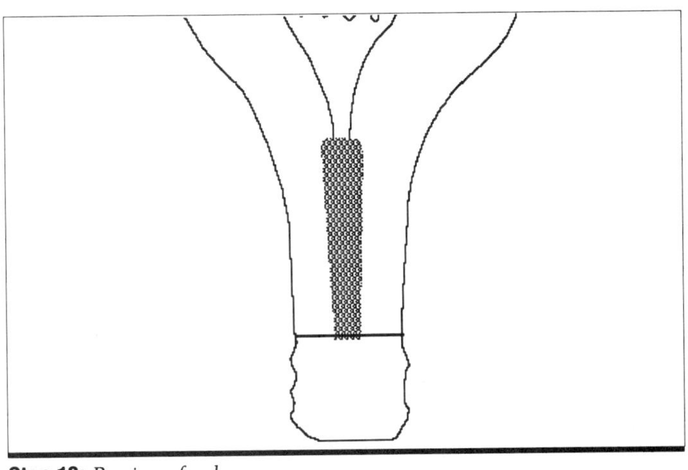

Step 18: *Preview of rod*

Figure 2.22: *Adding the rod (continued)*

5. Place the second anchor point in the center of the top of the rod and drag the direction point out enough to match the left corner curve.
6. Place the third anchor point down the right side of the rod, about opposite to the first anchor point, and again drag the direction point to match the corner curvature.

Figure 2.22 shows the placement of the three anchor points.

7. Press and hold down the space bar to access the hand tool and scroll down to display the bottom of the rod.
8. Position the cursor slightly below the top of the base and click once. Do not drag the direction point (you want to create a straight line from the last anchor point to this point).
9. Move across the rod to the other side.
10. Hold down the Shift key and click once again to force a perfectly horizontal straight line.
11. Scroll back up to display the beginning point on the screen, using the space bar to access the hand tool.
12. Place the cursor over the first point and click to create a straight line from the right bottom of the rod and close the rod figure.
13. Pull down the Style menu, select Paint, change Fill to 50% Black, and set Stroke to None.

If you preview this image, you will notice that the rod floats inside the bulb. You need to place a line across the bulb to separate the base of the bulb from the glass and rod.

14. Go back and select the pen tool if it is not still active.
15. Hold down the space bar and Command key and click the mouse to zoom in on the base and bottom of the rod until you have quite a bit of detail.
16. Draw a straight line across the bulb, above the base of the rod, using the Shift key to constrain the line to horizontal.
17. Pull down the Style menu, select Paint, and change Fill to 100% Black and the line weight to 2 points.

18. **Select Preview Illustration from the View menu. The image should look something like the one shown in Figure 2.22.**

Moving the Baseline

You will notice in our current light bulb artwork (Figure 2.22) that the base of the rod shows below the cutoff line that defines the base. We have to join the two ends together, so that nothing shows below the line, by moving the line to cover the base of the rod.

Let's assume that you still have the pen tool selected. You can do all the changing that is necessary without ever moving back to the toolbox.

1. **Move the cursor to a position on the line that you want to move, hold down the Option and Command keys simultaneously, and click.**

You have now selected the entire line, as shown by the two selected anchor points at each end of the line.

2. **Hold down only the Command key, and click and drag the line to the new position that covers the base of the rod—just down a short bit.**

As before, you will see the line in both the old and the new positions as you move it.

3. **Release the mouse button and then release the Command key to move the line to the new position and eliminate the old copy of the line.**

Suppose that the move hasn't gone right, or that you now see that you haven't moved the line correctly.

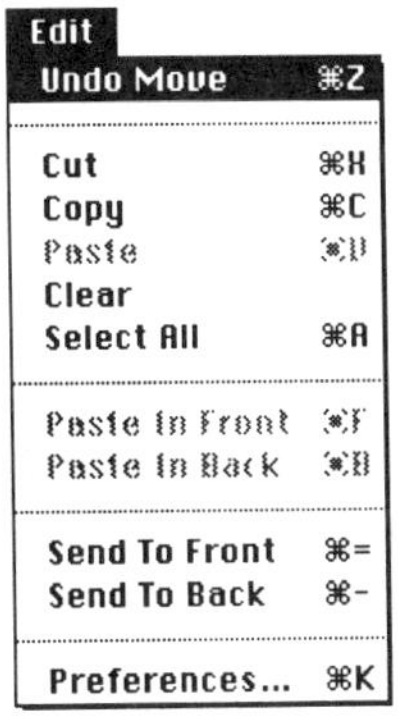

4. **Pull down the Edit menu and select Undo Move, which will be the first item in the menu.**

When you click on Undo Move, the line jumps back to its previous place. This is a perfect example of one way to correct errors.

5. **Adjust the positioning of the line. If the line was where you wanted it, select the first item on the Edit menu, which now says Redo Move, to put it back.**

6. **Select Preview Illustration from the View menu. The rod should end correctly at the baseline, as shown in Figure 2.23.**
7. **Select the Artwork & Template view and scroll up, holding down the space bar to access the hand tool, to show the filament and the top of the rod.**

You can see that the filament is not quite centered in the rod.

8. **Move the filament over by using the selection tool shortcut to select the filament as a unit and move it slightly to the right.**

It is important to select the entire object so it moves as a unit. That's why you must press the desired key or keys, then move and click the mouse, and then release the keys. Reversing the order may produce surprising results. If, for example, you continue to press the Option key while you move the selected graphic, you will copy the figure, not move it. If you only grab part of it, only that portion will move. If you make this kind of mistake, use the Undo Move option from the Edit menu.

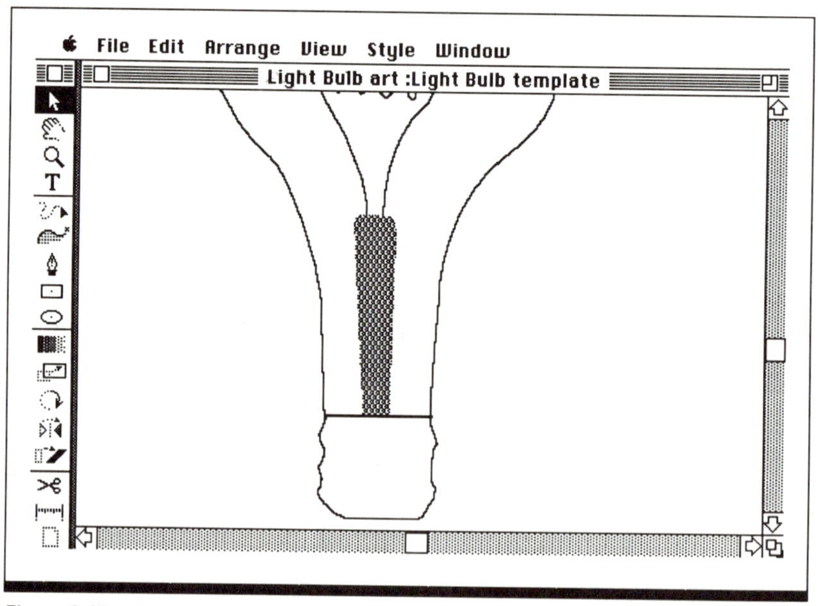

Figure 2.23: *Edited baseline and rod*

Filling in the Base

Our next refinement to the light bulb art will be to fill in the screw base. We could do this in a variety of ways; for example, we could draw thick individual lines, or we could outline each part of the screw lines at a high magnification to produce a more realistic image. However, we'll use a different technique here. To complete the screw base, we'll generate filled objects (ovals) to mimic the effect of the thick lines.

1. **Magnify the base of the light bulb until it fills a good portion of the screen.**

2. **Select the circle tool from the toolbox.**
3. **Starting about a quarter of the way inside the base, create four thin ovals that more or less match the four screw shadow lines on the template, as shown in Figure 2.24.**

We could use the ovals as they are to represent the screw lines. (You may even want to preview the artwork now to see how they look.) But let's go one step further and angle the ovals to make the artwork more closely match the template.

4. **Select the rotate tool from the toolbox.**

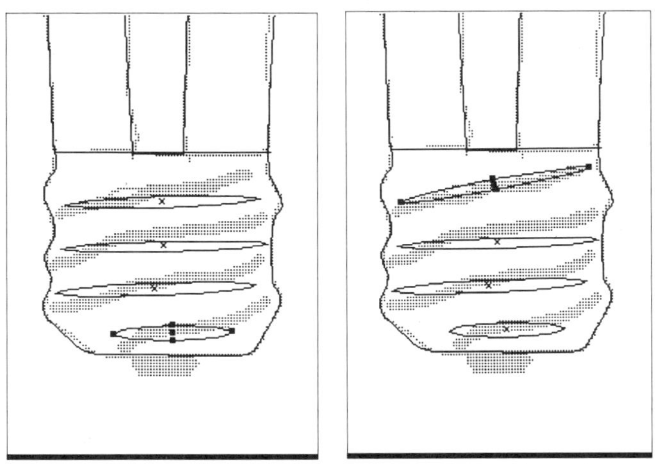

Step 3: *Drawing the ovals* **Step 8:** *Positioning first oval*

Figure 2.24: *Ovals on light bulb base*

This is the fourth tool from the bottom of the toolbox. It looks like a curved arrow between two lines. When you select it, the cursor becomes a +.

5. **Move the cursor to the end of the top oval.**
6. **Hold down the Command key and select the oval, and then click on a point just behind the left end of the oval.**

The cursor changes to an arrowhead shape to indicate that you should move the selected object.

7. **Position the arrowhead at the far right end of the oval, click, and move the oval up.**

You will see the oval rotate around the point that you first clicked as you move the arrowhead cursor.

8. **When the oval is in position (see Figure 2.24), release the mouse button.**

Now the cursor becomes a + again, and the oval is slanted more or less like the screw line.

9. **Use the selection tool to adjust the oval to its final position over the screw line, as shown in Figure 2.24.**
10. **Use the same technique to match the other three ovals to the lines on the template.**

We'll discuss rotation techniques in more detail later in the book (in Chapter 5).

Because we want the screw base ovals to be filled, we should set them to 100% Black Fill.

11. **Pull down the Style menu, select Paint, set Fill to 100% Black, and click on OK. (If Fill is already set to the default 100% Black, just click on OK.)**

You can preview the artwork to see how the filled ovals appear.

Positioning the Cap

To complete the light bulb, we'll add the small contact cap on the base. Again, there are several ways to approach this task. For example, we could simply draw the cap. Instead, we'll use the oval tool again.

1. **Select the circle tool from the toolbox and move the cursor to the base of the light bulb.**
2. **Magnify the base, if necessary, to get a good view of your working area.**
3. **Draw a relatively flat oval that matches the cap in width (don't worry about matching the height just yet).**
4. **Position this oval over the cap, as shown in Figure 2.25.**

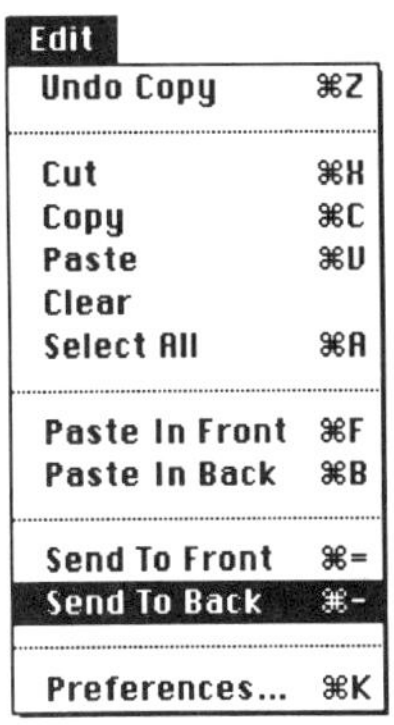

If you preview this image now, you will see that the base looks very close to how you want it, especially in a full-page view. However, we still need to adjust it so that only the portion of the oval that does not overlap the base shows.

5. **Select the cap oval, and then select Send To Back from the Edit menu.**

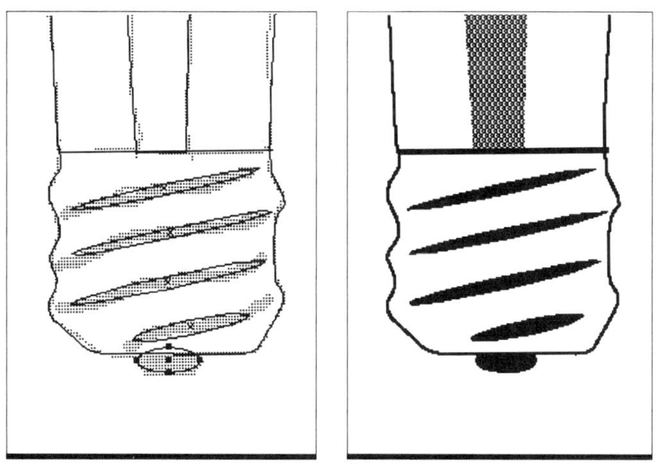

Step 4: *Positioning cap* **Step 7:** *Preview of cap*

Figure 2.25: *Positioning the contact cap*

If you are using Illustrator 1.1, you will have to cut the oval out of the artwork and then use Paste In Back from the Edit menu to reposition it. Send To Back and Bring To Front are just convenient shortcuts for cutting and pasting.

The oval is now placed behind the selected graphic—in this case, the light bulb outline. The oval will now be painted before the light bulb, so that the outline of the bulb will cover the oval. But we have to change one more thing to get the proper effect. We created a transparent light bulb outline (by choosing None for Fill from the Paint dialog screen), so now the base does not obscure the top of the contact cap. You must change the Fill option to get the right effect.

6. **Select the light bulb outline, select Paint from the Style menu, and change Fill to White. Figure 2.25 shows the result.**

You may wonder why the entire figure of the light bulb didn't fill with white and obscure the interior artwork (the filament and the rod). Actually, it did fill with white, but the filament and rod are still visible because they were created after the light bulb. By default, Illustrator paints objects in the order that they were created. You created the light bulb first, so it is the first object to be painted; the filament was created and painted next; and then the rod, followed by the base screws and contact. You deliberately forced the contact cap artwork to be painted before the light bulb; all the rest of the figures have retained their original order.

If you look carefully, you can see this same effect in the placement of the filament and the rod. A small portion of the filament actually extends down into the area painted by the rod. Yet, because of the paint order, the rod covers up the filament, even though the rod is 50% Black and the filament is 100% Black. Unless you have specifically selected None as the Fill option, the colors in Illustrator are entirely opaque.

Fast Track Chapter 3

88 **All fonts must be available**
to your output device (e.g., printer) before they can be used by Illustrator.

91 **To reduce or enlarge**
(scale) a selected object, click on a point of it with the scale tool and drag it into its position for the scaled version.

92 **To set scaling parameters,**
click on the scale origin (the fixed point for the scaling operation) with the scale tool while holding down the Option key. This accesses the Scale dialog box, in which you can specify scaling percentage, line weight scaling, and nonuniform scaling.

93 **To place type on a graphic,**
select the text tool and click on the text-entry point to access the text dialog box. Enter the text, select the font, and set the appropriate type size, leading, spacing, and alignment parameters.

103 **To revise the type parameters**
for an existing block of text, select that text block and choose Type from the Style menu (or press ⌘T) to access its text dialog box. Reset the parameters to change the text as necessary.

105 **To quickly make a copy of a figure,**
select it with the selection tool, hold down the Option key, and click and drag the figure to where you want the copy.

Chapter 3

ADDING TEXT TO GRAPHICS

Up to now, you have been absorbed in producing graphic images using the basic Illustrator tools and commands. Many graphics, however, require words as an integral part of the image, and Illustrator has facilities that enable you to place and edit such type. In this area, Illustrator falls in between drawing programs that treat letters just like all other graphics and provide no facilities for revising text and complete word-processing programs that provide extensive editing capabilities. Illustrator provides some text-revision capabilities, but it does not have extensive text-processing features. However, for most purposes, you will find the Illustrator facilities sufficient for integrating text with your graphics.

Text generation is one area where Illustrator is very closely connected to the PostScript language (the language of the program). Although we will discuss this important relationship in Appendix B, there will be several references to PostScript processing in this chapter as well.

WORKING WITH FONTS

Before we begin using Illustrator to place text, we'll review an essential element of text processing: fonts. A *font* is defined as a set of type—meaning a complete collection of characters and punctuation—in one style and size.

FONT FAMILIES AND NAMES

Fonts can be grouped in a variety of ways. The simplest and most obvious is by design, or *typeface*. Most of these designs have names, which represent a complete range of fonts with a common design but in different sizes and styles. Such a set of fonts is called a *font family*. Although a font, properly speaking, is only one size in a particular style of typeface design, I will use the term to refer to the whole font family of that particular typeface, unless a distinction should be made.

The font families can be classified into three basic categories:

- *Serif fonts* have small lines finishing off the major strokes of each letter, similar to the effect left by a chisel on stone, or a calligraphic pen on paper. The Times fonts, which you are probably familiar with from your local newspaper, are serif.
- *Sans-serif fonts* are distinguished by the absence of these small finishing lines. The Helvetica fonts are sans-serif. Generally, serif fonts look more traditional, while sans-serif fonts have a more modern appearance.
- *Typewriter fonts* are those that don't fall easily into either of the other two groups. One such font is Courier, which is primarily used for typewritten output.

FONT SIZES

Every character in a font has height and width. The width of a character within a font is called *pitch*. All characters in a typewriter font have a single width. Such fonts are called *fixed-pitch*, or *monospaced*, fonts. Characters in most fonts, however, have different widths depending on the shape of the individual character; these are called *variable-pitch*, or *proportional*, fonts.

Font height is generally given in points, just like the spacing on the page. The most usual size for reading type is 10 points, and 4-point type is about the smallest size that remains readable. There are 72 points in 1 inch, so 36-point type, for example, is approximately 1/2 inch high and proportionately wide.

FONT ACCESS

All fonts must be available to your output device before they can be used by Illustrator. There are several methods of making fonts available:

- Every PostScript output device has some built-in fonts, which are already available. At a minimum, all PostScript-equipped devices have the Times, Helvetica, and Courier fonts.

- You can send a copy of the font from your computer to the printer to be stored in the printer's electronic memory. This process is called *downloading*.
- You can create an entirely new font using PostScript operators or by making bit-mapped images of the necessary characters.

Each copy of a font requires memory within the printer controller, and each make and model of printer can hold a different amount of fonts in its memory. Sometimes there is a tradeoff between the number and size of the fonts and the size and complexity of the pages that can be handled by the printer.

In addition to being available to your printer, the fonts, or some approximation of them, must also be available for display on your screen. These *screen fonts* are important because Illustrator uses the same mechanism to generate the preview image as the printer uses to generate the image on the output page. If you don't have the screen fonts available for Illustrator to use, the screen image will not be the same as the printed output.

FONT SOURCES AND OWNERSHIP

Those that are not familiar with the world of printing and typesetting are usually surprised to discover that not all fonts are public property. In fact, almost all the high-quality, elegant fonts are private property; the designs are licensed to companies who want to incorporate the fonts into various devices. For example, Times-Roman and Helvetica are licensed fonts.

The type styles and sizes used in the exercises in this book are limited to those fonts that are built-in to every PostScript printer, so that every reader will be able to follow along. Feel free to use any other fonts that you have available. Similarly, if you would rather use different point sizes, go ahead.

ADDING TEXT TO ARTWORK

Now that we have established a common terminology for dealing with text, we can turn to using type and text in Illustrator images. In this section, we will add text to an image that we created in previous exercises.

CREATING A LETTERHEAD DESIGN

In Chapter 1, we created a simple logo for an imaginary company. Now we will add text to that artwork to make a complete letterhead. This is part of a process that will develop a complete page, using the logo and letterhead.

In order to make a letterhead out of the logo, we need to reduce the size of the logo artwork and add the company name and address. These steps can basically be done in two ways: you can do it to measure, or you can do it by eye. These methods are not exclusive; you can use both in combination, and this is what we will do in our exercise.

The original logo artwork is bordered by a frame 36 picas wide and 24 picas high. (If you have any questions about the ruler measures, check back to Table 2.1.) We want to reduce this to a box approximately 13.5 picas wide and 9 picas high.

Before we begin, bring the saved version of the logo artwork onto the Illustrator desktop. Reduce the image by one click and move it to the center of the screen. Also, set the rulers on, so that we can work to a fixed scale for those parts of the exercise that will be done to measure. At this point, your screen should look like Figure 3.1.

Reducing the Logo

The first step is to reduce the logo to an appropriate size. When we created the logo, we sized every piece to match every other piece, so the logo should be reduced exactly proportionately to maintain these relationships. Also, we will need to adjust the line width for the strokes that are used for the figures.

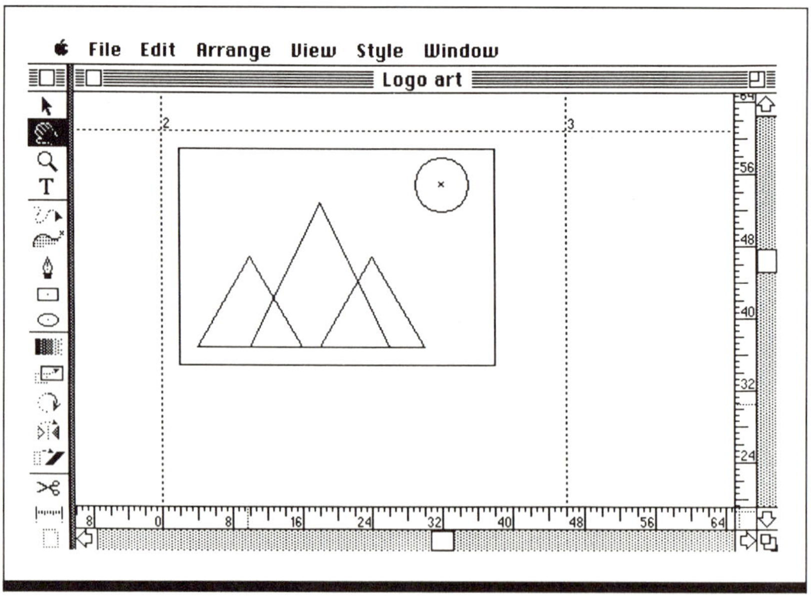

Figure 3.1: *Logo artwork revisited*

1. Pull down the Edit menu and choose Select All (or press ⌘A).

You could also use the selection tool, either by selecting it from the toolbox or by holding down the Command key, to select the entire figure. When you're done, every graphic on the page should be selected. This is shown by the presence of black squares at all the anchor points.

2. Select the scale tool from the toolbox.

This tool will reduce or enlarge selected objects in any way you wish. In this case, we want to shrink the logo artwork to a smaller version of itself in the upper-left corner of the page. Since the corner of the logo is already positioned there, you can just shrink the artwork evenly by moving the lower-right corner up and to the left.

3. Move the scale tool to the upper-left corner of the frame, and hold down the Option key.

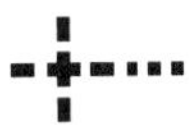

When you press the Option key, the cursor changes shape from a + to a sort of sideways t.

4. Click the mouse button to set the *scale origin* (the fixed point around which the scaling operation will occur). You will see the dialog box shown in Figure 3.2.

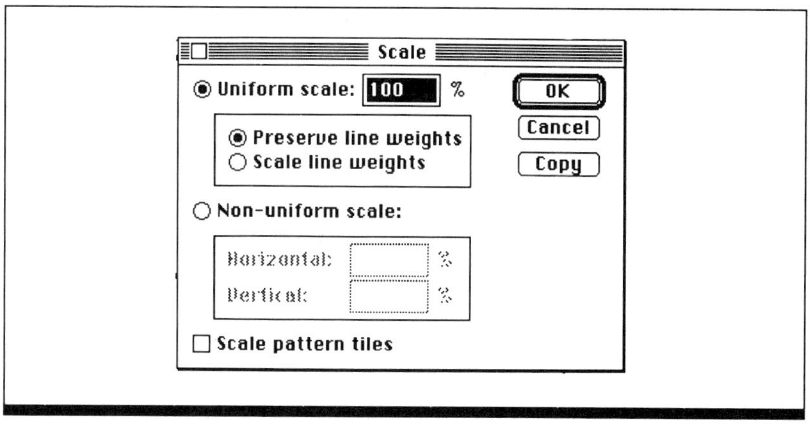

Figure 3.2: *Scale dialog box*

The Scale dialog box allows you to scale the line weights of the reduced artwork. You could scale the logo manually by dragging a point of it to create the scaled version (by using the scale tool without pressing the Option key), but with that method, the original line weights are preserved. We will discuss that option and other related tools and dialog boxes in more detail in Chapter 5. For now, we will use the option that scales the line weights along with the figure (for example, if you halve the size of the figure, you will also halve the thickness of its lines).

5. **Click on the button next to Scale line weights.**

There is also a sneaky way to get Illustrator to determine the scaling percentage for you. This method is discussed in Chapter 5 with the more advanced scaling and transformation features.

The dialog box also offers the options of scaling the figure either uniformly in both the x and y directions, or nonuniformly, by choosing different horizontal and vertical scaling factors. We want to scale this figure uniformly along both axes. This means that you must enter the precise percentage of reduction. In this case, it is just the ratio of the 9-point height you want to the existing 24-point height, which comes to 37.5 percent.

6. **Enter 37.5 in the box next to Uniform scale.**
7. **Click on OK to make the change. The result will look like Figure 3.3.**

The artwork is now an appropriate size for a logo on a letterhead. Let's ensure that we don't lose all this good work.

8. **Save the artwork with the name *Reduced Logo art*.**

Setting Up the Letterhead

Now we can proceed with the second step of adding text to the logo. We will add the name of the company, Mountain Sports Ltd., and its address and telephone numbers to the right of the logo. The name of the company will be larger than the address and telephone information. All the text should be approximately centered between the logo and the edge of the paper.

The company name should be placed about halfway up the logo artwork and halfway between the artwork and the right margin. The logo artwork is 9 picas high, as we calculated earlier, and 13.5 picas wide. The upper-left corner of the logo is at (2, 58), so the logo extends approximately to the 16-pica position on the x-axis and to the 49-pica

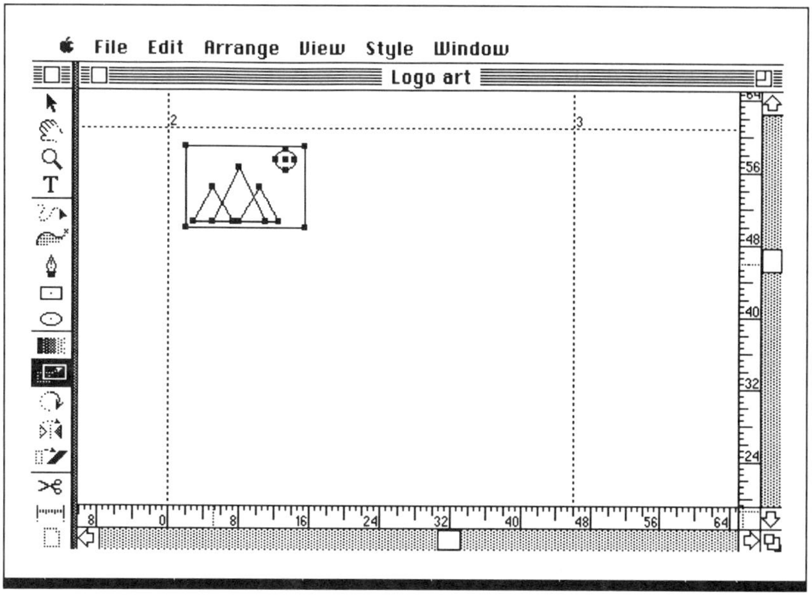

Figure 3.3: *Reduced logo*

position on the y-axis. You can verify this by checking the position of the bottom-left corner of the logo frame.

To position the text for the company name vertically, you want to be along the y-axis line at 53.5 picas, or 58 − 4.5 (half of the 9 picas). You want to center the text along the x-axis at a point halfway between the edge of the logo at 15.5 and the edge of the print area at 46. That would be at a point about 15 picas in, or at about 30 picas on the ruler.

PLACING TEXT ON THE LETTERHEAD

With the letterhead setup established, we can now place the text on the letterhead. We will do this in two stages. First we'll enter the company name in larger print, then we'll add the address and telephone numbers in smaller print.

Adding the Company Name

Here are the steps for placing the name on the logo:

1. **Select the text tool from the toolbox and position the text cursor on point (30, 53.5). Magnify the image around that point to display ruler divisions that show the exact coordinates.**

The cursor changes to a special text cursor, which may be familiar to you from other Macintosh applications. The small horizontal line in the center of the cursor represents the baseline of the type that you will place on the page. Wherever you place the cursor is the *text anchor point*. In some ways, this functions just like the anchor points for lines. In particular, the text anchor point changes color and shape to indicate that the associated text block is selected, and the anchor point is the fixed point around which the text is arranged or shaped.

2. Click the mouse, and you will see the text dialog box shown in Figure 3.4.

There are quite a few options to examine in this box, and we will discuss them all in the next section. For now, you can just complete the letterhead by a few simple actions.

3. Enter the words *MOUNTAIN SPORTS, LTD.* in the text box at the bottom of the dialog box and press Return.

This is where the text-insertion cursor is placed initially, so you can just type the text and it will go in the correct place.

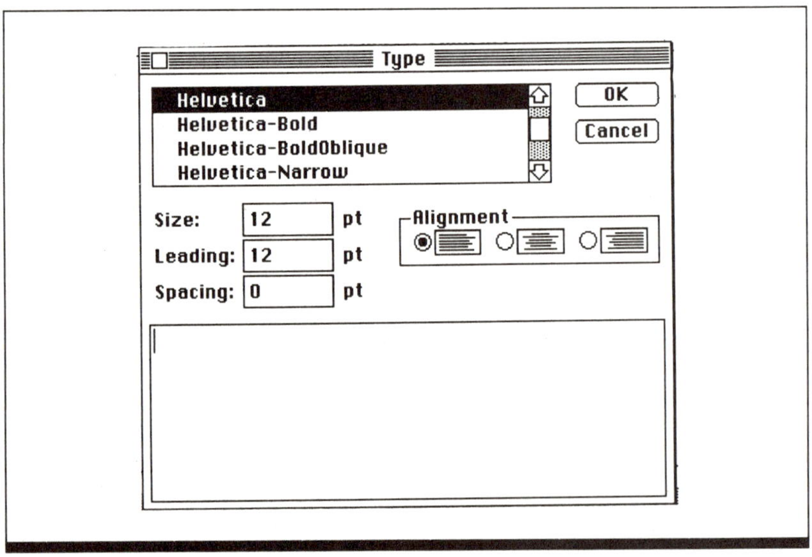

Figure 3.4: *Text dialog box*

4. **Move the cursor (the arrow) up to the top block of the box, which shows a list of available fonts.**
5. **Scroll down to Helvetica-BoldOblique and click on it.**

This establishes Helvetica-BoldOblique, which is basically a bold, italicized version of Helvetica, as the current font.

6. **Move the cursor to the Size box and change the size to 18.**
7. **Move the cursor down to the Leading box and change that entry to 18 also.**

Both size and leading are measured in points, as is typical in typesetting and printing.

8. **Move over to the Alignment section and click on the middle icon, which represents centered text.**

You have now entered a string of text, followed by a carriage return, to be printed in 18-point Helvetica BoldOblique, with 18 points between each line of text, and which is to be centered around the selected point.

9. **Click on OK.**

This will place the text string MOUNTAIN SPORTS, LTD. on the page, centered on point (30, 53.5). The result should look like Figure 3.5.

Adding the Address and Telephone Numbers

In entering the company name, we used a little trick to aid in placement of the next string, the address. In the steps above, we set the leading to 18 points, or $1/4$ inch, entered a carriage return, and then ended the block. The empty line is shown on the screen as a single dot, which is located 18 points below the first line of text because you specified a leading of 18 points. This is the point where we want to place the next line of text.

If the next line was going to be the same type style and size as the first, you could have simply entered multiple lines in the first block. However, we want the address and telephone numbers to be in smaller type, and not in the same font.

1. Place the cursor over the small dot under the first text line and click.

You will see the text dialog box again, with the values that you just entered.

2. Enter the address *123 Mountain Way, Chatsworth,* CA *91311* in the text box and press Return.

3. Enter the telephone number *(818) 882-8144*, press the space bar 15 times, and then type the telephone number *(213) 555-1212*. Do not press Return.

There are 15 spaces between the two telephone numbers for alignment. You could align them separately, but that would be quite time-consuming and no more effective.

4. Select Helvetica as the font.

5. Enter 10 as the Size and 12 as the Leading.

6. Leave the centered alignment selected and click on OK.

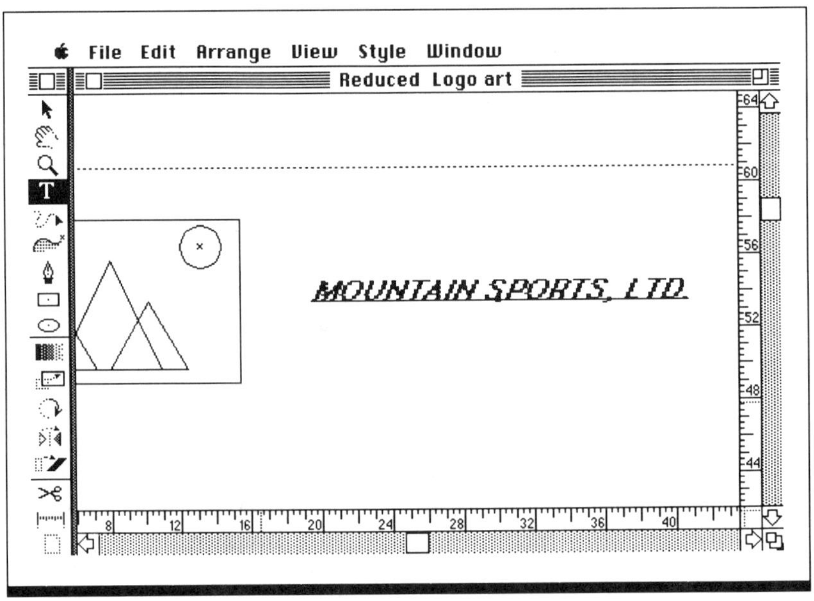

Figure 3.5: *First text placement*

You will see the address lines appear on the screen, centered along the same line as the company, as shown in Figure 3.6.

Removing the Logo Frame

Just one feature remains to take care of in this letterhead. The frame around the logo is unnecessary now that we have placed the graphic on the page. You can remove it as follows:

1. **Select the entire frame, using the selection tool and the Option key.**
2. **Pull down the Edit menu and select Clear.**

The frame is deleted from the page. Now let's see how the letterhead looks.

3. **Select Fit In Window and then Preview Illustration from the View menu.**

This is a little small to show any detail, but it gives you the placement of the letterhead on the page.

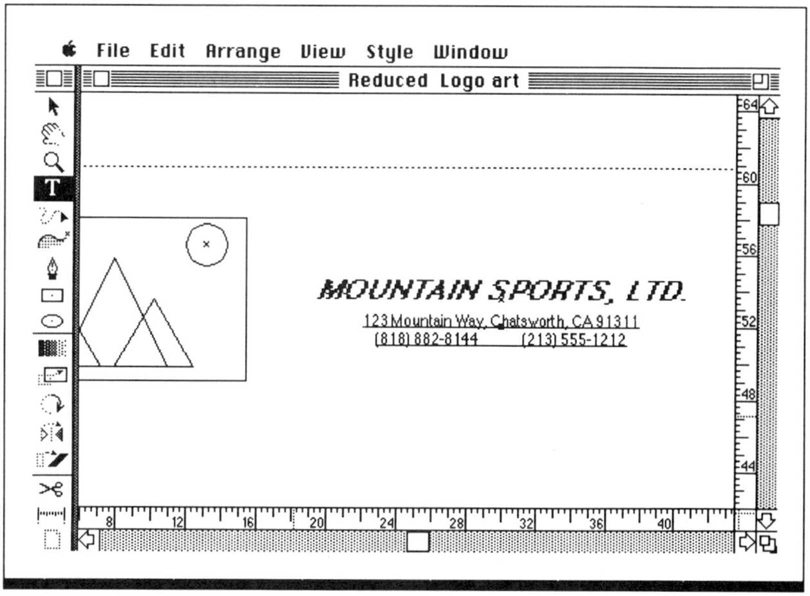

Figure 3.6: *Completed letterhead name and address*

4. **To get a full view, select Print from the File menu and print the page on your printer.**

The output should look like Figure 3.7 (except larger, of course).

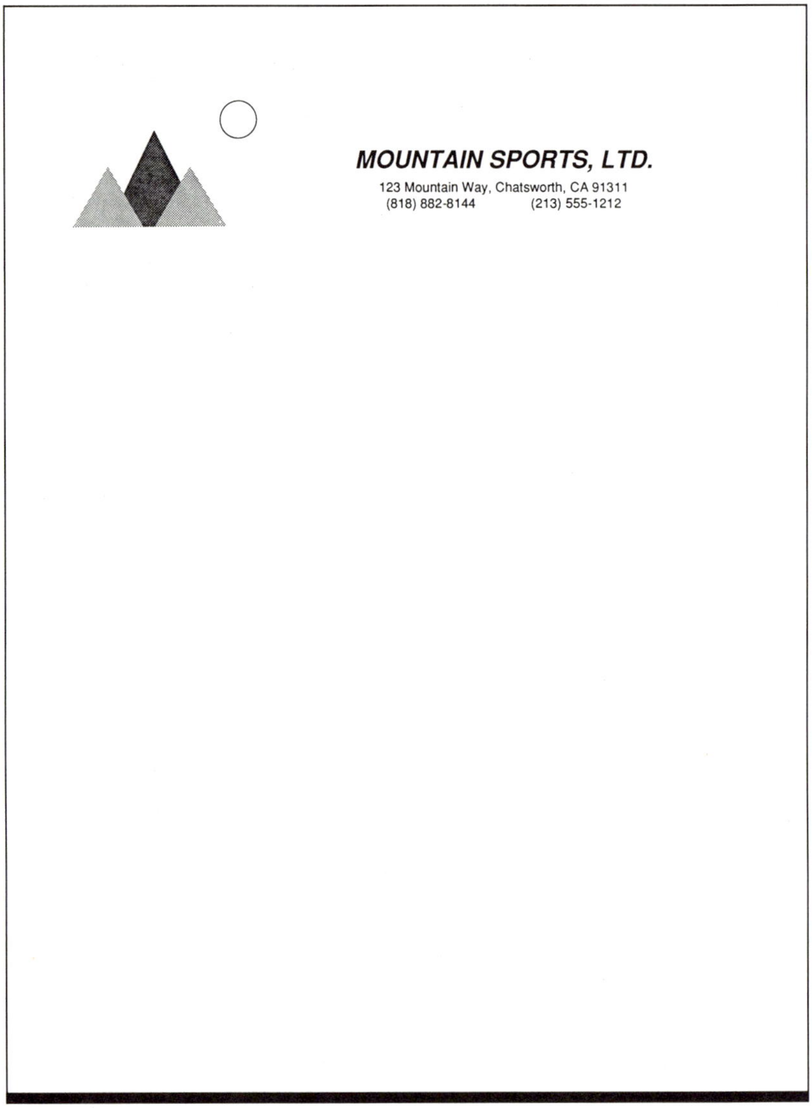

Figure 3.7: *Finished letterhead*

5. Save your work as *Letterhead art.*

We will continue to work with this artwork later in the chapter.

ILLUSTRATOR TEXT OPTIONS

Now that you have done some basic work combining text with Illustrator graphics, we will explore some of the options and operations of the text tool before we continue with another exercise.

All the text operations are accessed through the text dialog box (Figure 3.4). You can display this dialog box in three ways: by selecting the text tool and clicking on a specific point (as we did in our exercise), by selecting a block of existing text on the page and choosing Type from the Style menu, or by pressing ⌘T. When you use the latter method, the dialog box appears with the text string and parameters for the selected block. You can modify the text and parameters at any time (unlike other drawing programs, which do not let you make changes after the text is set).

AVAILABLE FONTS

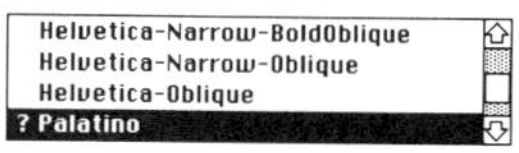

The top portion of the dialog box shows the list of fonts available on your system. The list can be scrolled by using the scroll bar, and the names are the standard PostScript names for the fonts. Some of the names in the list may be preceded by a bullet (•) or a question mark (?). The bullet indicates that the font has a matching screen font installed on your system, which means that the letters on your screen appear in the same shape as those on the printed output. Fonts that do not have a bullet in front of their name are available on the screen as a derivative of one of the available fonts. Illustrator modifies another font in the same font family to make an italic, bold, or narrow version, or whatever transformation may be appropriate.

A question mark in front of the font name means that Illustrator doesn't have that font available at all; there is no font that can be modified to display it correctly. Usually this is because you are working with an Illustrator artwork that was originally prepared on a system that had the font available, but which is not installed on your present system. When that happens, Illustrator uses the Macintosh system font (usually Chicago) to display the requested font on the screen.

When printing your text, Illustrator will always try to use the correct font; that is, the font that you requested from the list. Illustrator will download the fonts for you if they are available on your system but are not already resident on the printer. However, if the font is preceded by a question mark, Illustrator assumes that the printer will have the correct font available. If that font isn't resident on the printer, a default font will be used in its place (usually Courier).

Size, Leading, and Spacing Parameters

As you saw earlier, the Size and Leading parameters in the text dialog box specify, in points, the size of the requested type and the distance between two successive lines of type, respectively. The leading is used only on successive lines within the same text block (those lines in the text box of the dialog box). It does not apply to successive lines of text created and positioned separately.

In Illustrator 1.1, the Spacing box is labeled Kerning. This kerning is really the same as spacing and should not be confused with the more usual typesetter's notion of kerning, which is adjustment of the position of certain pairs of letters to make a more pleasing appearance. Illustrator simply adjusts all letters in the text block by an equal amount; it has no provisions for individual letter pair kerning.

Leading the same as type size is the minimum necessary to avoid overlapping letters on successive lines. If you enter a leading value of zero, the lines of type will overlap completely. If you use negative values for leading, the second line of type will appear above the first line by the specified leading amount.

The Spacing box specifies the distance between letters in the text block, in points. The default spacing value of zero spaces letters according to their usual width in the font. Any higher spacing values add space to the usual font spacing. As for leading, you can enter negative spacing values. Such values will move the letters closer together and may result in overlapping, depending on the point size, the specific letter sizes, and the negative spacing value.

Alignment Options

The Alignment box offers three selections for aligning the text in relation to the selected anchor point. The leftmost icon provides left-justification for the text, which is the default alignment. Selecting the middle icon will center the text around the anchor point, and selecting the rightmost icon provides right-justification with a ragged-left margin. Illustrator does not provide a true justification, with even margins on both sides of the text.

The bottom part of the text dialog box is the box for inserting the actual text. Illustrator allows a maximum of 255 characters in this box; that is, each block of text can have no more than 255 characters. If you need to use more characters, you must divide the text into two or more blocks.

USING OTHER TOOLS WITH TEXT

Because type characters are just another graphic object from Illustrator's (and PostScript's) viewpoint, most of the other tools in the toolbox can be used with text blocks. Indeed, only the pen, square, and circle tools are not applicable to text manipulation. All the other tools, particularly the transformation tools (such as the rotate and shear tools) can produce interesting effects. You will see a number of examples of using text with the transformation tools in Chapter 5.

In addition, text can be filled and painted like any other graphic object. Keep in mind that anything you can do to a square or a circle, you can do to type.

TEXT EFFECTS

Because the characters in PostScript fonts can be stroked or filled as required, they can also be modified through the Paint dialog screen. All these selections are available and applicable to type. You can use the Fill option to make the type show on the page in the usual range of black to white. You could adjust this setting to show white lettering against a dark or patterned background, for example. You can also use the Stroke options to change the letters to outline form; for example, you can set Fill to White and Stroke to 100% Black with a thin line width to generate letter outlines.

EXAMPLES OF TEXT FEATURES

Now we'll experiment with some of the text functions. first open a new Illustrator drawing surface. You don't have to exit your current document (if you have one up); just select New from the File menu to bring up a new drawing surface. The old one is still there and open, but now it is located behind the new surface that you see.

A NOTE ABOUT MULTIPLE WINDOWS

Like most Macintosh applications, Illustrator supports multiple windows. You can use all the usual Macintosh window controls to manipulate the windows: the size box, the zoom box, and the title bar (for moving the window).

In addition, Illustrator allows you to choose which window to make active by bringing it to the front. The active window is always the one in front. You control the windows through the Windows menu. The bottom section of this menu lists the available windows. The currently active window has a checkmark next to its name. To make another window active, select its name from this menu. You might try that now to see the previous window that you were working on and then again to switch back to the new window.

INSERTING MULTIPLE LINES OF TEXT

To begin, we'll enter three long lines of text.

1. **Select the text tool, pull down the View menu, and select Show Rulers to set the rulers on.**
2. **Select Preferences from the Edit menu (or press ⌘K).**

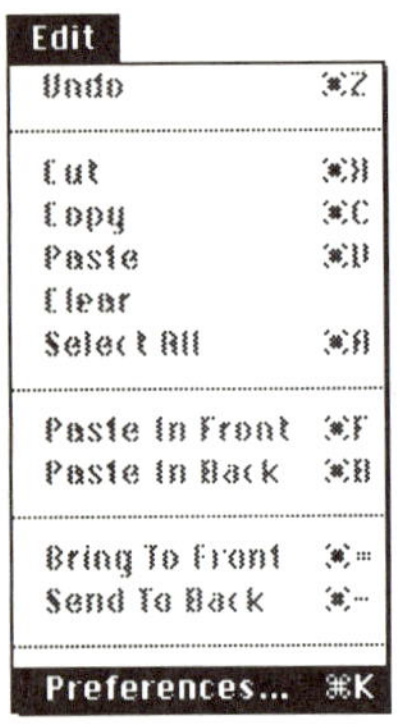

This displays the Preferences dialog box, as shown in Figure 3.8. The Preferences function allows you to adjust a variety of Illustrator parameters. In particular, you can choose whether the rulers display measurements in centimeters, inches, or the more traditional picas and points. We will use inches to simplify moving this text block around on the desktop.

3. **Click on the button next to Inches in the Ruler units box and then click on OK.**
4. **Move the text cursor to point (1/2, 9) and click.**

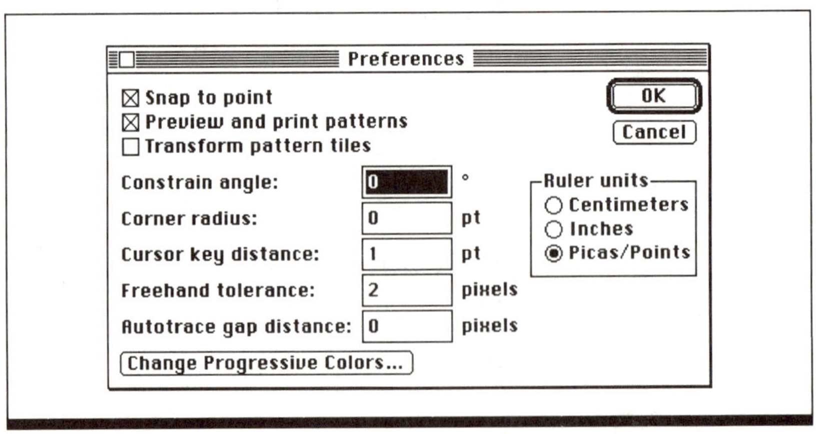

Figure 3.8: *Preferences dialog box*

You'll see that the last settings that you used for text are preserved in the text dialog box. In particular, if you are continuing from the last exercise, you will find Helvetica still selected and set to 10-point size. Notice that text values are still in points, even though the rulers display inches.

5. **Select the Helvetica font, with Size and Leading both set to 10 points and Spacing to 0, and click on left alignment.**
6. **Enter the text *Now is the time for all good men to come to the aid of the party.***

The line of text is longer than the box and it wraps automatically around so it remains visible within the box. Don't be fooled by this display; the text remains one single line on the output.

7. **Click on OK and you will see the entire line placed on the page.**

The anchor point for the line of text is a filled black square, and the line of text is underlined. When you click on the anchor point of a text block to select it, this is how Illustrator shows the selected text and its anchor point.

8. **Pull down the Style menu and select Type.**

You see the text dialog box for the selected text block.

9. **Position the cursor behind the period in the text line and click.**
10. **Press Return and enter *—and for quick brown foxes to jump over lazy dogs.***
11. **Press Return and enter *This block is set in 10 point Helvetica with 10 point leading and 0 spacing.***

There are approximately seven lines of text (five lines if you have version 1.1) shown in the text box. Unlike most Macintosh application boxes, the text box provides only limited scrolling capabilities. To move up and down within the box, you must use the cursor-movement keys (the arrows). As you move the cursor into a portion of the text that is not shown, the window shifts to keep the cursor in view.

12. Click on OK to set the three lines of text, as shown in Figure 3.9.

Notice that there is still only one anchor point for the entire block, but that all three lines are underlined. At a glance, you can tell that the text block is three lines long and that it is left-aligned.

ALIGNING TEXT

Before we start to work on variations of point size, leading, and spacing, we'll test the three alignment options. In all of the following work, you can always use ⌘T to quickly access the text dialog box.

1. Pull down the Style menu, select Type, and click on the icon for centered alignment.

The anchor point stays where you set it, at point (1/2, 9), but the text is now centered around that point instead of extending to the right as it did previously. If you move the screen to the left, you can see that the string now extends off the page on the left and is ragged on both ends.

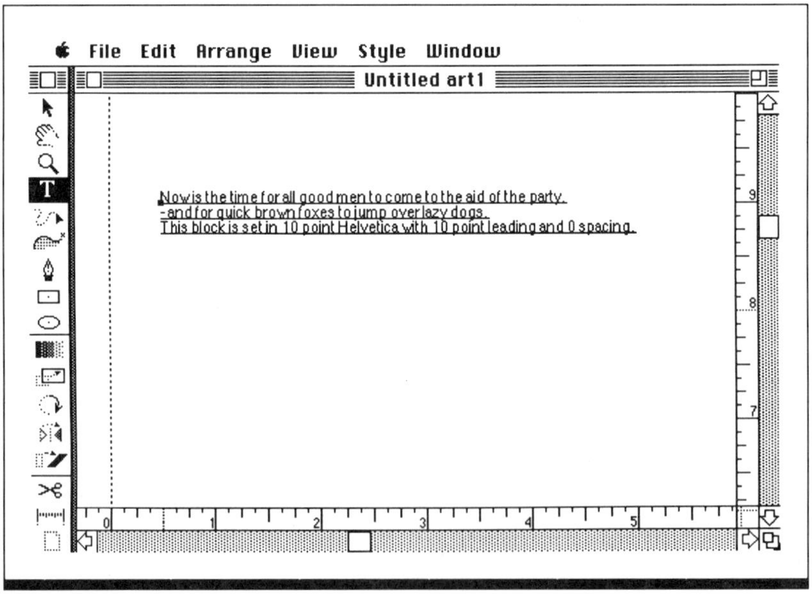

Figure 3.9: *Setting multiple lines of text*

2. **Pull down the Style menu, select Type, and click on the alignment icon for right-justification.**

Here you see the text justified on the right with the anchor point still in the same place. The text extends quite far off the page on the left and, while the right edge is now aligned, the left edge is ragged.

3. **Pull down the Style menu, select Type, and reset the text to left-justified.**

This text is the basic string that we will use to explore some of the combinations of point size, leading, and spacing. To see the effects of changing various parameters, we'll keep the first two lines of text the same and only adjust the last line to reflect the current settings.

Changing Leading, Point Size, and Spacing

Now we'll see the effects of changing the text parameter settings.

1. **Use the selection tool to select the text block.**
2. **Hold down the Option key, click on the anchor point with the selection arrow and drag it to point (1/2, 8).**

Don't worry if the text image lags behind the movement of the cursor; Illustrator will catch up with the image before it stops moving.

Using the Option key during a move is a handy way to make copies. Instead of moving the selected object to a new location, the old version remains, and the new version is a copy of the old version instead of a replacement. Notice that the copy is now selected and the original is deselected.

Remember to hold down the Option key until you have released the mouse button. If you don't, you will move the block instead of copy it. If that happens, pull down the Edit menu and select Undo Move, which will move the text block back to where you started. Then try again. Also, you may have some trouble selecting the text block. If the block is already selected when you start to move it, clicking the mouse sometimes causes the block to be deselected, as indicated by the change in the anchor point from a black square to an x and by the disappearance of the underlines. Just go back and click on the anchor point again if that happens.

3. **Either select Type from the Style menu or press ⌘T to display the dialog box associated with the selected text.**
4. **Change the leading from 10 to 12 points, change the last line of text to read *...with 12 point leading...*, and click on OK.**

You could use the same method to move the anchor point manually to whatever point you want. In this case, however, we want to move each successive text block a precise distance. There is a much faster and easier way to do this, using some more options in the Preference dialog box.

5. **Access the Preference dialog box again by selecting Preferences from the Edit menu (or by pressing ⌘K).**

All the control values in the dialog box that were previously points are now inches. We want to move each successive copy of the text block 1 inch down the page. You can do that more quickly and accurately by setting the cursor key distance and then using those keys.

6. **Change the value in the box labeled Cursor key distance to 1 and click on OK.**

This means that any time you press a cursor-movement key (arrow), you will move exactly 1 inch in the direction indicated by the arrow.

7. **Copy the text block to its new location (1/2, 7) by holding down the Option key and pressing the down-arrow.**

You will see the clock icon for a second, and then a copy of the text block will appear 1 inch below the previously selected block.

8. **Use the Type selection on the Style menu (or ⌘T) to set the point size to 12. Once again, change the last line of the text to display the current point size.**
9. **Use the same method to copy the 12-point type with 12-point leading 1 inch lower, but this time set the spacing to 2. Change the last line of the text block to reflect the spacing value you have just set.**

This actually would be a most unusually large value to use in ordinary work with 12-point type; it represents more than one-sixth of the maximum height of the type. We used it here as an exaggerated example of the effect of the spacing value on the type.

10. Copy two more blocks: one with 12-point type on 14-point leading and 0 spacing, and another with 12-point type, 14-point leading, and spacing at 4. Move the blocks a sufficient distance to avoid running over one another and make the appropriate changes to each last line of text to indicate the settings for the type of block.

This gives you some feeling for the effects of changing leading and spacing. In particular, you can see how the additional leading adds to readability. Generally, you will find that leading of 1 or 2 points greater than the type size looks the best.

11. Pull down the View menu and select Fit In Window to view the entire page, as shown in Figure 3.10.

You will see that the two lines with the exaggerated spacing have run past the edge of the sheet. The tiling effect (mentioned in Chapter 2) indicates that this text will not fit on a single printed page.

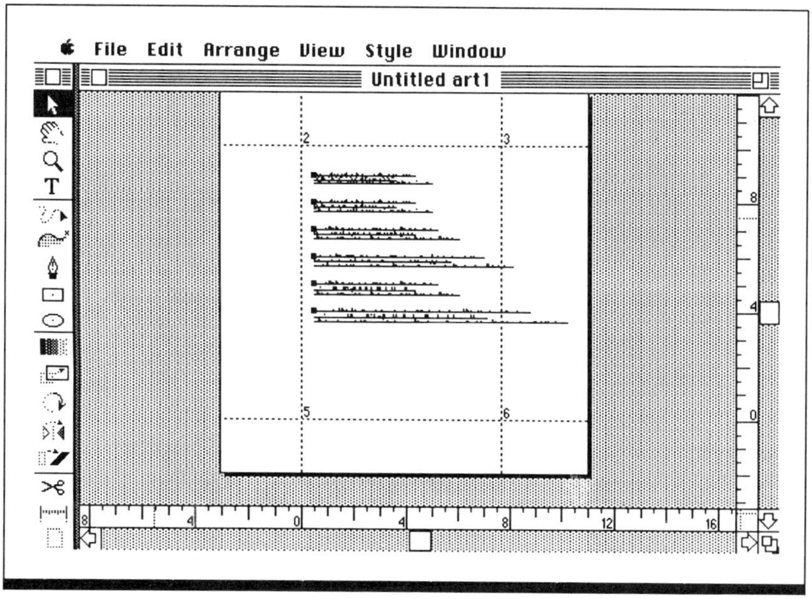

Figure 3.10: *Text shown on full-page display*

PRINTING TEXT

If you printed our text example, you would get two pages of output. You may want to do this to get an idea of how Illustrator matches printed pages to the tiles shown on the desktop. If you wanted to print only the main page, you could specify a single page number (as well as a range of page numbers) to print in the Print dialog box. However, the central page is not page 1 in Illustrator's page-numbering system. Illustrator numbers pages from the upper-left corner, as illustrated in Figure 3.11. You can see the page numbers on the Fit In Window screen display (the small numbers in the lower-left corner of the pages).

In this case, to print only the central page, you would specify page 5. The result of printing from page 5 to page 5 is shown in Figure 3.12.

If you specify a print range from page 1 to page 1 for the sample text, you will not get any output at all. Because the page is empty, Illustrator will not generate any code that will result in output. This is not to say that you can't print a blank page; you can, but the page must be blank—with actual blank characters on it—not empty without any characters at all.

CREATING A BUSINESS FORM

We have reviewed all the basic text operations and can now proceed to a practical example. For our next exercise, we'll take the letterhead design we created at the beginning of the chapter and add some additional graphics and information to make an invoice form.

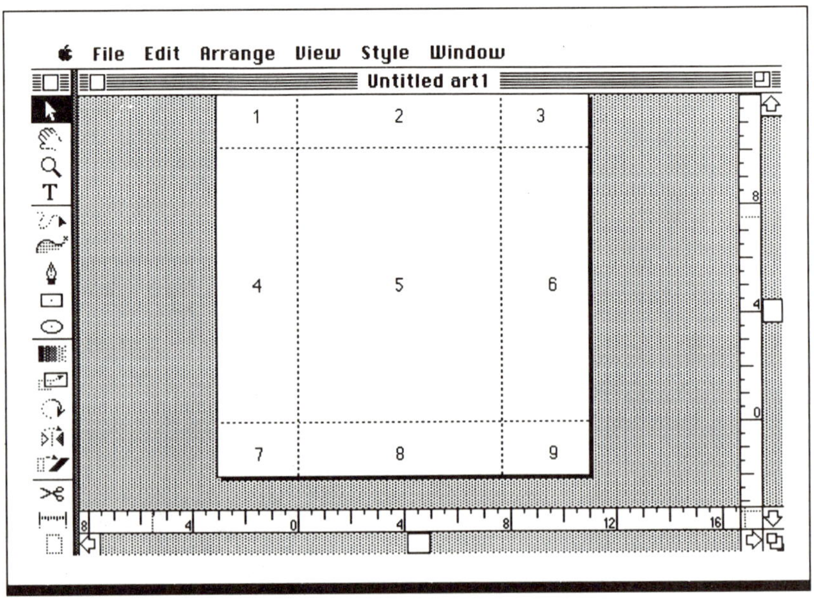

Figure 3.11: *Page numbering for printed output*

THE FORM TEMPLATE

Designing a form usually requires a certain amount of time. You have to consider how it will be used, what data it will have on it, and how it needs to fit into other processes both within and outside the company. You also need to make aesthetic choices about the form's appearance.

Typically, you would go through a process of trial and error to generate the exact specifications for a new form. With Illustrator, you could also scan in an existing form to make a template for your new form, or use a form produced in some other acceptable way. For our example, we will use the form shown in Figure 3.13. This form was prepared in MacDraw and saved in PICT format for use as an Illustrator template. Create this template and name it Invoice template. If you can't generate such a template, you can use the ruler coordinates to establish the correct location of lines and text on the form.

PLACING THE LETTERHEAD ART

First we need to place a copy of our letterhead artwork at the top of the invoice template.

Now is the time for all good men to come to the aid of the party.
- and for quick brown foxes to jump over lazy dogs.
This block is set in 10 point Helvetica with 10 point leading and 0 spacing.

Now is the time for all good men to come to the aid of the party.
- and for quick brown foxes to jump over lazy dogs.
This block is set in 10 point Helvetica with 12 point leading and 0 spacing.

Now is the time for all good men to come to the aid of the party.
- and for quick brown foxes to jump over lazy dogs.
This block is set in 12 point Helvetica with 12 point leading and 0 spacing.

Now is the time for all good men to come to the aid of the party.
- and for quick brown foxes to jump over lazy dogs.
This block is set in 12 point Helvetica with 12 point leading and 0 spac

Now is the time for all good men to come to the aid of the party.
- and for quick brown foxes to jump over lazy dogs.
This block is set in 12 point Helvetica with 14 point leading and 0 spacing.

Now is the time for all good men to come to the aid of tl
- and for quick brown foxes to jump over lazy dogs.
This block is set in 12 point Helvetica with 14 point lea

Figure 3.12: *A page of text output*

1. Open the Letterhead art document.
2. Select the entire letterhead artwork, either by using the selection tool, the Select All option on the Edit menu, or ⌘A.
3. Pull down the Edit menu and choose Copy.

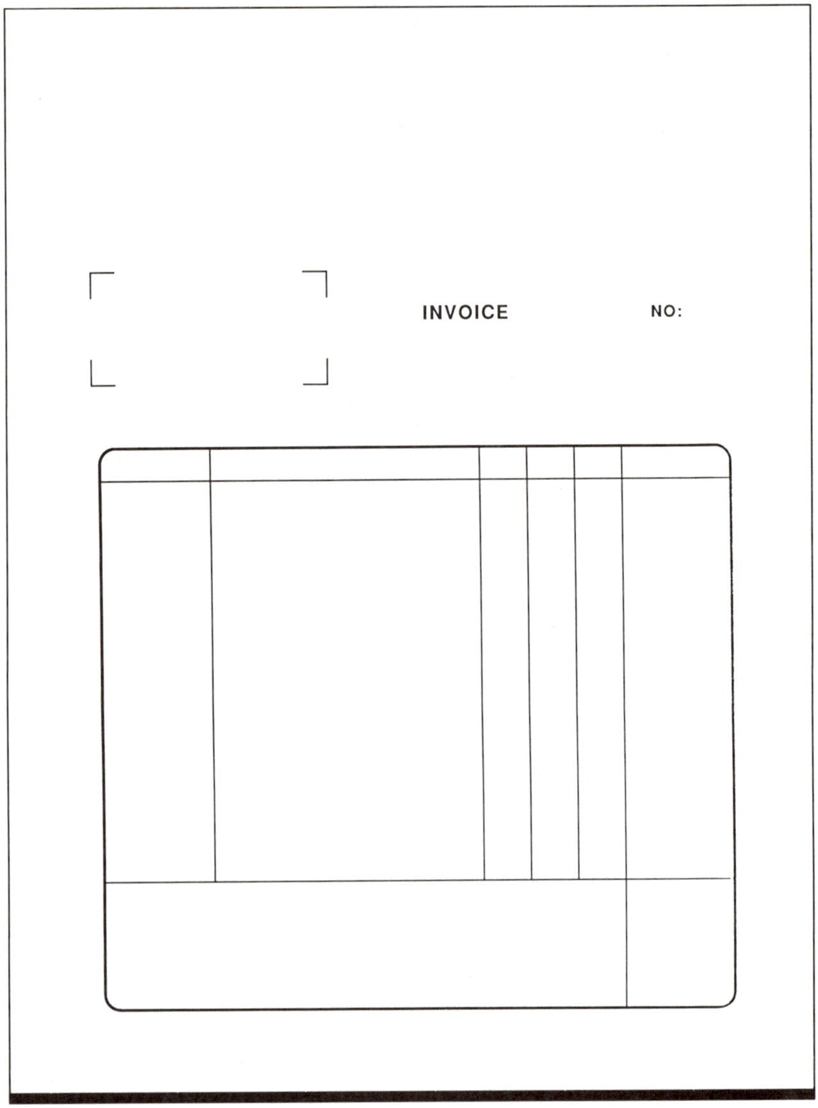

Figure 3.13: *Invoice form template*

This puts a copy of the letterhead on the clipboard.

4. **Select New from the File menu and click on Invoice template.**
5. **Select Fit In Window from the View menu to display the entire page on the screen.**
6. **Paste the saved letterhead from the clipboard onto the new drawing, as shown in Figure 3.14.**

You will probably have to move the letterhead around to position it at the top of the template in the space provided for it.

Tracing the Form

With the letterhead in place, we're ready to draw the form.

1. **Trace the name and address box, which is the rectangle outlined by four small corners on the upper-left side of the page. In the Paint dialog screen, set Stroke to 100% Black, Fill to None, and the line weight to 1 point.**

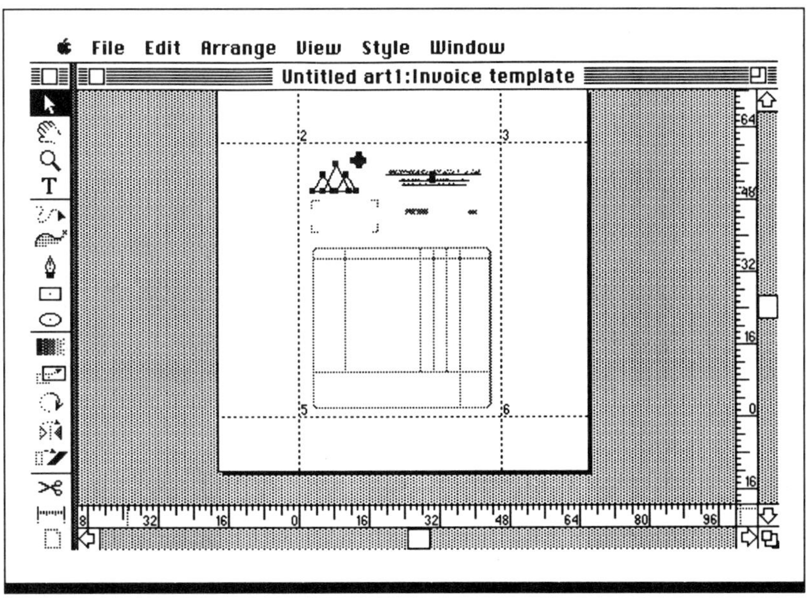

Figure 3.14: *Letterhead art on the invoice template*

Each line segment is 2 picas wide, and the four corners are at points (3, 48), (18, 48), (18, 41), and (3, 41). Remember to return to the pen tool after you complete each corner so that you don't continue the line across the figure inadvertently. Be attentive to the shape of your cursor!

Next you should create the large outside box that will enclose the data. This has rounded corners, so you will need to combine straight lines, along the sides, with curves at each of the corners.

2. Reduce the image by two clicks to fit the entire box on the screen.

The top and bottom of the box are at lines 37 and 2; the left and right sides are at lines 3 and 44. Start at the top left of the box a short distance from the corner. Use the Shift key to constrain the sides and keep them straight.

3. Select the pen tool, move the cursor over to the top-right side of the outline, and click once while holding down the Shift key.

This generates a straight line for the top of the form.

4. Click again on the anchor point you just created, and drag the direction point out in a straight line to about the line that you are going to draw down.

This moves the direction point on that side of the anchor point out so that the curve can be constructed.

5. Move the cursor around the corner about the same distance down as the distance from the previous anchor point to the corner, and click and drag the direction point to match the curved corner.

Figure 3.15 shows an enlarged view of the corner just after making the curve. Notice how the direction point on the top of the curve is positioned; this is the key to getting a smooth, rounded corner.

6. Continue on around the form, using the same technique on each of the corners.

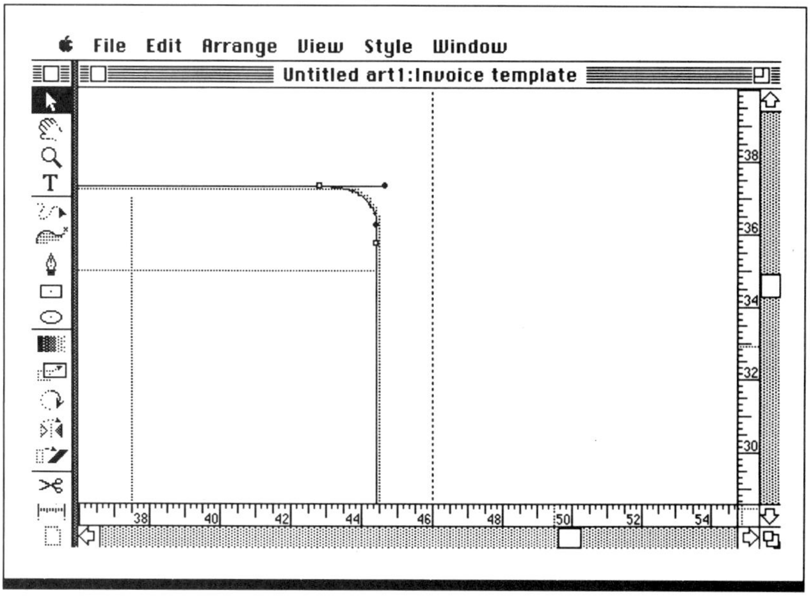

Figure 3.15: *Rounded corner construction*

Illustrator 88 provides an alternative method for making a box with rounded corners. You can set a corner radius in the Preferences dialog box. Then, whenever you draw a box using the rectangle tool, the box will have corners rounded to the radius you specify. This method is faster and more precise than the method you used here. To produce the same result, however, you would need to ungroup the resulting figure and delete the center point in the box. We will cover these techniques in a later chapter.

The important points are to use the Shift key to ensure that the sides are straight and to round the corners by using the procedure described above: set the anchor point for a side and then click once on the anchor point and drag the resulting direction point straight out, as though you were extending the line you just finished, about to where you want the next side to be.

7. **When you finish tracing the form, set the Stroke to 100% Black, Fill to None, and line weight to 2 points.**
8. **Add the horizontal and vertical lines that divide the form into the required areas for headings, data, totals, and so on. Set the line weight for the two horizonal lines and the rightmost vertical line (which is the only one that extends all the way down to the bottom of the form) to 1. Set the line weight for the other four vertical lines to .5.**

These are all just straight lines, otherwise unconnected. Remember to use the Shift key to constrain them to be exactly horizontal or vertical. The two horizontal lines are along the y-coordinates 35 and 10; the five vertical lines, from left to right, are at x-coordinates 10.5, 27.5, 30.5,

33.5, and 37.5. The complete outline of the body of the form is shown in Figure 3.16.

ADDING TEXT TO THE FORM

We have now finished the preliminary work to make the form. You have placed the letterhead and added the graphic elements that make up the invoice. Now we have to insert some type to label the divisions on the form and to title it.

The title of the form, INVOICE, and the associated label, NO:, have a suggested position on the invoice template, so you might start with these.

1. **Select the text tool, position the text cursor at (24, 45) to set the title, and click.**
2. **Set the text *INVOICE* in Helvetica-Bold, 15 point, left-aligned, and with a leading and spacing of 0.**
3. **Set the label *NO:* at point (38, 45), also in Helvetica-Bold, but with a point size of 12 (all the other parameters remain the same).**

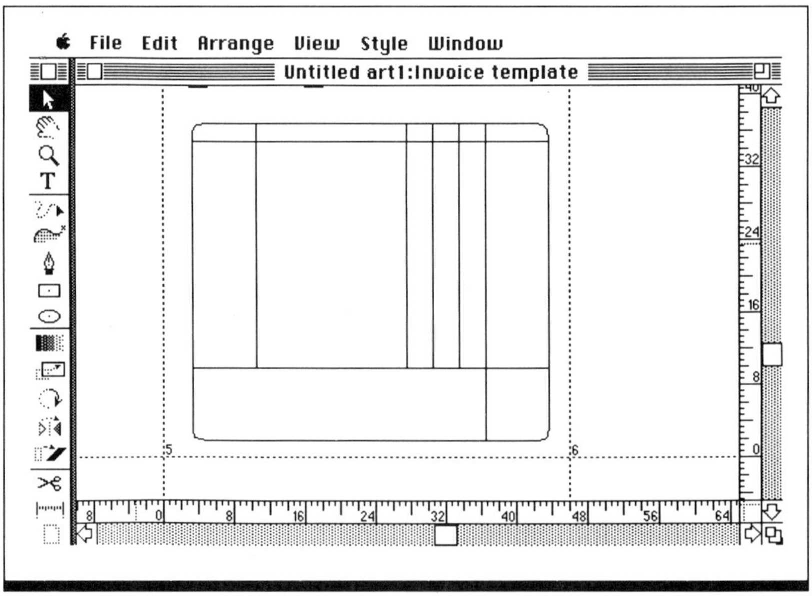

Figure 3.16: *Completed form body*

Now we can set the column headings in the data box.

4. **Enlarge the picture to Actual Size, if it's not already in that view.**

The titles are all set along a common baseline, which is 35.5 on the y-axis of the template that is shown here. The important points are that the titles be approximately centered vertically in the boxes and that they appear on a common baseline.

5. **Set the column headings at the points listed below. Choose the Helvetica font, and set the point size to 10, the leading and initial spacing to 0, and left-alignment.**

ITEM NO.	5.5
DESCRIPTION	16.0
ORDER	27.5
SHIP	31.0
UNIT #	33.75
EXT. PRICE	37.5

This results in a set of column headings that should look something like Figure 3.17. Two of these, however, can be noticeably improved by adjusting their spacing values. First, the DESCRIPTION heading seems a bit lost in the midst of such a large block. We could improve the form by spreading out this word a bit.

6. **Select the anchor point for DESCRIPTION, pull down the Style menu, and select Type.**
7. **Set the spacing value to 1 and click on OK.**

Next notice that the heading ORDER really doesn't fit in the box available for it. We can improve this by using a negative spacing value to compress the letters. We will use a small, fractional negative spacing value to squeeze the word just a little without losing legibility.

8. **Click on ORDER to select it and press ⌘T to display the text dialog box.**

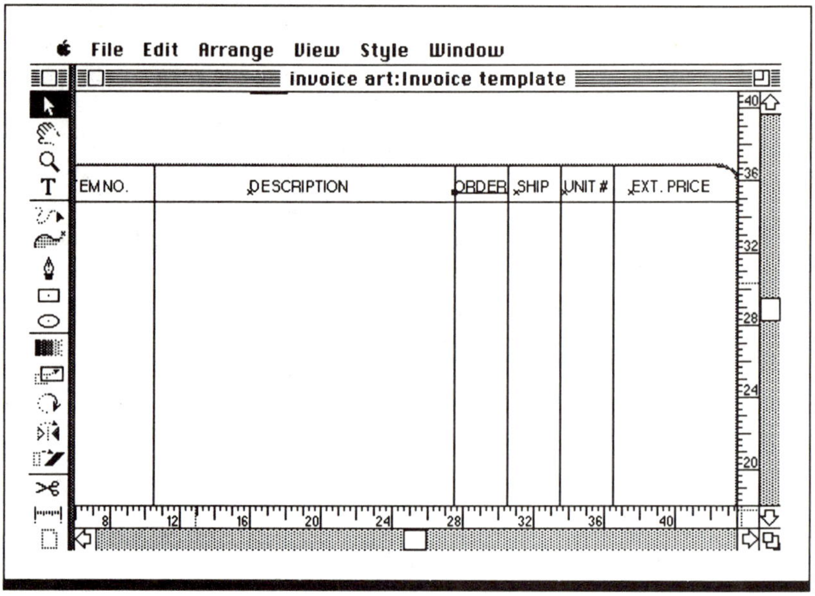

Figure 3.17: *Column headings before adjustment*

9. Set the spacing value to – 0.15 and click on OK.

Finally, we need to add the labels that define the entries beneath the interior box.

10. Add the labels *SUBTOTAL:*, *SALES TAX:*, *SHIPPING:*, and *TOTAL:*. Set them in Helvetica-Bold, 10 point, right-aligned (against the 36 x-coordinate), and with 0 leading and 1 spacing.

These labels are positioned at 9, 7, 5, and 3 on the y-axis, respectively. The final result is a form that looks like Figure 3.18 when printed out

11. Save the artwork under the name *Invoice art*.

Actually, I saved the form several times along the way. It's a good habit to save your work periodically, so that you don't have to redo a lot of exacting and time-consuming labor if something goes wrong. I know you've heard that a zillion times, but it's true, and bears one more repetition. For work like Illustrator especially, where placement and sizing are so important, it can be very frustrating to lose work already completed to your satisfaction, since it may be impossible to remember

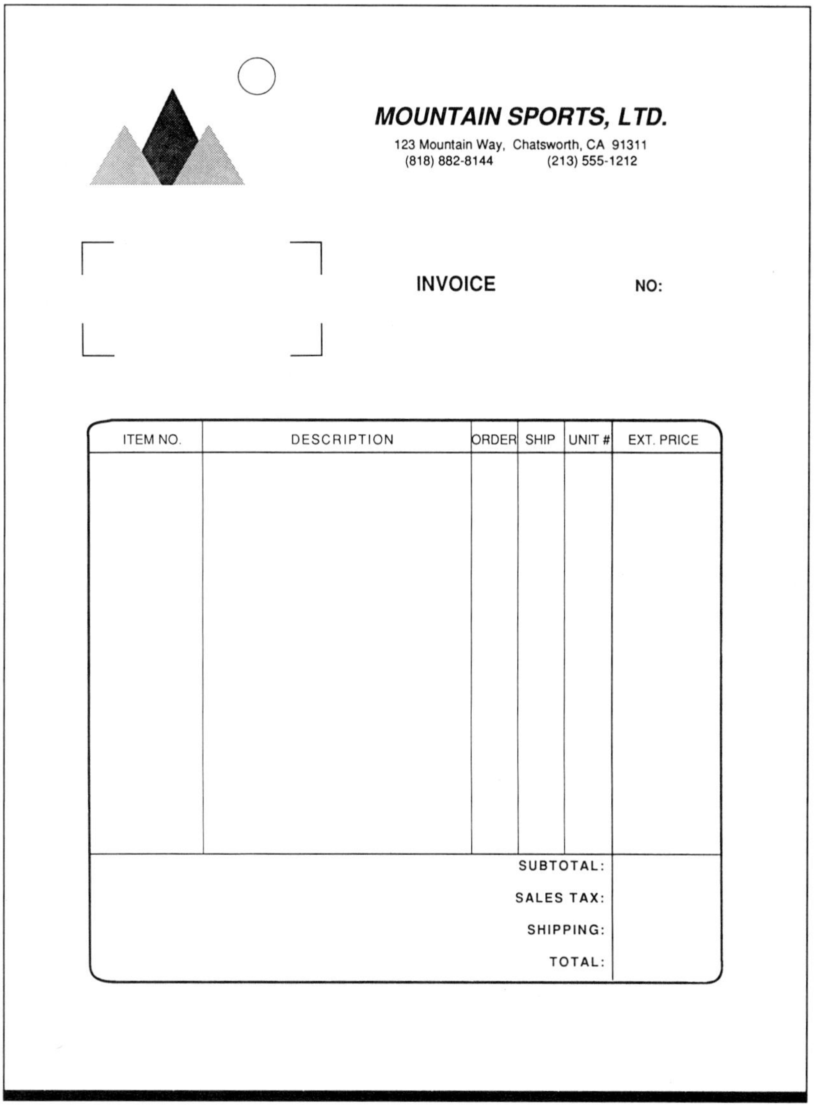

MOUNTAIN SPORTS, LTD.
123 Mountain Way, Chatsworth, CA 91311
(818) 882-8144 (213) 555-1212

INVOICE NO:

ITEM NO.	DESCRIPTION	ORDER	SHIP	UNIT #	EXT. PRICE

SUBTOTAL:
SALES TAX:
SHIPPING:
TOTAL:

Figure 3.18: *Finished invoice form*

exactly where you placed the anchor points or positioned the text block to get that nifty effect.

This example gives you some idea of how you can use Illustrator in a working context. Ordinary business work can also benefit from a dose of computer assistance. The advantage of this form made by Illustrator over forms produced by other tools, such as MacDraw, is that it is ready for electronic publication. You can either send it to a printer and have thousands made up, or you can, with the appropriate software, have it electronically filled in by an application program and print finished invoices that are ready to mail.

Illustrator provides other ways to take a template and logo, such as the ones presented here, and combine them very quickly and conveniently into a page of output. This involves using advanced techniques and auxiliary programs, which we will discuss in Chapter 6. Although these advanced tools can help you get the same job done more easily, the hands-on techniques that you have learned and practiced here form the basis of all other methods.

Fast Track Chapter 4

123 **To form a curved corner,**
return to the anchor point of the corner and click on it while you hold down the Option key. Then drag the direction point to draw the corner.

124 **To associate a new template with existing artwork,**
use the Copy option from the Edit menu to copy the artwork, close the original, and choose New from the File menu. Select the new template from the template selection screen; and then paste the copy onto the new desktop.

128 **To change from a curve to a straight line,**
and vice versa, return to the anchor point where the change should occur, and click on it. To form a straight line, next move the cursor to where you want that segment's anchor point and click again. For a curve, drag the direction point into position.

149 **To alter existing artwork,**
select it and use the scissors tool to either cut out the portion you want to modify or cut into the artwork to create a space for the new work.

160 **To group figures**
so that they can be worked with as a single unit, select all the figures and then choose Group from the Arrange menu. You cannot access the individual anchor points of grouped figures.

163 **To ungroup objects,**
including Illustrator's automatically grouped shapes such as circles and squares, select the group and then choose Ungroup from the Arrange menu.

170 **To reposition the screen display**
and printed page tiling, use the page tool. You can have Illustrator display and print the desktop in as few as four tiles, up to nine tiles (the default).

Fast Track

174 To move the coordinate system
displayed on the rulers (shift the origin), click on the scale box in the lower-right corner of the rulers and drag the crosshairs to where you want the new origin, (point 0,0).

175 To see multiple views
of a page, open the document, put it in one view, and then select New Window from the Window menu. Use the window size and position controls to rearrange the windows.

178 To reposition an inactive window
without making it active, hold down the Command key and click on its title bar as you move it.

Chapter

4

Working with Graphics: Shaping, Altering, & Grouping

Illustrator provides many powerful tools for bending and shaping graphics. You will want to use them to create special effects, as well as to change some existing graphic into a new image.

In this chapter, you'll learn how to create curved corners, make basic modifications to existing artwork, and work with "groups" of figures. We'll also discuss the manipulation of pages as a unit.

FORMING CURVED CORNERS

In the exercises so far, you have drawn two kinds of corners: those joining straight lines together and those joining curved lines to straight lines. However, you have not formed any corners that join curved lines.

As you have seen, Illustrator curves move smoothly toward and away from each anchor point. The default direction points are symmetrical around the anchor point in both length and direction. You learned earlier how to modify a direction point to change the length of the line from the anchor point. But in all our exercises, both direction points and the anchor point between them lay on a single, straight line. If you want the curve to bend in a different direction, to form a curved corner like an arch, you need to alter that relationship so that the two direction points no longer lie on a single line. Instead, there should be two lines: one from one direction point to one side of the anchor point, and another from the anchor point to the direction point on the other side.

The two lines formed by the two direction points and the anchor point are still tangent to the curve at the anchor point, but now the curve no longer has to move smoothly toward and away from the anchor point. Instead, it can become a corner.

Creating two distinct lines outward from the anchor point to the direction points is the basic technique for forming curved corners. To create this new line from the anchor point, you move the cursor back to the anchor point and, while holding down the Option key, click on the direction point and drag it to where you want it. As before, the real trick to this is placing the direction point so that the curve moves the right way. You can use the one-third rule (make the distance from an anchor point to the direction point about one-third of the total distance to the next anchor point) as a guide, but the best way to learn proper placement is by practice. As a beginning, we'll add a stem and leaf—figures that have curved corners—to the simple apple artwork we created in Chapter 2.

ADDING CURVED CORNERS TO ARTWORK

Instead of modifying the original apple template, you may choose to use a new apple template, including the additional features, and start all your artwork over. Or, you may want to work without a template and build from your previous apple artwork.

For this exercise, you need a modified version of the Simple Apple template you used in Chapter 2. Use MacPaint (or another drawing program) to add a leaf and stem to the apple template, as shown in Figure 4.1. Name it Revised Apple template.

ASSOCIATING A NEW TEMPLATE WITH EXISTING ARTWORK

Now we want to copy the previous artwork onto the new template and then create a new piece of artwork. As we discussed earlier, you cannot simply associate the new template with the existing artwork. You could give the new template the same name as the old one and erase the original template, but then you could never return to the old artwork and template combination. For our example, we'll use another method. We'll associate the new template with a copy of the existing artwork, and we won't change the original template.

1. **Open the Simple Apple art document.**
2. **Select the selection tool, place the pointer in the upper-left corner of the page—both above and to the left of all the artwork—and click and drag to the bottom-right corner of the page.**

You will see a selection marquee, made up of dotted lines, enclosing the entire artwork.

Figure 4.1: *Revised apple template*

Another way to select everything on the page, rather than just all the art in a certain region, is to choose the Select All option from the Edit menu (or press ⌘A).

3. When the selection marquee encloses all the artwork, release the mouse button.

Everything within the selection marquee is selected (all the anchor points appear as black squares). A selection marquee always selects everything within the box.

4. Pull down the Edit menu and choose Copy.

Now a copy of the apple artwork is on the clipboard.

5. **Close the old artwork and select New from the File menu.**
6. **As the template, select Revised Apple. Your screen should look like Figure 4.2.**
7. **Select Paste from the Edit menu.**

This places the artwork from the clipboard in the center of the screen of the current desktop. This isn't exactly where we want it, but you can make the adjustments easily because the entire artwork is already selected.

8. **Use the selection pointer to move the artwork so that it is correctly placed over the matching parts of the new template, as shown in Figure 4.3.**

You may want to magnify or reduce the page appropriately to get the correct placement.

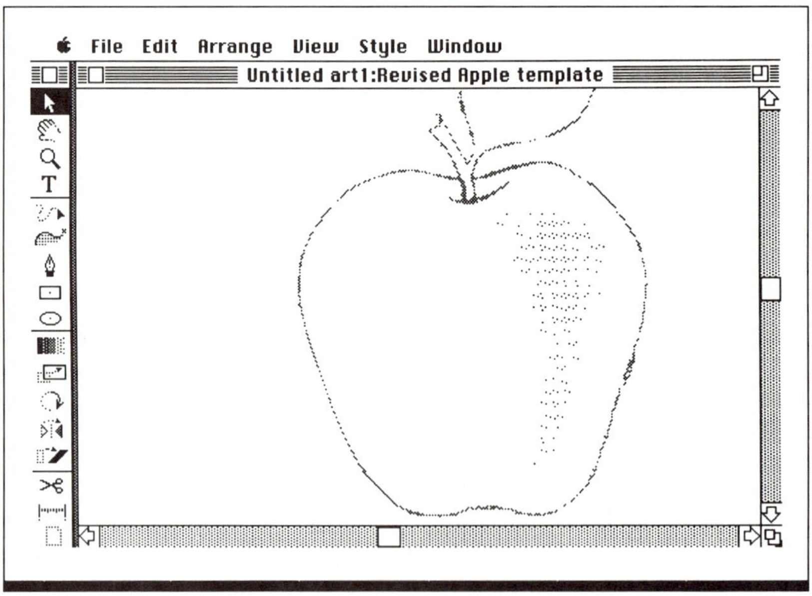

Figure 4.2: *Illustrator with Revised Apple template*

TRACING A CURVED CORNER

Our additions to the apple will actually require two curved corners: the tip of the leaf and the leaf and stem junction.

Drawing the Leaf

You are now ready to begin tracing the leaf and stem for the apple. In order to accurately follow the new parts of this template, you will need to magnify the view of the template and move around some to keep the current work in focus.

1. **Use the zoom tool to magnify the base of the stem by one click to 200%.**

2. **Select the pen tool and, beginning at the right base of the stem, trace the stem and leaf until you reach the first serration on the leaf.**

In the screen showing the beginning of the leaf and stem artwork (Figure 4.4), I moved the artwork so that you can see all the anchor points that have been placed so far. When you actually do the work, the direction point at the top must be on the screen.

Remember the bump rule, and notice that there are just two bumps between the base of the stem and the beginning of the serration. At this point, your artwork should look something like the first screen in Figure 4.4.

3. **Magnify the serrated part of the leaf.**

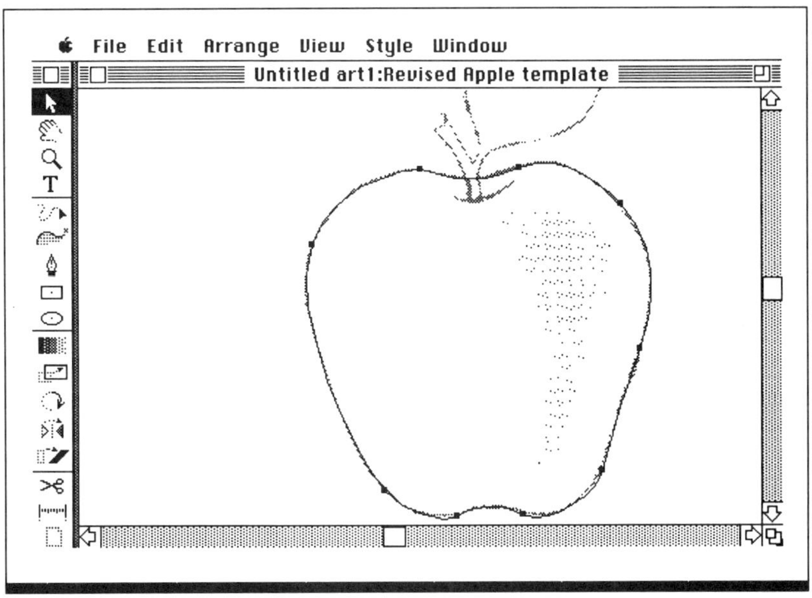

Figure 4.3: *Matched artwork and template*

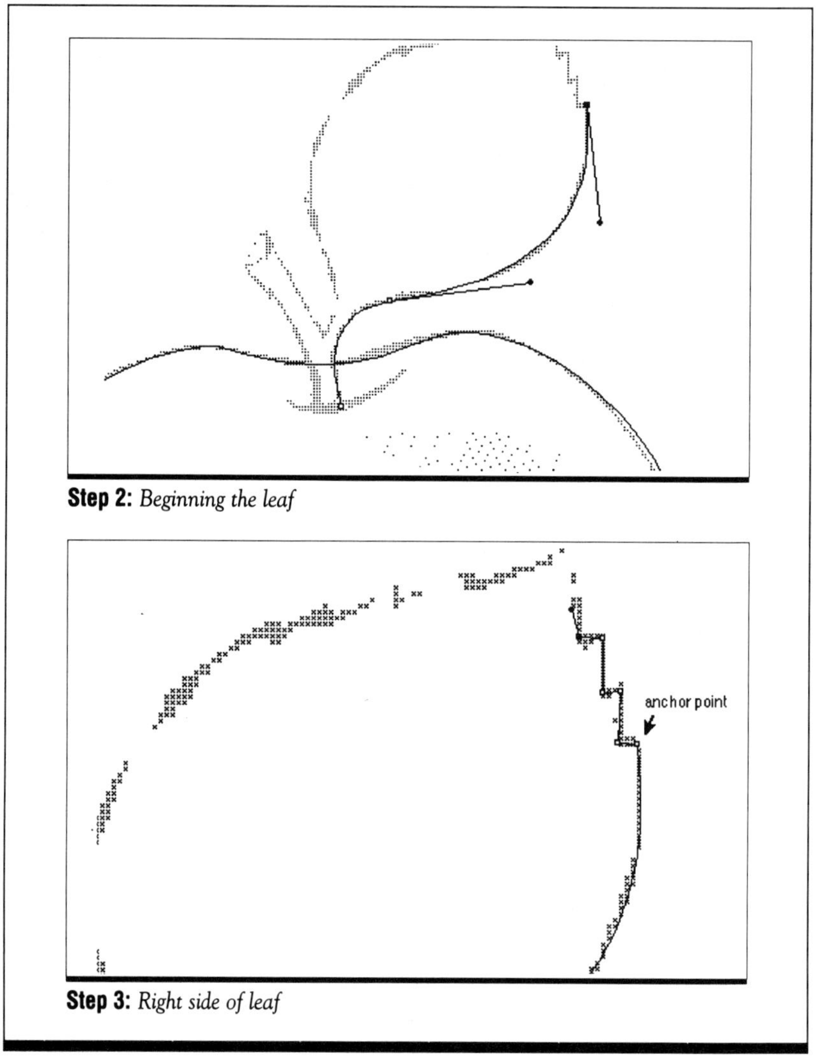

Step 2: *Beginning the leaf*

Step 3: *Right side of leaf*

Figure 4.4: *Tracing the first leaf tip (continues)*

You'll see that the first serrations on this side of the leaf are best represented as a series of straight lines (see Figure 4.4).

4. **Change from an arc to a straight line by returning to the anchor point where the change occurs and clicking on it.**

This will eliminate the direction point on the side of the curve that you are working on and make the next line a straight line from the chosen

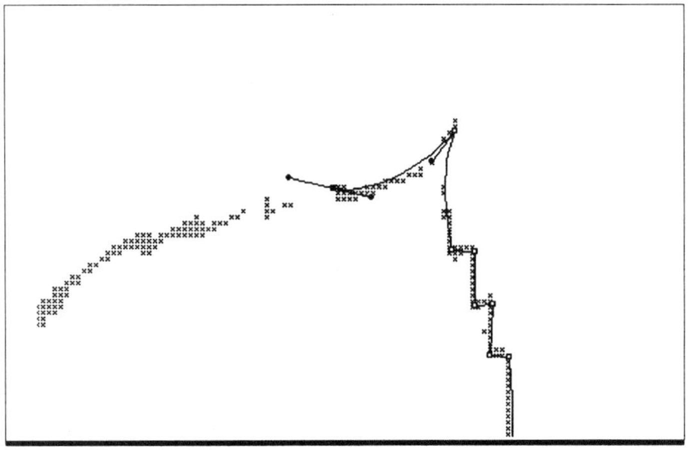

Step 8: *Corner anchor point*

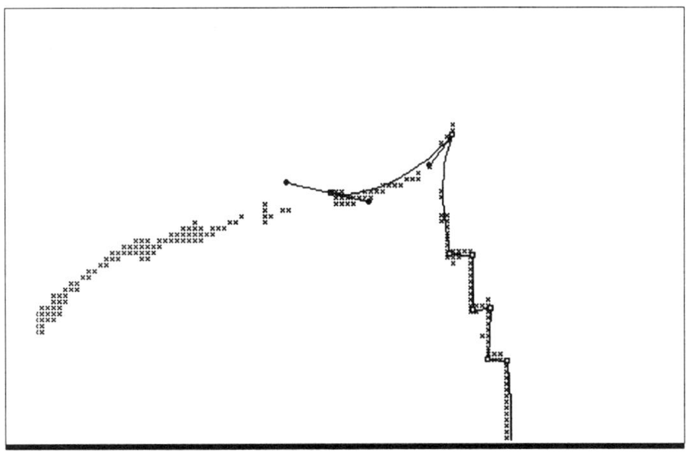

Step 9: *Finished leaf tip*

Figure 4.4: *Tracing the first leaf tip (continued)*

anchor point (see Figure 4.4). Now we want to continue the end of the leaf with a curve, leading to the tip of the leaf, which will be a corner anchor point.

5. **Position the cursor on the tip and drag the direction point up, away from the leaf and out, to make the edge of the leaf curve inward.**

6. **Return the cursor to the anchor point at the tip and click on it while you hold down the Option key.**
7. **Continue to drag the direction point from the anchor point down toward the leaf, to the final position around the tip (see Figure 4.4).**

The delta cursor that you see shows about how far to pull down the new direction point. You could move it anywhere at this point, but since the leaf is more or less symmetrical at the tip, the correct estimate is to make the new direction point similar to the first direction point in length and angle from the anchor point.

8. **Move down to the next serration on the top of the leaf and click and drag in the ordinary fashion to finish creating the curved corner point at the tip of the leaf, as shown in Figure 4.4.**

After you have formed the curved corner, you can use Illustrator's full range of editing and movement controls. For example, if you want to move the corner anchor point in toward the leaf, you can just press the Command key to activate the selection tool and then move this anchor point as you would any other. Similarly, you can move the direction points to alter the shape of the curve. However, you will notice that any movement of the direction point on one side of the corner anchor point will not affect the other side because you have effectively uncoupled one side of the anchor point from the other.

9. **Continue the leaf edge by making the serrations using straight lines.**

Remember that to change from a curve, such as the leaf tip, to a straight line (or vice versa), just return to the anchor point and click on it. Then move the cursor to where you want the next anchor point for the straight segment and click again. If you want to change to a curved segment, click and drag to set the direction point.

10. **When you come to the last serration, use the technique discussed above to change from a straight line to a curve.**
11. **Reduce the magnification by one click so that you can see most of the leaf and finish the rest of the leaf to where it joins the stem again.**

When you're done, your artwork should look something like Figure 4.5.

Drawing the Stem

As you can see, the leaf and stem junction is another corner anchor point. In this case, you are going to turn the curve back up toward the top of the stem, and so you need to change directions.

1. **Move the cursor to the anchor point, hold down the Option key, and click and drag the direction point upward, remaining tangent to the curve shown on the template (see Figure 4.6).**
2. **Move the cursor to the top of the stem (at the point of the oval that forms the cut end), hold down the Option key, click, and drag to create a curve that matches the template for the top of the stem.**

Because this point is also a corner point, you have to use the Option-click-drag combination once again to get the direction point to move toward the other corner of the oval.

3. **Create another anchor point at the opposite end of the oval to complete the top of the stem.**

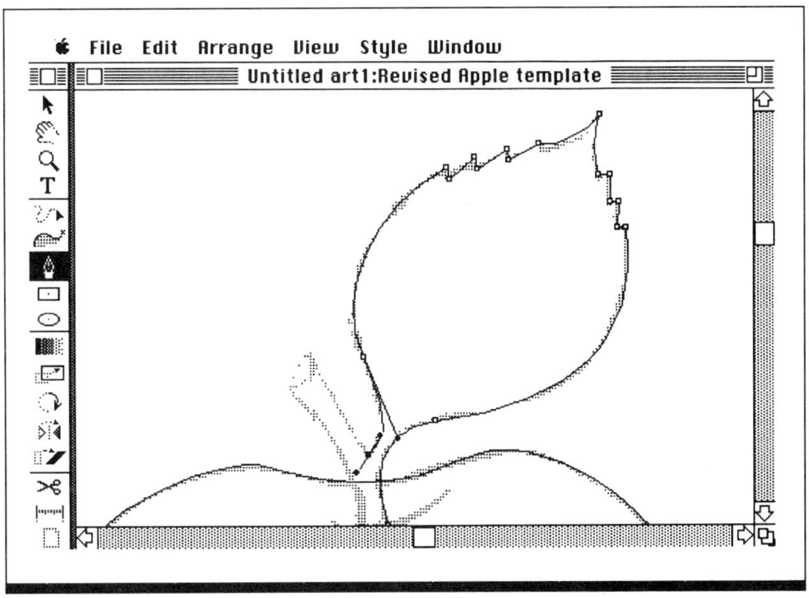

Figure 4.5: *Finished leaf*

This will leave you positioned to finish the stem. Don't worry for now about the rest of the oval that forms the cut end at the top of the stem.

4. **Continue down toward the base of the stem in one arc, and then close the figure with a straight line across to the starting anchor point, as shown in Figure 4.6.**

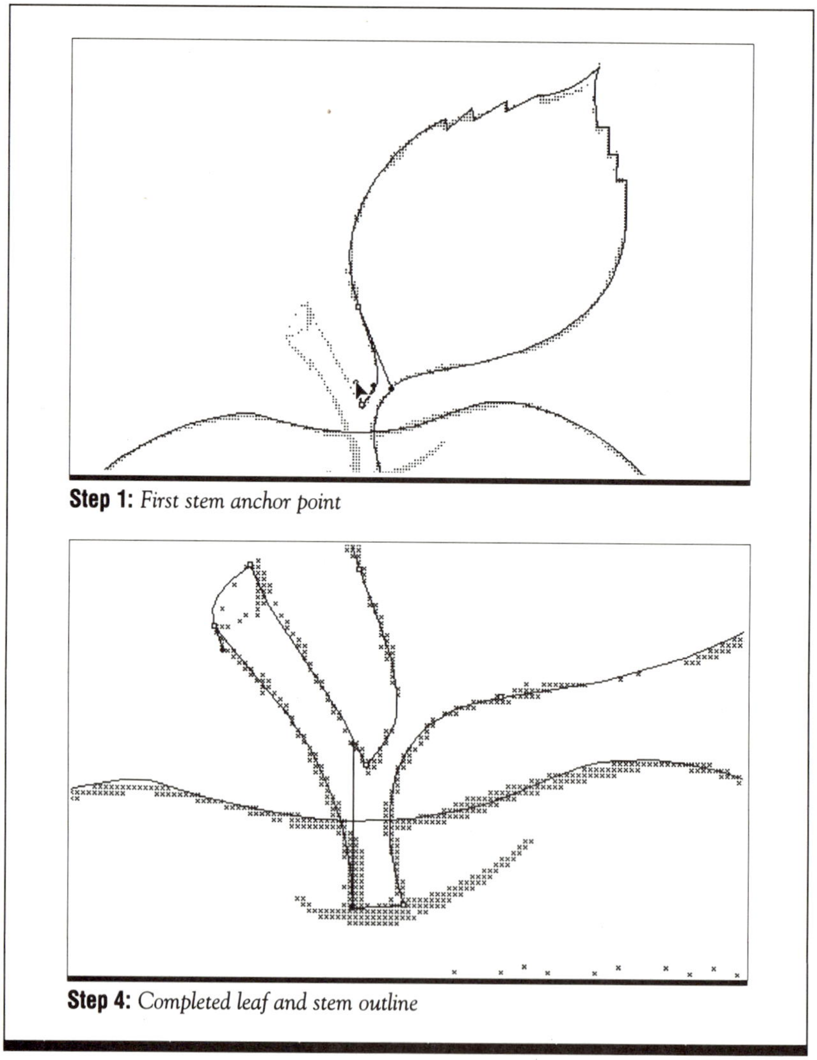

Step 1: *First stem anchor point*

Step 4: *Completed leaf and stem outline*

Figure 4.6: *Leaf and stem outline completed*

5. Pull down the View menu and select Preview Illustration.

You will see the new artwork filled in with black, while the old artwork is still in the gray shade that we set for it earlier.

6. Return to the Artwork & Template view of the desktop and select the new artwork.

7. Select Paint from the Style menu, and set Fill to White, Stroke to 100% Black, and the line weight to 1.

We set Fill to White instead of None so that the stem outline overlays the apple. If you used None, the stem would be transparent, and the apple would show through.

8. Zoom in on the oval at the top of the stem.

We still need to add the bottom of the oval to finish the stem.

9. Select the pen tool again and position it on top of the first anchor point at the top of the oval.

10. Click and drag a direction point tangent to the bottom curve of the oval.

11. Move down to the anchor point at the bottom of the oval and click to complete the bottom of the curve.

12. Drag the direction point out to match the bottom of the oval.

Figure 4.7 shows the completed stem top.

Adding Detail

To finish off this exercise, let's add the small depression at the base of the apple's stem. This is particularly interesting because both ends of the arc will require rather acute corner points.

1. Start at either end and form the bottom of the arc first.

The curve is easiest to match at the bottom. As you place the second point, use the techniques that you have learned for creating the point of a curved corner. This one has a sharp corner, and the curve lies above the tangent line.

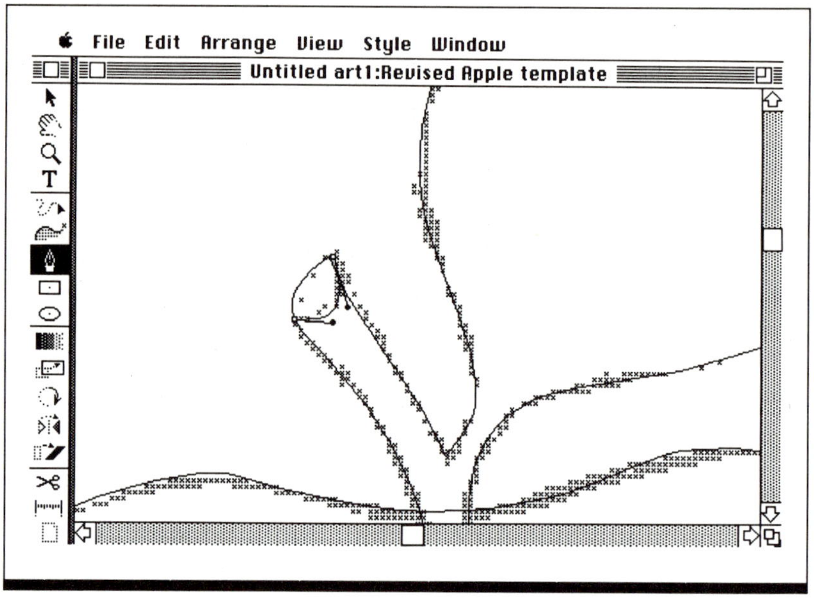

Figure 4.7: *Completed top of stem*

2. **Complete the arc by holding down the Option key while clicking on the first point to close the path.**

Notice as you do this how sensitive the curve is; if you move the mouse much in any direction, you will see the curve move wildly. Also notice that the delta cursor that you are dragging is moving by itself out away from the direction point that it controls. Just use small increments and let the top of the arc fall naturally. Figure 4.8 shows the final result.

Giving the artwork a name to match the template is a good habit to get into. Of course, Illustrator will always remember the original template association, but if you lose, rename, or otherwise misplace the template, you may have some trouble getting it back if you haven't kept to some naming scheme.

3. **Select Paint from the Style menu and set Fill to 100% Black.**
4. **Select Actual Size from the View menu and then preview the artwork.**

The apple should look like Figure 4.9 at this point. Notice how the arc overlays the base of the stem, so that the stem appears to run down into the core of the apple.

5. **Save the artwork under the name *Revised Apple art.***

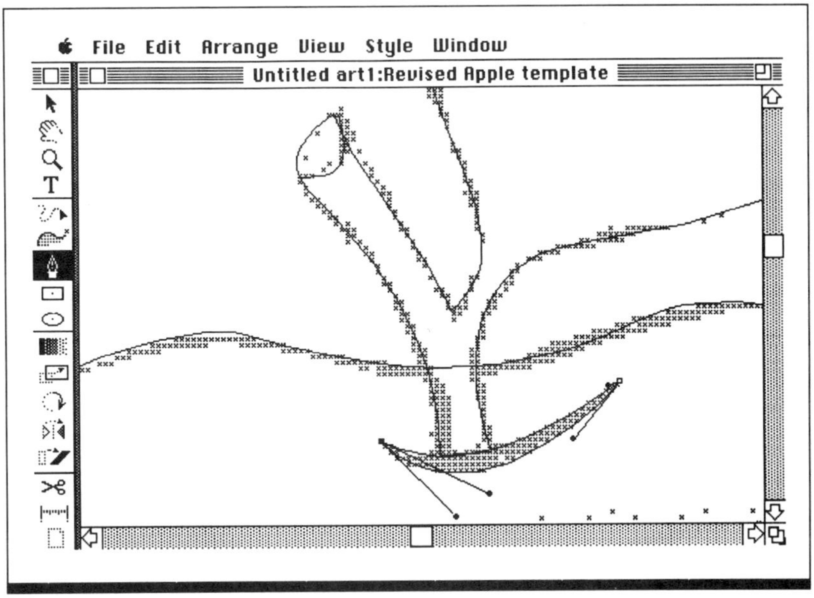

Figure 4.8: *Arc at stem base completed*

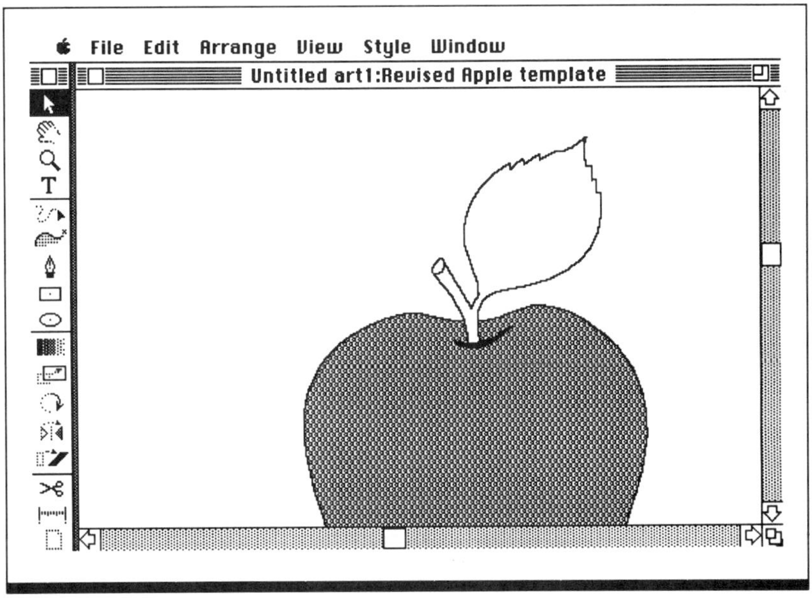

Figure 4.9: *Completed apple with leaf and stem*

We'll return to the apple artwork later in the chapter. Now we can combine some of these techniques to create some interesting graphic effects.

Creating the Cover Artwork

You can combine many of the techniques that we've covered up to this point to create a part of the artwork used for the graphic on the cover of this book. We'll draw the man's head and his hands holding a fork and a torch. The entire image is framed by a box and has a patterned background. The template for this artwork is shown in Figure 4.10. If you don't have a prepared template, you can use MacPaint (or any other drawing program) to prepare a similar image for this exercise or follow the exercise without a template.

Figure 4.10: *Somba Man template*

Drawing the Head

As you can see, the entire graphic image is composed of thick and thin lines. We will begin by tracing the outline of the head itself.

1. **Select the pen tool and start to follow the template from the base of the neck.**

The first segment is a short, straight line that forms the neck.

2. **Click on the anchor point at the top of the neck while holding down the Option key and drag the direction point out tangent to the curve of the head to form the corner between the straight line and the curved segment (see Figure 4.11).**

As you see, this is just a special case of the general method for creating corners on curves. The anchor points for a straight line, remember, can be thought of as having direction points that are on top of the anchor point. In that sense, you are pulling one of the direction points away from the anchor point in the same way that you made the curved corners for the apple leaf artwork earlier.

3. **Continue the curve around the head to the eyebrow. Make the last anchor point for the curve at the eyebrow.**
4. **Click on this anchor point again with the pen tool. Then move down to the bottom of the nose and click again to create a straight line from the previous anchor point.**
5. **Finish the nose with another straight line.**
6. **Change to the Artwork Only view. Your figure should look something like the one shown in Figure 4.11.**

This is another way to connect a straight line segment to a curved one. Because you are continuing with a straight line from the curve, it isn't necessary to use the Option key and reset the direction point. Just clicking again on the anchor point with the pen tool resets the direction point for a straight line continuation.

7. **Select Paint from the Style menu and set the Fill to None and Stroke to 100% Black with a line weight of 7 points.**

8. **Continue by making the line that forms the eyebrow. This is just a straight line and has the same Paint attributes as the previous line.**
9. **Start at the eyebrow and make a straight line down to the chin.**
10. **Form the chin and the neck with small straight line segments, as shown in Figure 4.11.**

Notice that we have not yet added the last anchor point to the neck and shoulder. Also, we traced down the neck, not up along the chin. This line is slightly thinner in stroke width than the lines that form the head, which you have already made, and the lines that form the chin, which you will do in a moment. You can't mix stroke widths on a single line segment, so we want to form the segment that is all one width at one time.

11. **Once again, click the pen tool on the anchor point while holding down the Option key to create a short, curved line to form the top of the shoulder.**

Figure 4.11 shows the anchor points and the direction point for this segment.

12. **Select Paint from the Style menu and again set Fill to None and Stroke to 100% Black, but this time use a line weight of 5.**
13. **Continue the figure by tracing the ear.**

This is a simple curved segment that is formed by three anchor points, using the bump rule. The bottom of the ear is itself a small bump, and so the entire ear cannot quite be formed in one single curve. If you are willing to form a somewhat smoother, rounder ear than the template, you can do it with two anchor points instead of three.

14. **Select Paint and set the line weight for the ear to 7 points.**
15. **Finish the jaw line with a single curved line segment that connects the ear to the rest of the jaw that you drew earlier.**

The artwork at this point should look something like the outline shown in Figure 4.11.

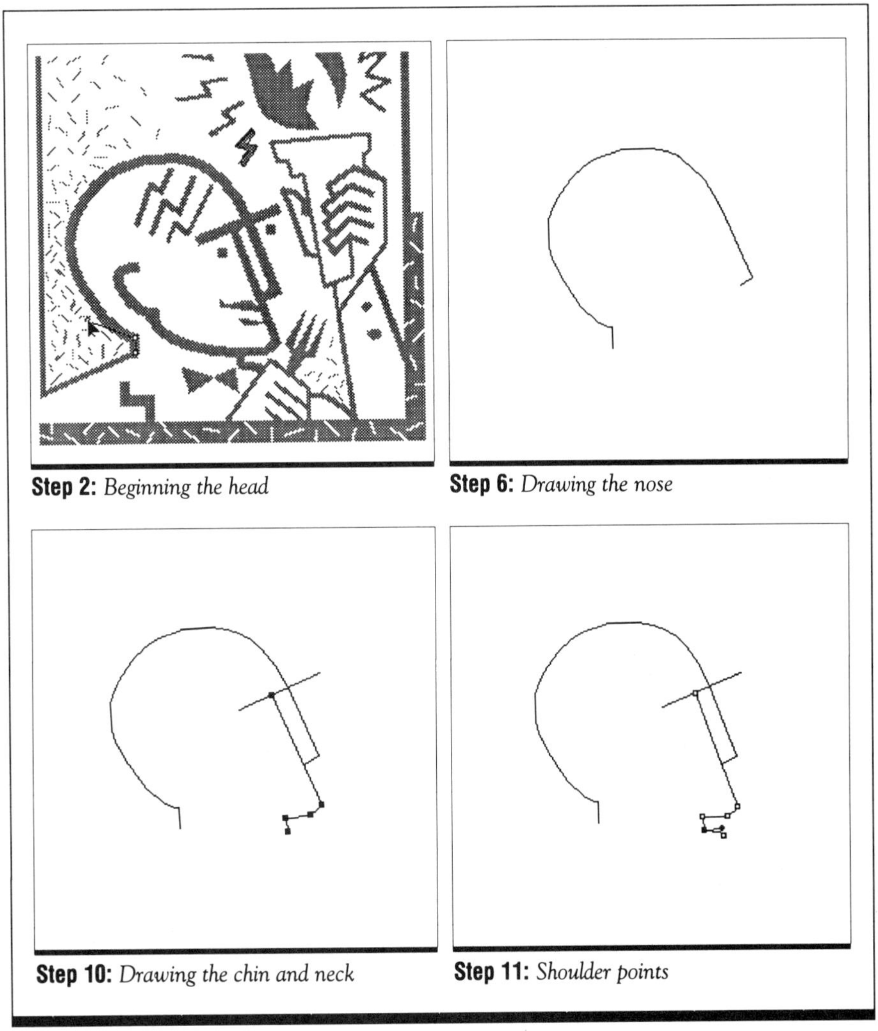

Figure 4.11: *Somba Man head (continues)*

Adding Details

Now we want to add some details to the head. We will add the hair, eyes, and lips. We will begin with the hair, which is just three zig-zag lines, again drawn with a relatively heavy line weight.

1. **Start by magnifying the head by one click and centering the hair in the frame (see Figure 4.12).**

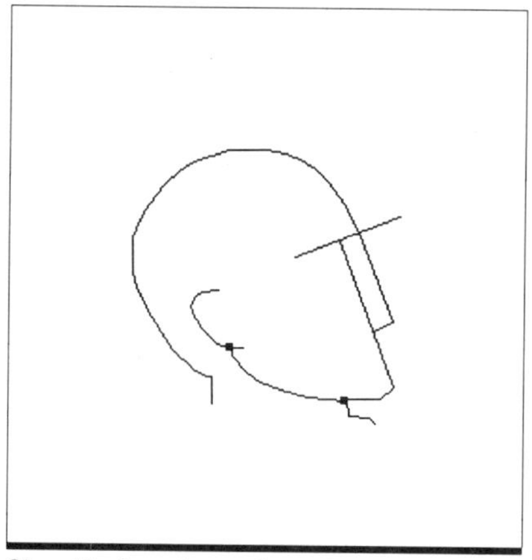

Step 15: *Completing the outline*

Figure 4.11: *Somba Man head (continued)*

2. **Each line of the hair is three straight line segments in a zig-zag form. Use the pen tool to create the first line.**
3. **Set the Paint attributes of Fill to None, Stroke to 100% Black, and a line weight of 4 points.**
4. **Create each of the other lines in the same fashion (see Figure 4.12).**

Now we want to make the eyes. These are just two small squares, filled in with black.

5. **Select the square tool and draw a box that matches the left eye.**
6. **Select Paint from the Style menu and set Fill to 100% Black and Stroke to None.**
7. **Make a matching box for the right eye (see Figure 4.12).**

The mouth is added next. This is a little more complex, although it also consists primarily of straight lines. All of these parts of the figure are filled with 100% Black and no Stroke. You have already set these Paint attributes, so the rest of the objects won't need to be set individually. You may want to magnify this portion of the template by one more click to help with placement.

8. **Draw the lower lip. This consists of a small triangle to match the template.**
9. **Begin the upper lip at the line that forms the front of the face. Use straight lines to follow the line of the upper lip and close the figure by returning to the first anchor point. The last line will lie along the line that forms the front of the face, as shown in Figure 4.12.**

Now we can continue to add details to the figure. Next we will draw the bow tie and the lapel of the coat.

10. **The bow tie consists of straight lines that form two triangles joined at their common apex. Start at one corner, and connect each corner and the center with straight lines, as shown in Figure 4.12.**

This is still a filled shape, so you don't have to worry about the Paint settings; they remain the same as before.

11. **Create the lapel using a zig-zag straight line.**
12. **Set the Paint attributes of Fill to None, Stroke to 100% Black, and a line weight of 7 points.**
13. **Return to the Actual Size view and preview the artwork to this point. Figure 4.12 shows how far we have come.**

Drawing the Hand and Fork

Now we are ready to proceed to the hand and fork. The hand is made up of straight lines, but some curved lines are used to form the bottom of the tines.

1. **Magnify the hand two clicks so that you can see the detail necessary for accurate line placement.**
2. **Use the pen tool to make the straight-line segments that form the outline of the hand.**
3. **Set the Paint attributes for the line to no Fill, 100% Black Stroke, and a line weight of 3 points.**

This makes the hand somewhat lighter than the line of the chin but still gives it good definition.

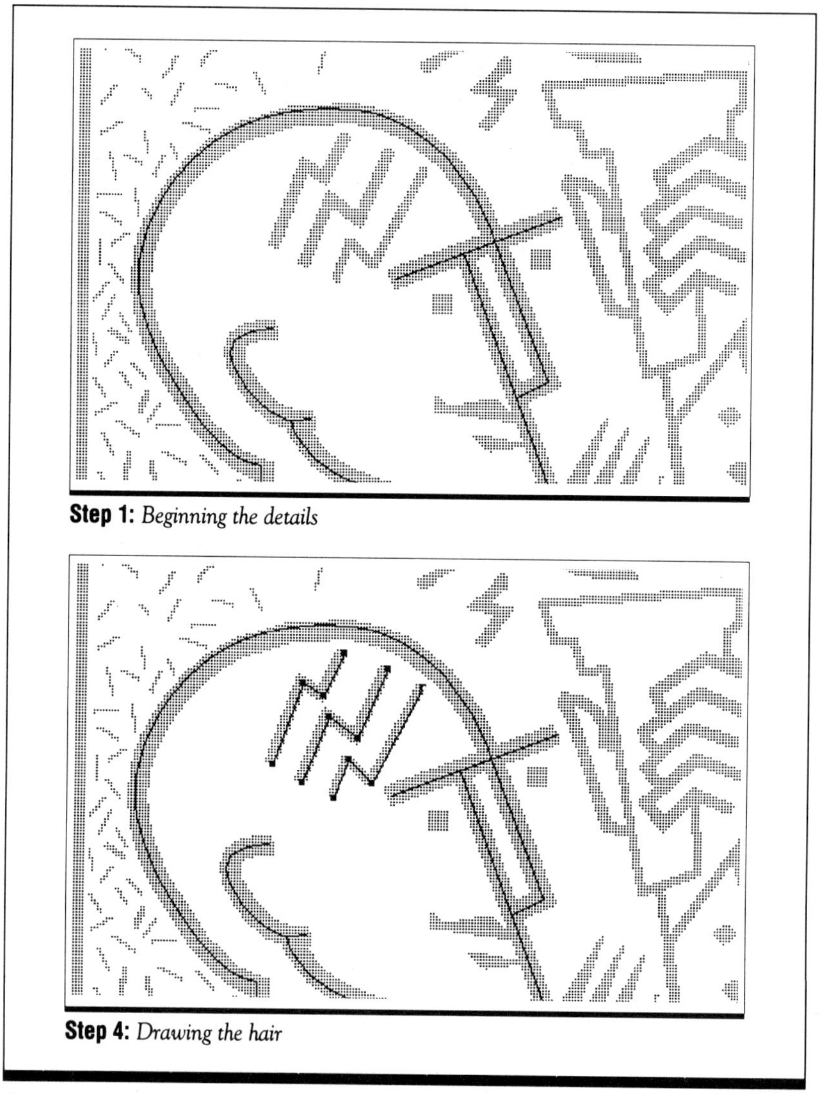

Step 1: *Beginning the details*

Step 4: *Drawing the hair*

Figure 4.12: *Somba Man head features (continues)*

4. **Next make straight lines for each of the fingers (see Figure 4.13).**

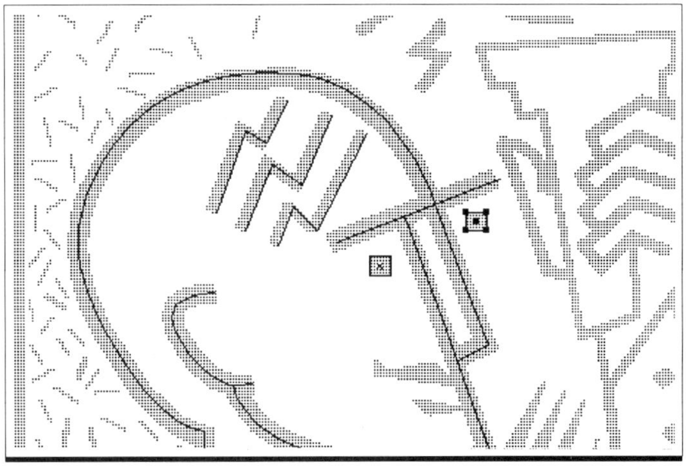

Step 7: *Drawing the eyes*

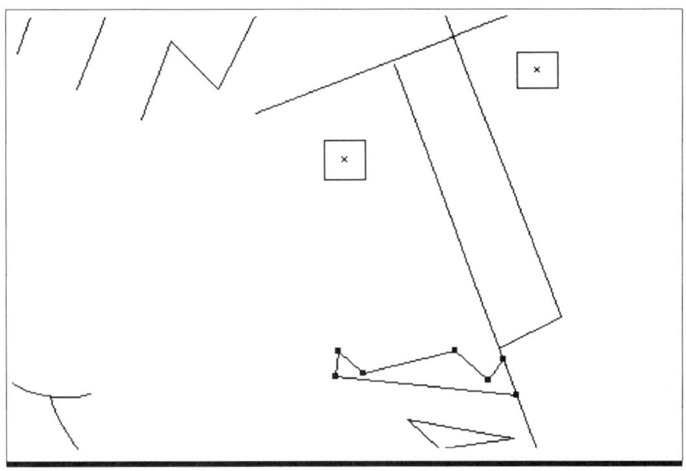

Step 9: *Drawing the lips*

Figure 4.12: *Somba Man head features (continues)*

Note that the middle finger is composed of two line segments to give a slight bend to the image, while the other two fingers are single lines. We will use the same Paint attributes for these lines, so you don't need to make any changes in the Paint dialog box.

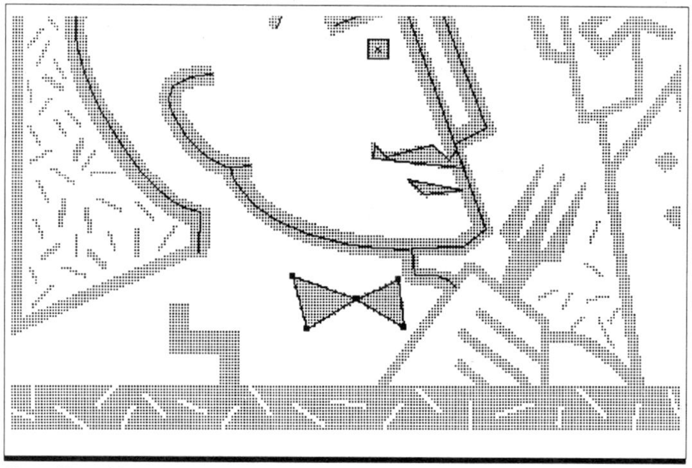

Step 10: *Adding the bow tie*

Step 13: *Preview of art*

Figure 4.12: *Somba Man head features (continued)*

5. Use the hand tool to scroll the fork portion of the template into the center of the screen (see Figure 4.13).
6. Use the pen tool to construct straight lines to form the top of the fork and the first tine, but not quite to the bottom of the tine.

To make the fork lighter and more regular in shape, we are going to create rounded spaces between the tines.

7. **Click again on the last anchor point while you hold down the Option key, and drag the direction point down to form a rounded curve along the bottom of the space between the tines (see Figure 4.13).**
8. **Move about the same distance up the second tine and finish the curve (see Figure 4.13).**
9. **Click again on the anchor point to force a continuation as a straight line.**
10. **Make the top and side of the second tine with straight lines.**
11. **Use the same technique as you did on the first tine to make a rounded space between the second and third tines.**
12. **Finish the fork off using straight line segments. Continue on around the fork and close the figure, as shown in Figure 4.13.**

The use of the rounded curves between the tines makes the separation of each tine more distinct. If you use straight lines, the space between the tines does not show up as well, and the fork looks larger and heavier.

13. **Set the Paint attributes of Fill to 100% Black and Stroke to None.**
14. **Reduce the magnification by one click and preview the image.**

The result looks like the preview in Figure 4.13.

Adding the Border

Although, as you can see from the template, there is a certain amount of texure and patterning in the border as well as the background of the figure, we will just do a simple, solid border for now. Later in the book, we will return to this artwork and add the patterning and texture features. The bottom and right side border are all one piece of work, consisting of straight lines.

1. **Start at the bottom-left corner of the border and trace bottom and right side borders with the pen tool.**

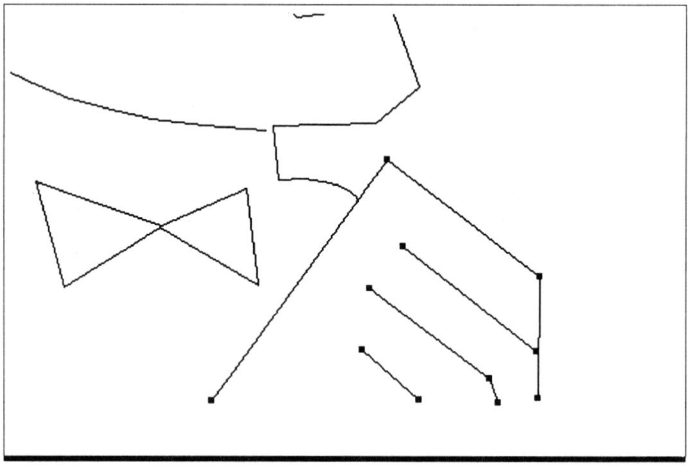

Step 4: *Drawing the hand*

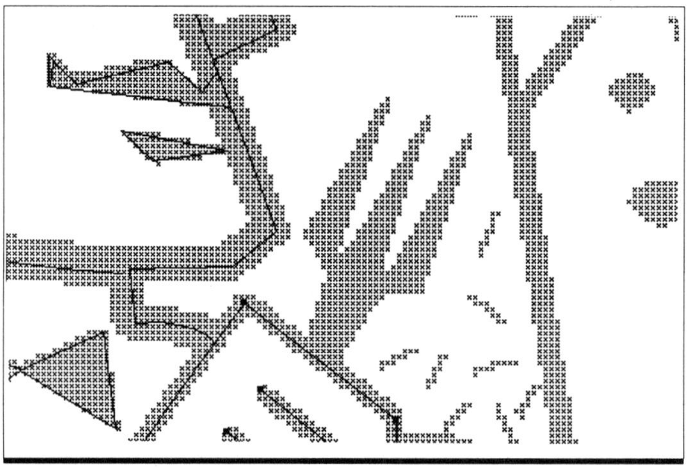

Step 5: *Beginning the fork*

Figure 4.13: *Somba Man hand and fork (continues)*

2. **Set the Paint attributes of Fill to 100% Black and Stroke to None.**
3. **Change to the Artwork Only view.**

You should see a figure that looks something like the first one in Figure 4.14.

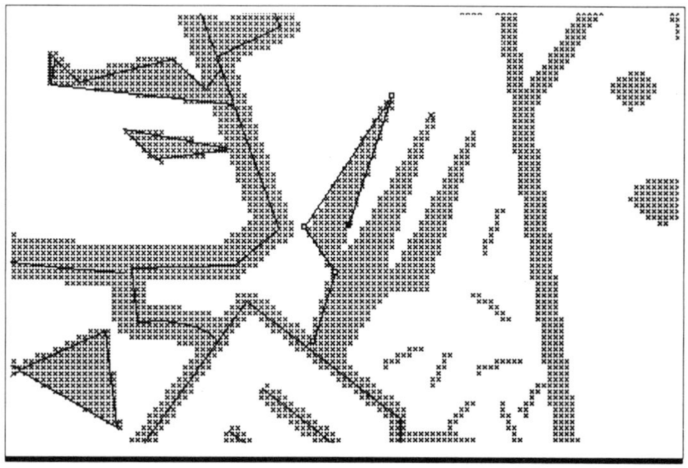

Step 7: *Drawing the first tine*

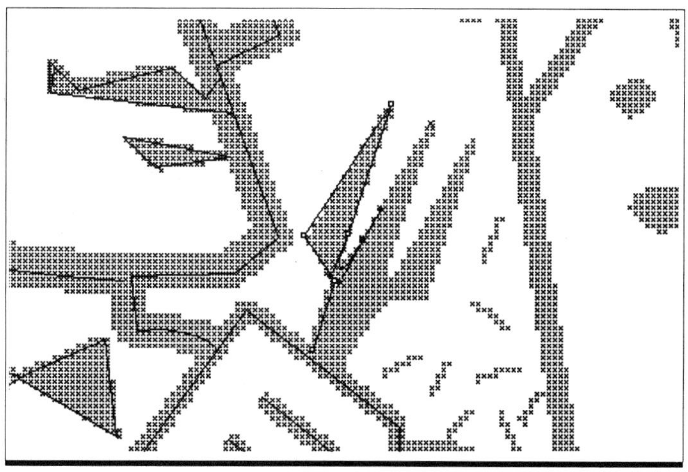

Step 8: *Drawing the second tine*

Figure 4.13: *Somba Man hand and fork (continues)*

4. Change to the Artwork & Template view and scroll up so that the top of the figure is in view.
5. Make the shoulder and left side border in two straight line segments, continuing the top of the line to the top of the top border (see Figure 4.14).

Step 12: *Completing the fork*

Step 14: *Preview of hand and fork*

Figure 4.13: *Somba Man hand and fork (continued)*

6. **Set the Paint attributes of Fill to None, Stroke to 100% Black, and a line weight of 4 points.**

This provides a intermediate-weight line that joins the shoulder and border as a unit.

7. **Select the square tool and complete the top border with a rectangle.**

The upper-left corner of the rectangle should be identical to the top of the left border that we just drew, as shown in the Artwork Only view presented in Figure 4.14.

8. **Paint the box with a Fill of 100% Black and no Stroke.**
9. **Preview the artwork, which should look something like the preview shown in Figure 4.14.**

This completes the first part of the cover artwork. As you have seen, this is an interesting graphic that can be created with basic Illustrator tools and concepts. It is a good example of the powerful tools and operations that Illustrator places at your fingertips. Now we'll move on to our next main topic: modifications.

ALTERING ARTWORK

Generally, you will often want to alter an existing artwork image for a new use. You already know a number of ways to change the shape of art with Illustrator: moving anchor points, changing direction points, and so on. Now we will discuss ways to add to artwork without modifying the existing points.

You can insert new art into an existing artwork or modify a portion of the original artwork. For both operations, you begin by selecting and "cutting" a portion of the existing artwork.

CUTTING INTO ARTWORK

You use the scissors tool to either create a space for new artwork to be added or to cut out the portion of the existing artwork that you want to modify. You can cut an Illustrator graphic at almost any point of the figure, except the cut must be made along a segment or at an anchor point that is not an endpoint.

Cutting in the middle of a line produces the effect that you would expect: you divide the segment into two pieces. Each piece has an endpoint at the point where you cut, and these two points exactly overlap. If the segment is a curve, each anchor point will have direction points suitable to the arc of the curve at that point. If the line is straight, of course, the anchor point will have no visible direction points.

Step 3: *Beginning the border*

Step 5: *New anchor points*

Figure 4.14: *Borders for Somba Man (continues)*

Cutting on an anchor point also creates two overlapping anchor points where there was only one before. This technique allows you to cut off an entire line segment and move it somewhere else without affecting the remainder of the figure.

Step 7: *Drawing the top border*

Step 9: *Preview of art*

Figure 4.14: *Borders for Somba Man (continued)*

MODIFYING THE LOGO BORDER

As our first use of the scissors tool, we'll modify the logo that we created for the imaginary Mountain Sports, Ltd. company. This logo now has a border of straight lines. We will alter the border to have rounded corners.

1. **Open the Logo art document (the full size logo).**
2. **Move to the top-left corner of the artwork.**
3. **Pull down the View menu and set the rulers on so that you can make matching modifications to all the corners.**

4. **Select the scissors tool.**

As you move the scissors onto the drawing surface, the cursor changes to a + to mark the exact point that you will cut.

5. **Move the cursor to point (2, 56), which is below the top-left corner, and click the mouse.**

You will see a new anchor point appear under the cursor.

6. **Move the cursor to (4, 58) and click again.**

You now have created two new anchor points, each two units away from the corner at (2, 58), as shown in Figure 4.15.

7. **Select the selection tool, place it on the corner point, hold down the Option key, and click.**

The three anchor points (the corner point and the two new anchor points that you created) are all black squares to show they are selected.

8. **Use the selection pointer to move the corner away from the artwork, as shown in Figure 4.15.**

Each cut that you made with the scissors separated the line into two segments at the newly defined anchor points. This allows you to remove the cut portion and replace it with a round edge.

9. **Click on the anchor point that is at position (2, 56).**

This anchor point is now selected, and the anchor point at (4, 58) is shown as an open box because it has become the other endpoint of the border, which is no longer a closed figure.

10. **Select the pen tool and start a new line at point (2, 56), dragging the direction point straight up to point (2, 58).**

11. **Move the cursor over to the other endpoint at (4, 58), click, and drag until the cursor is at (6, 58) and the matching direction point lies over point (2, 58) also.**
12. **Select the selection tool again and click anywhere outside the figure.**

This deselects the artwork and allows you to see what you have done more clearly. You have created a smooth, rounded corner (see Figure 4.15).

13. **Use the selection tool with the Option key to select all of the leftover segment of the previous corner. Then choose Clear from the Edit menu to remove it.**
14. **Use the same technique to replace the other three corners. For the corner at (38, 58), make your cuts at (36, 58) and (38, 56); the corner at (38, 34) should be cut at (36, 34) and (38, 36); and the corner at (2, 34) should be cut at (4, 34) and (2, 36).**
15. **Preview the final result.**

At this magnification, the logo border corners may look ragged or uneven. This is because of the screen resolution limitations. If you printed the logo, you would see that the corners are, in fact, quite smooth.

You will see the logo graphic with rounded corners on the border, as shown in Figure 4.15.

MODIFYING THE APPLE ART

Ultimately, you may want to create a library of basic Illustrator images that you can modify for different graphics.

Now we will continue on with a somewhat more complex exercise using the scissors tool. We'll add a second leaf to our revised apple. This is a good example of how you can use the Illustrator tools to create a new figure from old artwork.

1. **Open the Revised Apple art document.**
2. **Scroll up until the leaf and stem are in the center of the screen, then use the zoom tool to magnify the junction of the stem and leaf, as shown in Figure 4.16.**

You are going to cut the entire leaf off of the stem and copy it.

3. **Select the scissors tool, move it onto the drawing surface, and click exactly on top of the anchor point at the top of the leaf and stem junction.**

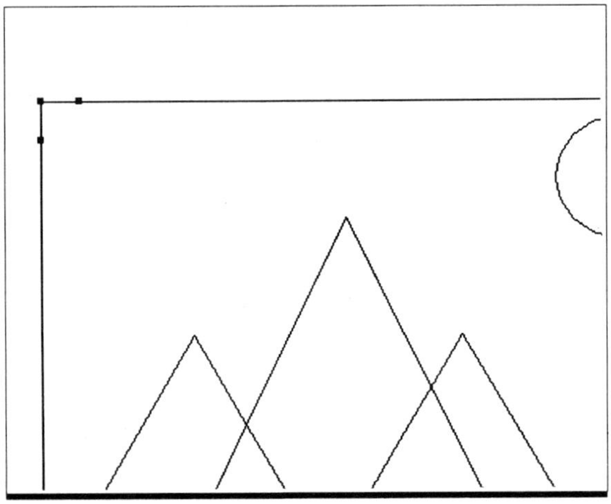

Step 12: *Placing the rounded corner*

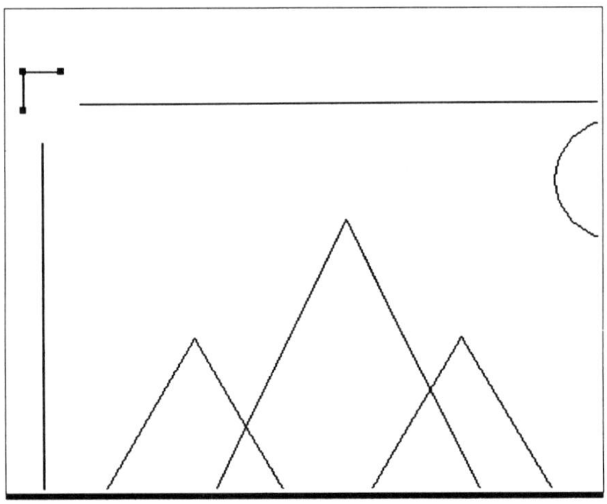

Step 15: *Modified logo*

Figure 4.15: *Modifying the logo art (continues)*

You may find this step easier if you use the Artwork Only view (we are not following a template for this part of the exercise at all). After the cut, the previous anchor point and both segments, on either side, will be selected.

4. **Move the cursor down to the curve below the stem and leaf junction and click again.**

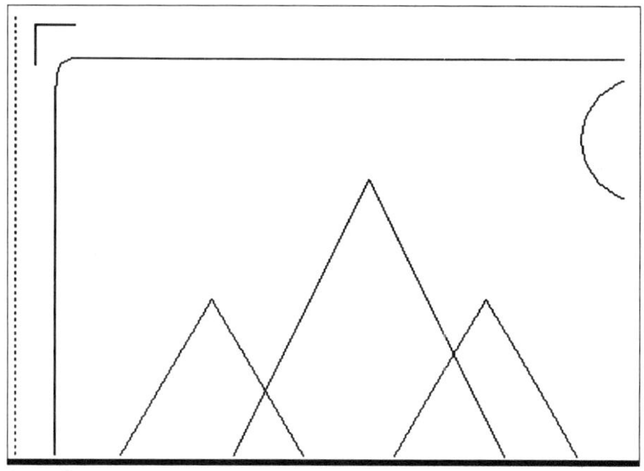

Step 6: *Drawing the left border*

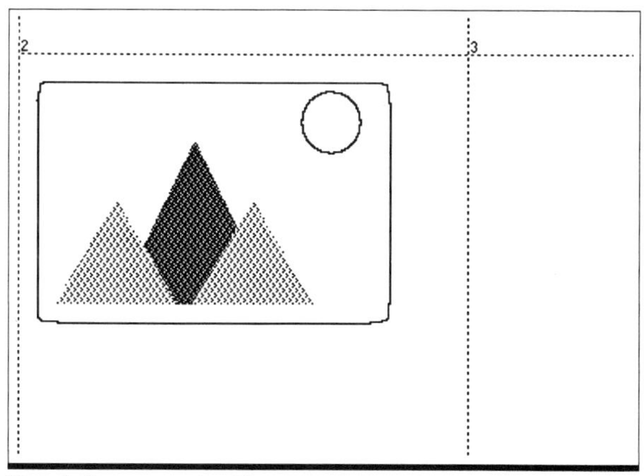

Step 8: *Removing the old corner*

Figure 4.15: *Modifying the logo art (continued)*

This makes a second cut and now divides the leaf image from the stem. The first cut appears as an open box, and the second cut shows as a selected anchor point, as shown in Figure 4.16. Now you are ready to duplicate the leaf.

5. **Move back out from the close-up view about two clicks so that you can see the entire leaf and stem.**

6. Use the selection tool and the Option key to select the entire leaf.

If you see that all the anchor points around the leaf are selected, but none of the stem points are selected (as shown in Figure 4.16), your cuts have been made correctly.

7. Place the selection pointer anywhere on the leaf, click, hold down the Option key, and drag to move a copy of the leaf image away from the apple artwork.

We'll use this copy as the second leaf. Notice that the copy is automatically selected.

8. Select the rotate tool.

We want to rotate the leaf copy to a new position before reattaching it to the stem. The rotation cursor looks like a + to start with.

9. Move the rotation cursor to the anchor point at the base of the leaf copy and click.

This sets the center of rotation at the base of the leaf, which means that this point will be relatively stationary while the top of the leaf is moving. The rotation cursor changes into a delta shape to indicate that the next action will be to move the selected graphic around the center of rotation.

If, for some reason, the copy of the leaf isn't automatically selected, select it before you use the rotate tool. The rotation won't work if nothing is selected; even worse, if the wrong artwork is selected, you'll have a real surprise on your hands. So be attentive when you use these techniques.

10. Position the cursor at the topmost point of the leaf and move it counterclockwise.

Notice that the old image of the leaf copy remains visible. This allows you to use the copy as a guide for how much rotation looks appropriate and realistic. Figure 4.16 shows the copy of the leaf at about a 30° rotation, along with the starting position of the copy before the rotation. When you release the mouse button, the copy of the leaf moves from its original position to the rotated position.

11. Use the selection tool to move the rotated copy over to the stem. Position the second leaf so that the connection to the stem fits correctly onto the stem (overlaying the original junction of the leaf and stem).

Now the two leaves are in exactly the same relationship as you saw during the rotation. This leaves only one difficulty. The second leaf, being the last object placed on the drawing, will paint in front of all the other objects in the artwork, but we want the second leaf in the background.

Users of version 1.1 will have to select Cut from the Edit menu, move the new leaf to the clipboard, and then select Paste In Back from the Edit menu.

12. Select Send To Back from the Edit menu.

This moves the second leaf to the rear plane of the graphic, so that the stem and the first leaf paint over it. Figure 4.16 shows how the result looks in preview mode.

ADDING ANCHOR POINTS

You can also use the scissors tool to add an anchor point to a line segment without cutting the segment, a technique that gives you more control of a line segment. We'll use this method to modify the second leaf on the apple so that the leaves are slightly different.

1. **Use the zoom tool to magnify the top of the second leaf, as shown in Figure 4.17 (you should still see the Artwork Only view).**

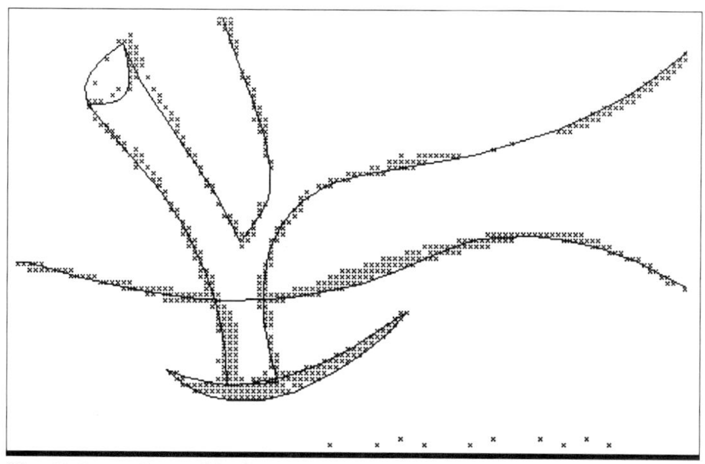

Step 2: *Start of second leaf*

Figure 4.16: *Adding a second leaf to the apple (continues)*

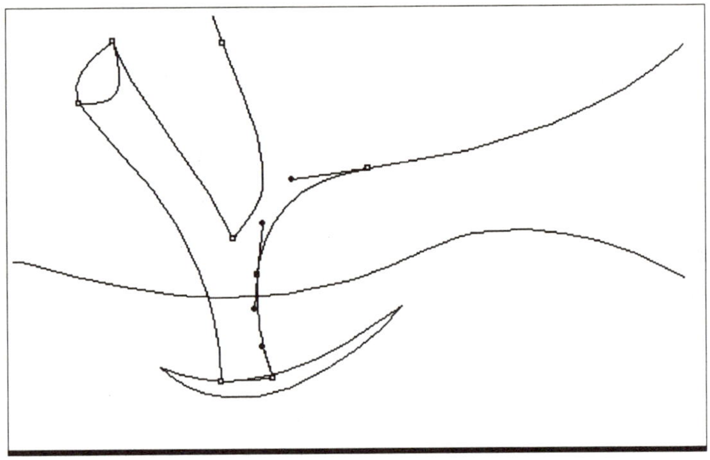

Step 4: *Cuts for moving the leaf*

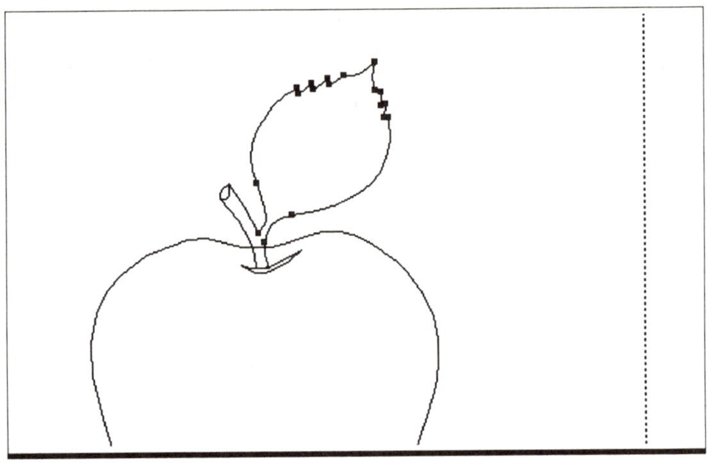

Step 6: *Selected cut leaf*

Figure 4.16: *Adding a second leaf to the apple (continues)*

2. Select the scissors tool and move the cursor over to the top-left side of the second leaf.

3. Position the cursor along the curved segment that arcs down from the tip of the leaf (just a small distance above the anchor point), hold down the Option key, and click.

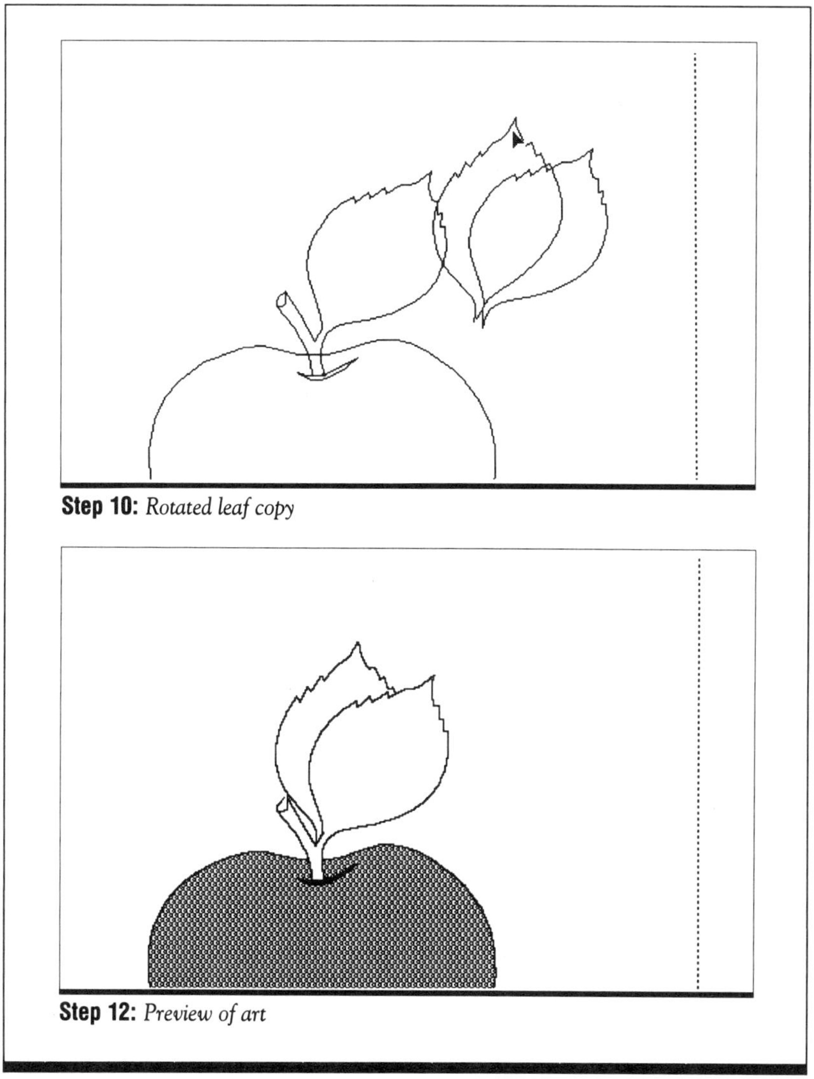

Step 10: *Rotated leaf copy*

Step 12: *Preview of art*

Figure 4.16: *Adding a second leaf to the apple (continued)*

Using the Option key creates a single new anchor point rather than cutting the line segment and creating two overlapping anchor points. As shown in Figure 4.17, the new anchor point has the correct direction points to define the existing curve between the two previous anchor points; in other words, the curve is unchanged by the addition of a new anchor point. But this new point gives you the capability to move any of the points that define the leaf's serration.

4. **Move the anchor point that is just below the new anchor point up to create another serration on the edge.**

Notice that the direction points stay just as they were, even while you move the anchor point. If this becomes a problem, you will have to do the process in two steps: first move the anchor point and then adjust the direction point. Figure 4.17 shows the changed edge of the second leaf.

MANIPULATING GROUPS OF GRAPHICS

As you know, most of Illustrator's tools and menu options operate on selected portions of your artwork. You also know that you can select an entire figure as a unit by clicking the selection tool pointer on any portion of it while holding down the Option key. This type of selection allows you to move, transform, edit, and restore a whole figure, without having to select each anchor point individually. Illustrator also provides a way for you to do this with more than one figure. You can select two or more related objects by grouping the figures into one unit.

The selected *group* (as it is called) can be used as though all the anchor points were attached to a single figure. You can move and adjust the unit without worrying about destroying the relationships between the various figures that make up the group, as well as rotate, transform, cut, and paste the group as one unit. In short, you can do all the things to a group that you can do to an individual graphic.

Grouping anchor points in no way connects them graphically. If you made a set of discrete points on the page, for example, and then grouped them, you would still have just a set of points—there wouldn't be any lines created between the points by the group function.

DEFINING A GROUP

Fundamentally, any set of anchor points can be logically joined together to make a group. A group is just an internal connection that relates the selected anchor points to one another.

The difference between defining anchor points as a group and just selecting groups of points (through the selection marquee or the Select All option on the Edit menu) is that the association of the grouped points is permanent; they remain associated until you "ungroup" them. You cannot access individual points in a group. When you select one point, all points in the group are automatically selected.

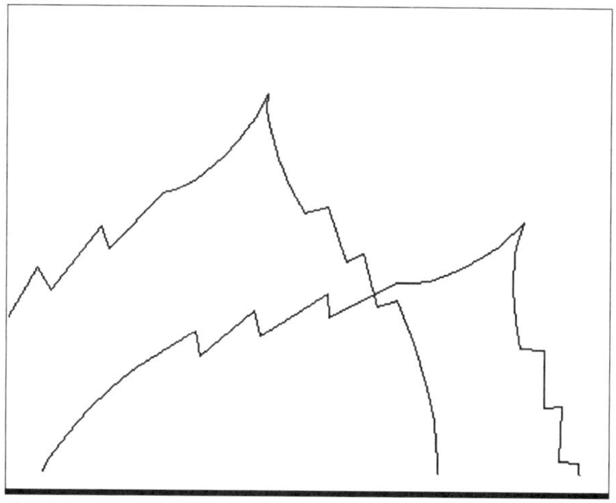

Step 1: *Start of modification*

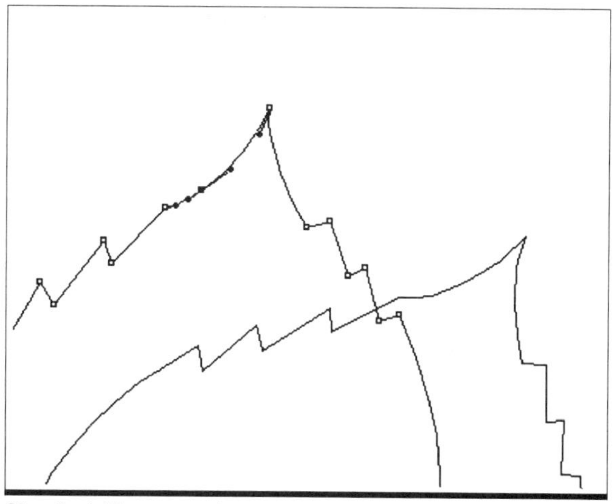

Step 3: *Adding an anchor point*

Figure 4.17: *Modifying the second leaf (continues)*

Grouping the Logo

As an example, we'll define the logo graphic as a group. This is practical because the completed logo will be used as a single unit, not as a separate collection of Illustrator objects. Grouping the points will make it easier to work with, as well as ensure that no part of it is altered accidentally.

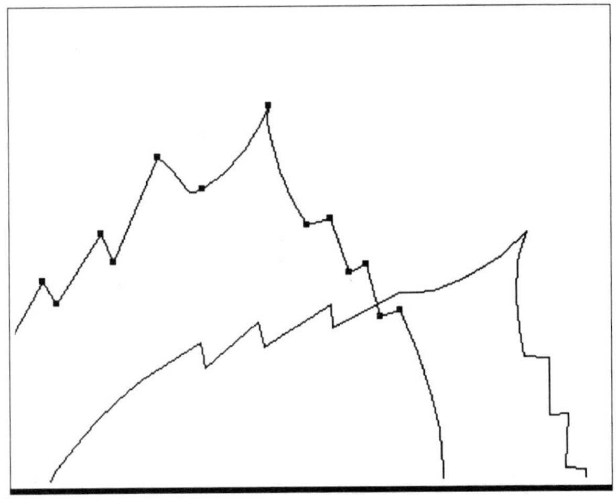

Step 4: *Revised leaf edge*

Figure 4.17: *Modifying the second leaf (continued)*

1. **Open the Logo art document.**
2. **Select Fit In Window from the View menu. Your screen should look like Figure 4.18.**
3. **Use the selection tool to form a selection marquee around the entire logo artwork, excluding the border around the logo.**

Start the selection process in the upper-right corner of the graphic to be sure that you encompass the sun. Be careful not to touch any of the border or you will include it in the selection process. When you are done, all the points that make up the three mountains and the sun should be selected.

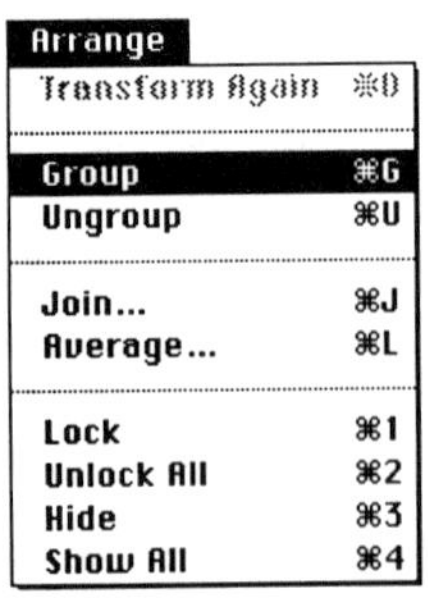

4. **Pull down the Arrange menu and select Group.**

This simple action makes all the selected points a group. To see for yourself, move the selection pointer anywhere off of the graphic and click to deselect the points. Now move the selection pointer back onto any part of the grouped logo and click. Immediately, all the grouped points become selected as a unit. If you want to experiment with the grouped

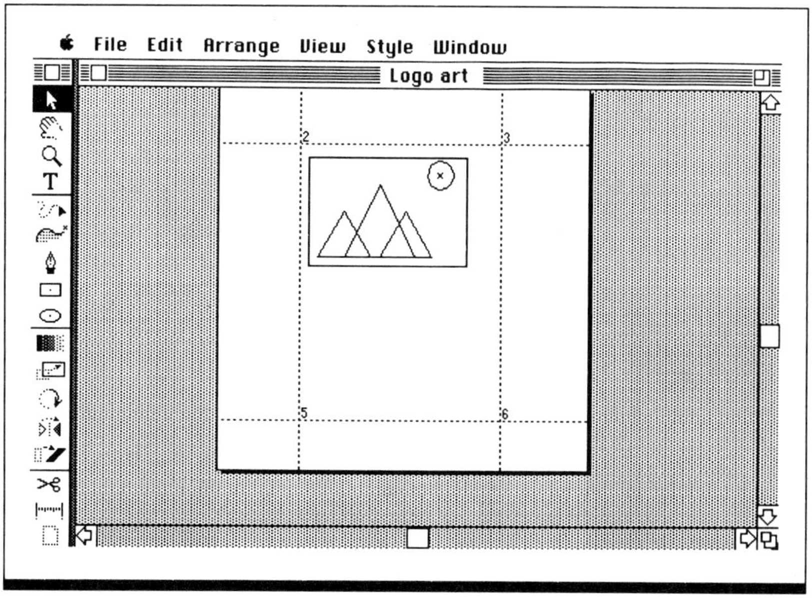

Figure 4.18: *Logo artwork ready for grouping*

logo graphic, move it around the page, make a copy of it, or try some other sort of transformation.

UNGROUPING TO WORK WITH INDIVIDUAL POINTS

Although you can't modify an artwork's individual elements while they are grouped, you can reverse the effect so that single points can be manipulated again. In fact, you can even ungroup objects that Illustrator automatically groups, such as the figures produced by the circle and square tools.

As an example, we'll use the circle tool, and then change the shape to a half circle.

1. **Open an empty desktop, and do not select a template to use with it.**
2. **Select Show Rulers from the View menu.**
3. **Click the circle tool and move it onto the center of the desktop.**
4. **Draw a circle with the center at about (22, 28).**

The circle has five grouped anchor points: four around the edges and one at the center. Actually, the circle is constructed of four arcs, each defined by two anchor points. The center point is for your convenience in working with the graphic; it is not essential to the construction of the circle itself.

To form a half circle, we need to cut off the bottom portion of the circle and draw a straight line connecting the two side points. However, as it is currently structured, you cannot alter any portion of the circle. Let's see what happens when you try to make a change.

5. Select the scissors tool and cut the circle at one of the side anchor points.

You will see an error screen, as shown in Figure 4.19.

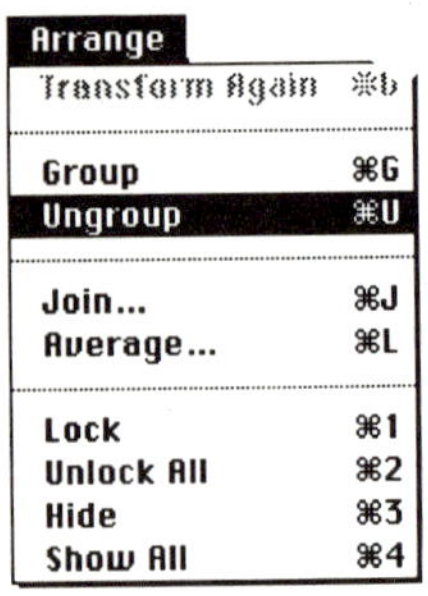

6. With the circle selected, pull down the Arrange menu and select Ungroup.

7. Move the selection tool to deselect the circle, and then move it back onto any part of the circle and click.

You will now see the individual anchor and direction points, as with any typical artwork object (see Figure 4.20).

8. Use the scissors tool to cut the circle at each of the two side points into two halves.

9. Use the selection tool and Option key to select the bottom half, and move it a short distance away from the upper half of the circle, as shown in Figure 4.20.

10. Select Clear from the Edit menu to remove the bottom half of the circle.

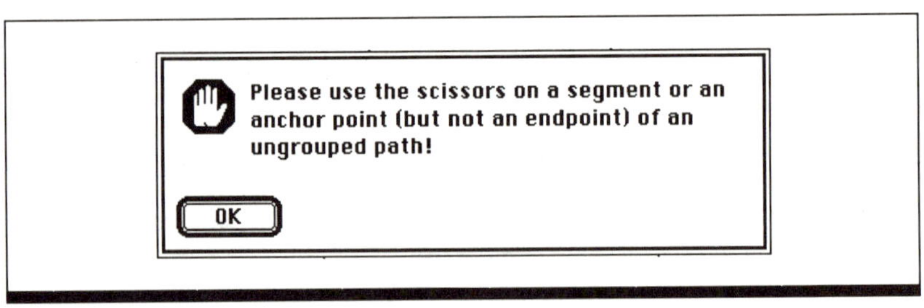

Figure 4.19: *Error screen for using the scissors on a group*

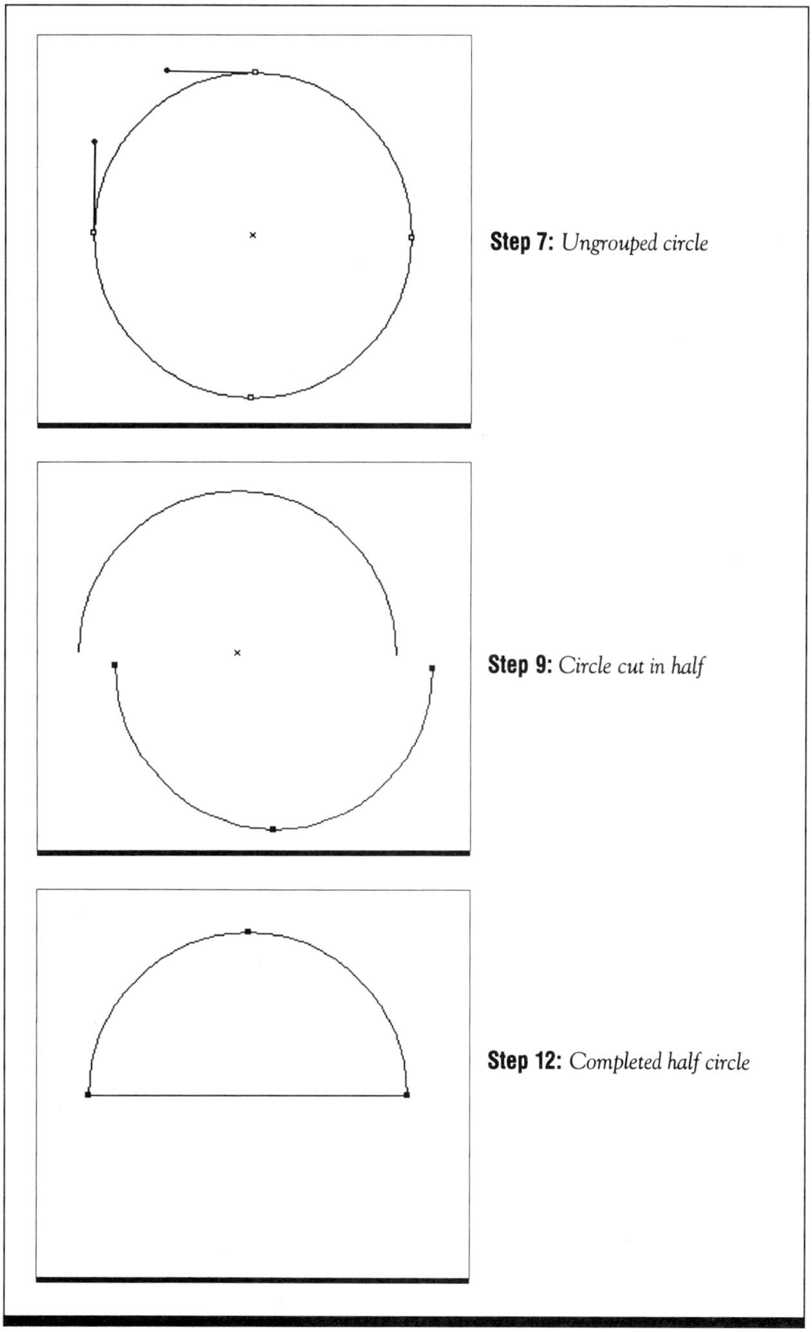

Figure 4.20: *Ungrouping to form a half circle*

11. **Use the pen tool to draw the line across the bottom of the remaining half circle.**

You may want to select the upper half of the circle before you start, so that the precise endpoints show on the screen. When you complete the bottom line, the cursor changes back to the starting line form (the x). Illustrator has closed the arc into a half circle for you automatically and considers the new line to be part of the completed artwork.

12. **Select and clear the center point of the original circle.**

There may be situations where you would want to keep the point as a positioning guide for some other purpose, but generally the center point is no longer useful after you have ungrouped the artwork.

The final result is shown in Figure 4.20. This half circle will paint a solid black, as you can see if you view it in the preview mode.

Duplicating and Centering Groups

As another example of the usefulness of both grouping and ungrouping, we'll create a graphic of a target seen through a gunsight. All the elements of this artwork are circles, squares, and rectangles.

1. **Start again on an empty desktop, with the rulers on.**
2. **Select the square tool and create a rectangle from (16, 36) at the upper-left corner to (30, 24) at the lower-right corner.**
3. **Select the rectangle and use the Ungroup option on the Arrange menu.**
4. **Use the scissors tool to cut off the top line of the rectangle, and then clear it (see Figure 4.21).**
5. **Connect each of the upper-corner points—the ones that you just removed the line between—to the center point with straight lines.**

This creates a notched figure that will represent the rear gunsight.

6. **Select the circle tool and position a small circle in the center of the notch.**

You can constrain the shape to a circle by holding down the Shift key. You can also use the Option key to draw the circle from the center outward rather than from one edge to the other. In this case, since you want the center of the circle precisely placed over the center of the notch, this is an extremely useful technique. Of course, if you don't get the position quite right the first time, you can always relocate the circle, using the centerpoint and the ruler coordinates to ensure proper positioning.

7. **Use the square tool to draw a rectangle that is the width of the circle and extends from the bottom half of the circle to the base of the notch (see Figure 4.21).**

If you previewed the artwork now, you would see it painted black and the ball on the front of the gunsight partially obscured by the rectangle.

If you have version 1.1, use the usual cut and paste technique to move the circle to the front.

8. **Select the circle, and then select Bring To Front from the Edit menu.**
9. **Select Paint from the Style menu and set Fill to 10% Black and Stroke to 100% Black.**

The preview image of the gunsight portion of artwork is shown in Figure 4.21. Before we go on to create the target artwork, let's stop and consider the final effect we want. Obviously, the target will be behind the gunsight and must, therefore, paint after the current graphic. We will ultimately have to move this artwork as a unit in front of the target that we will draw. Here is where grouping can be a real advantage. We should group these objects now because we know we will need to manipulate them as a unit later.

10. **Choose Select All from the Edit menu and then Group from the Arrange menu.**

Now we can proceed to create the target. The target will take the traditional form of concentric circles of varying shades of gray. We will create the circles off to one side of the existing artwork. This will help you select the target as a unit when it is done and will allow you to position it as a unit over the gunsight. Remember to use the Shift key to constrain the circle to be exactly round—you don't want to generate a lopsided target, and, as you will see, any inaccuracy will be compounded as you proceed.

11. Create a large circle, about 24 units in diameter.

When you make the circle, be sure that its center is well outside the edge of the previous artwork (the reason for this will become obvious in a moment).

12. Select Paint from the Style menu and set Fill to 70% Black and Stroke to None.

13. Select the scale tool, position the cursor over the centerpoint, and hold down the Option key.

As when we scaled the logo (in Chapter 3), you will see the cursor change from a + to a sort of sideways *t*, with the horizontal bar stretched out to the right of the cursor.

14. Click on the center point, and you will see the Scale dialog box.

15. Set the value for Uniform Scale to 70%, select Preserve line weights (if it is not already selected), and click on Copy.

This creates a copy of the existing circle centered on the same point, reduced to 70 percent of its original size, and with the same line weight if you were stroking it (not relevant for this exercise, but you should keep it set as the default value).

16. Select Paint from the Style menu and set Fill to 50% Black for this circle.

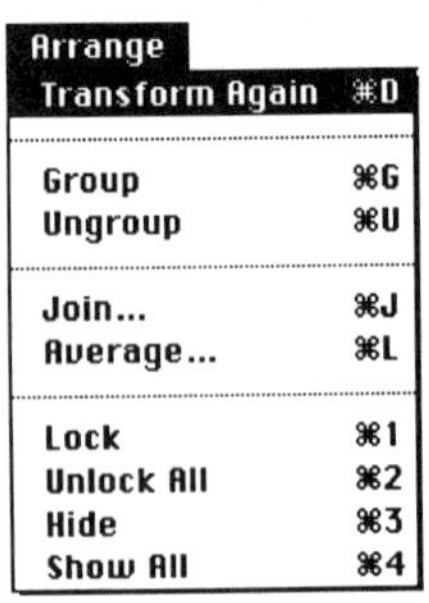

17. Select Transform Again from the Arrange menu.

This produces another 70 percent scale copy of the same circle.

18. Select Paint from the Style menu and set Fill to White for this copy.

19. Use the Transform Again option (or ⌘D) to create another copy, and fill this with 100% Black.

20. Make two more duplicates, and fill the inner one with 20% Black.

You may have noticed that you didn't set a new Fill value for the ring just outside the center. The reason is that, as you can see on the screen, the circles are beginning to appear too close together, which is a natural result of taking a continuous 70 percent reduction. As the circles become smaller, 70 percent of the figure becomes a greater absolute number. For example, if you take 70 percent of 10 inches you get 7 inches; you have cut off 3 inches. But if you take 70 percent of the 7 inches, you only take off 2.1 inches, to go down to 4.9 inches, and so on. To compensate for this, we will delete the second ring.

21. Select the selection tool, move it to the second ring, and select that circle.

22. Use Clear from the Edit menu to erase the circle.

This leaves a target of five concentric circles, each with a different color value, as shown in Figure 4.21.

Whenever possible, create objects in the order that you want them to paint.

We worked from the outermost ring to the center for a very practical reason. If you worked from the center outward (as you certainly might think to do), each larger circle would overlay the earlier, smaller circles and obscure them. In that case, you would have to send each of the successive circles to the back.

Notice that the gunsight we drew earlier paints behind the target graphic. We now want to move the target into position over the gunsight and place the gunsight on top. To move the graphic, we need to group it. This can be done quite easily, using a simple trick.

23. Select the selection tool and draw a small selection marquee around the common center point for all the circles.

As you see, this has the effect of selecting all the circles at once. Each circle has a center point, and all the center points lie on the same point but are actually distinct, being associated with different graphics. When you use the selection marquee, you are telling Illustrator to select everything within it. Even though the points overlap, Illustrator selects them all at once, and, with the center points, all the rest of the circle comes too, since each is part of a group.

24. Choose Group from the Arrange menu (or use ⌘G) to create this group of groups.

25. Move the target artwork over the gunsight until the second circle just rests on the edges of the notch.

This should put the center of the target in line with the center of the circle and rectangle that form the front gunsight element, as shown in Figure 4.21.

Again, users of version 1.1 will have to cut and paste to move the gunsight in front of the target.

26. Select the gunsight and select Bring To Front from the Edit menu. Then preview the finished artwork.

The finished artwork should resemble the preview image shown in Figure 4.21.

WORKING WITH PAGES

Along with grouping for the kinds of exercises we've just done, you can manipulate entire pages of graphics as a single entity. This process is more conceptual than actual; that is, there is no actual grouping that goes on. Instead, certain functions and processes in Illustrator are constructed to use the entire page as a unit. We will discuss these techniques in the remainder of this chapter.

MOVING GRAPHICS ON A PAGE

There are several ways to move Illustrator artwork on a page. The most obvious is to select the entire artwork and simply move it to wherever you want on the page surface. In this case, you would use the Fit In Window view to be sure that the artwork went where you wanted it to go.

But what if the artwork is larger than one output page? As you look at the output surface, you remember that the entire Illustrator drawing area is 14-inches by 14-inches. For output purposes, this area is tiled into nine output areas, as shown in the Fit In Window display. If you have a large graphic that you want to display, you may want to adjust the tiling so that certain portions of the artwork appear together on a single page (tile).

The page tool allows you to adjust the tiling of the drawing surface so that you can have the artwork print across page junctions at any point. This gives you complete control over the tiling process.

The easiest way to see how this facility works is to watch it on the screen.

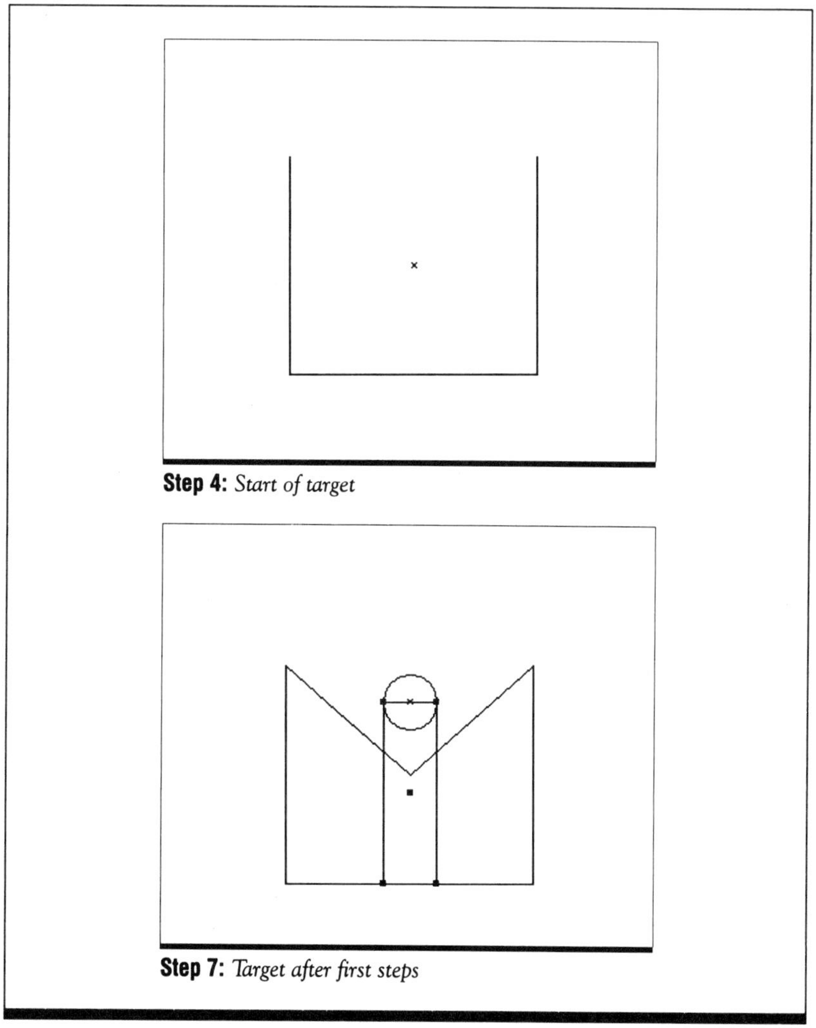

Step 4: *Start of target*

Step 7: *Target after first steps*

Figure 4.21: *Creating target art with groups (continues)*

1. **Open a blank desktop.**
2. **Select Fit In Window from the View menu.**

3. **Select the page tool from the toolbox.**

When you move the cursor out onto the drawing surface, it is shaped like a +.

Step 9: *Preview of gunsight*

Step 22: *Preview of target*

Figure 4.21: *Creating target art with groups (continues)*

4. **Click the mouse button, and the + becomes the bottom-left corner of the primary output page.**

The entire page is shown as a dotted outline, and you can reposition this page anywhere on the surface. Figure 4.22 shows this process.

When you release the mouse button, the position of the primary output page is fixed, and the remainder of the drawing surface is tiled

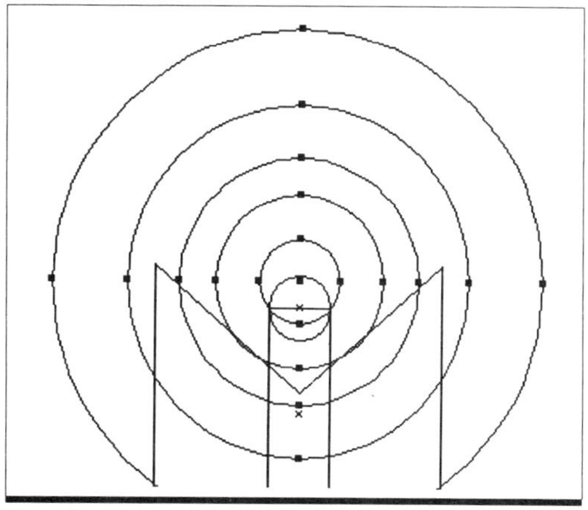

Step 26: *Preview of target and gunsight*

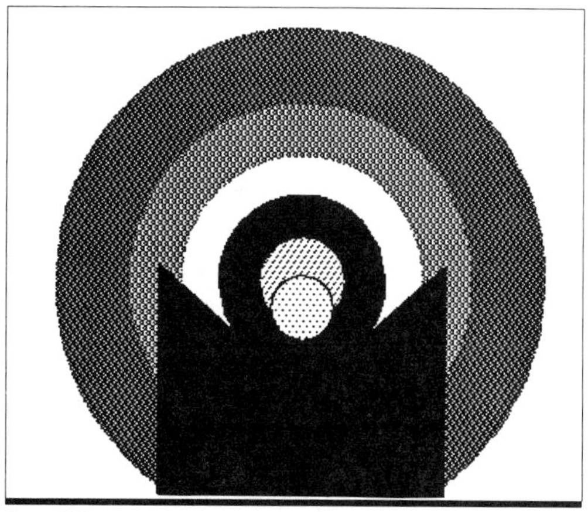

Step 25: *Target and gunsight*

Figure 4.21: *Creating target art with groups (continued)*

If you have a graphic that requires the entire 14 by 14 inch surface, you might well prefer to tile it into four pieces rather than nine. However, for most work, when one page of output is sufficient, it is most convenient to have the output page in the center of the surface rather than a corner, as provided by the default nine-page tiling.

accordingly. You can continue to experiment with this mechanism here, on a blank surface, to see how the process works.

The entire drawing surface can be tiled in as little as four tiles or as many as nine. Four-tile coverage results when the primary output page is at one of the corners; you will get nine tiles when the primary output page is in the center of the drawing surface, which is the default positioning.

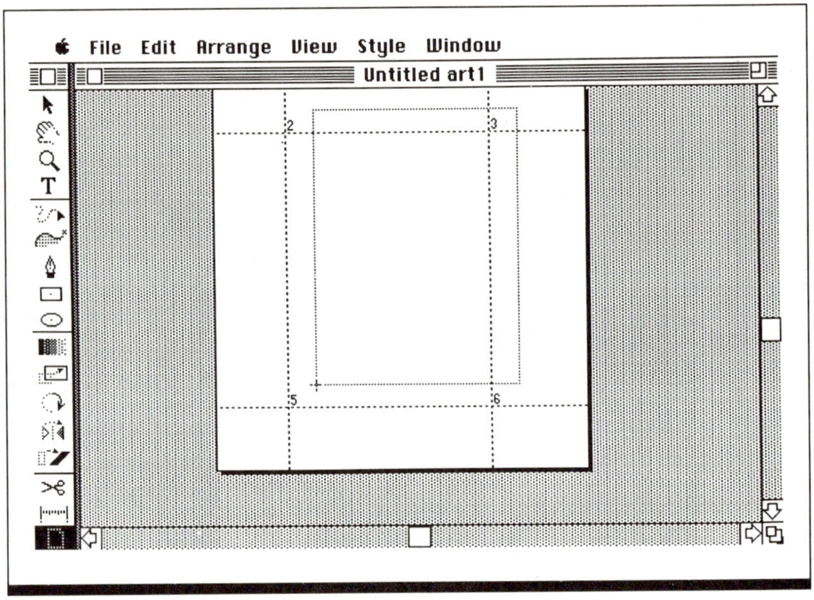

Figure 4.22: *Page repositioning with the page tool*

If you have the rulers on as you move the primary page around, you may notice that they do not move with the page. Point (0, 0) remains in the same place even when you move the page tiles. This is because your graphic has been drawn with a given set of coordinates, and there is no reason to change those; the only requirement is to change the coordinates to match an output page.

To move the coordinate system, you move the origin, (0, 0), to the new location. When you do that, all the coordinates on your artwork will be changed to match, so don't be surprised if there is a certain amount of reading and writing from your disk if you use this technique with artwork already on the drawing surface.

You can move the origin by clicking on the scale box in the lower-right corner of the rulers and dragging the crosshairs to any position on the page, as shown in Figure 4.23. The center of the crosshairs represents the point that will become the new origin, (0, 0), when you release the mouse button. This process does not move the page tiles. If you want to move both the origin and the tiling to match one another, you must do each step separately.

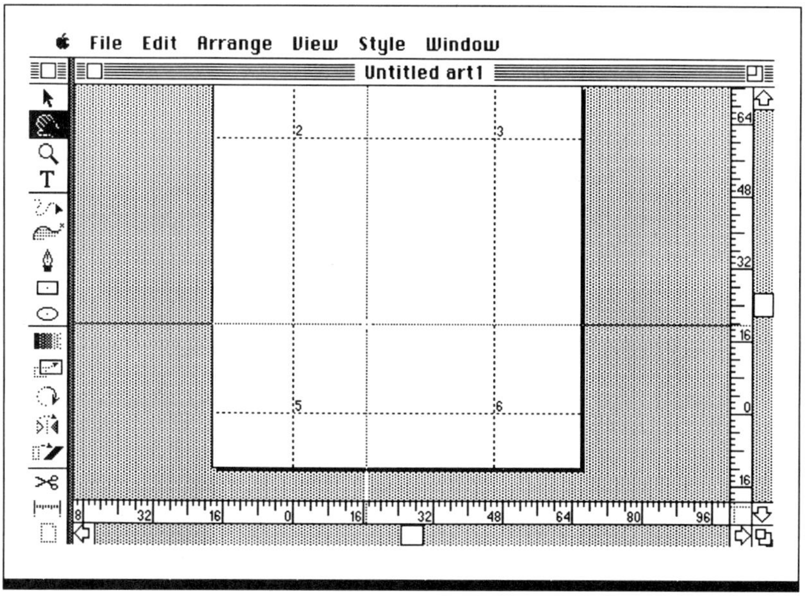

Figure 4.23: *Adjusting the page origin*

SEEING MULTIPLE VIEWS OF A PAGE

Another feature of Illustrator is its capability to open multiple views of the same page at the same time. This is most useful for large screen displays because you really can't see much of several views on smaller screens. Nevertheless, let's take a look at how this works in practice, even on a small display.

1. **Open the Revised Apple art document (or any other artwork that you prefer; we are not going to make any permanent changes).**
2. **Move it to the left of the screen and select Preview Illustration as the viewing mode (see Figure 4.24).**
3. **Select New Window from the Window menu.**

Immediately, a new image, identical to the previous one, replaces the first screen. The only visible difference is that the title of the screen now has *:2* added to it, which indicates that you are looking at the second view of the named artwork and template.

4. **Change the view back to Artwork & Template.**
5. **Use the window size box and the window position controls to resize and move the second window to the upper-right corner of the desktop.**

At this point, you can see both windows at once (although only a portion of each), as shown in Figure 4.24.

6. **Use the selection tool and the Option key to select the apple in the second window.**
7. **Select Paint from the Style menu and change the Fill for the apple in the second window from 50% Black to 80% Black.**
8. **Click on OK and return to the desktop.**

You will see the preview version of the apple in the first window change to reflect the new value. This is one valuable use for multiple views: they allow you to see the preview at the same time that you are working on the artwork.

Step 2: *Preview of apple*

Figure 4.24: *Opening multiple views (continues)*

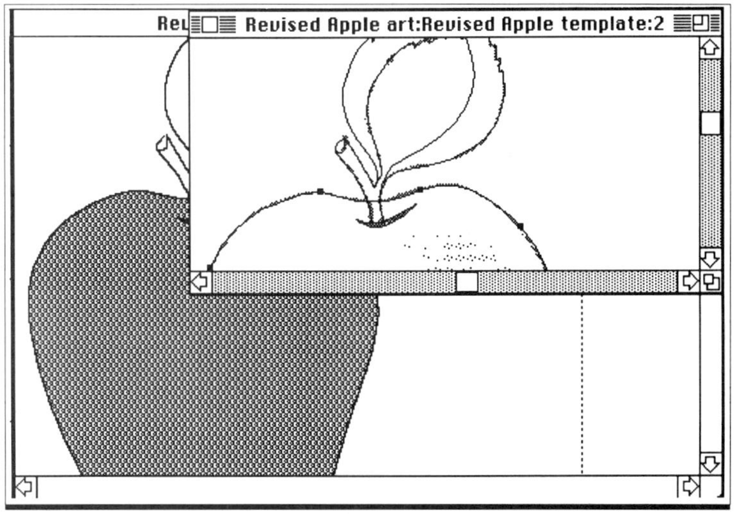

Step 5: *Both views displayed*

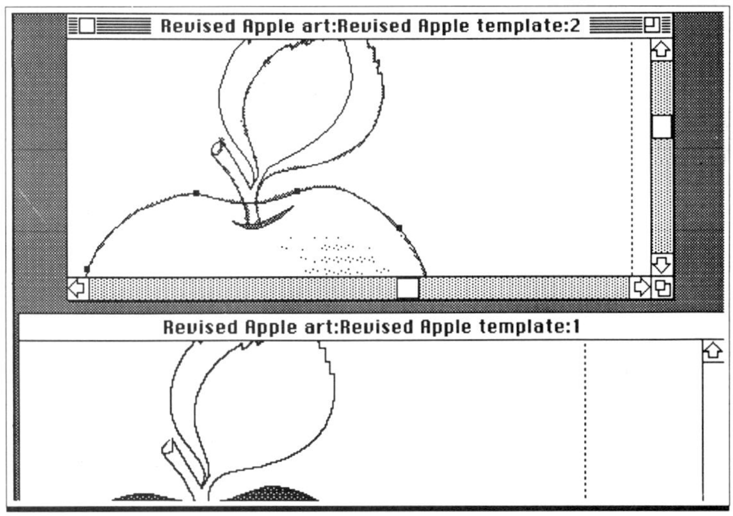

Step 9: *Moving inactive windows*

Figure 4.24: *Opening multiple views (continued)*

Generally, all Illustrator windows are managed in the same ways as other Macintosh windows. All the usual controls are available, such as those you just used to move and resize the second view window. In addition, Illustrator has certain features that you can use for managing its windows. You can reposition an inactive window by holding down the Command key and clicking on the title bar of the inactive window as you move it. This will move the window but allow it to remain inactive.

9. Hold down the Command key, click on the title bar of the first window, and move it down behind the second, currently active window so that you can see the title bar, as shown in Figure 4.24.

If you have version 1.1, you can send an active window to the back of the other windows, making it inactive and hiding it if the other window fills the screen, by holding down the Command key and clicking on the title bar of the active window.

As usual, if you click anywhere in an inactive window, it becomes active and moves to the front of the desktop. When it does, it may completely cover other windows. If that happens, you can use the Window menu to reselect the active window display. This makes the current window inactive and sends it to the back of the set of windows.

There are two points to notice about these multiple views. First, the title of the window will always have the number of the view appended to the usual title information. If the window contains only artwork, for instance, the title will be *xyz art:2*, *:3*, or whatever number is correct. As described above, the windows are displayed in sequence, and if any window is closed, the remaining windows are renumbered accordingly.

Second, all these windows, or views, represent a single artwork. Changes to any one of the windows will change all the other windows at the same time. The point here is that the multiple views are just that: multiple visions of the same object. This means that if you save the document from any window, you save it for all the windows. By the same token, if you close a window without saving any changes you made to it while there are still others open, you will not lose those changes. You only have to save the changes when you close the final view.

You now have seen how to use groups and move pages of art around as a unit in various ways to generate new page structures. You also learned about multiple views of the desktop and how to manipulate them. In the next chapter, we will discuss in more detail how to transform artwork into a variety of shapes and sizes to accomplish some of the more unusual and interesting Illustrator effects.

Fast Track Chapter 5

189 To move an object a precise amount,
select the object and then access the Move dialog box by holding down the Option key while you click on the selection tool icon in the toolbox.

190 Precise scaling effects
can be made using the optional dialog box accessed by holding down the Option key when you set the scale origin. The box also shows the precise values for the most recent use of the scale transformation.

191 To blend one image into another,
select one point on each image and then click on each point with the blend tool. Enter the desired number of blending steps into the dialog box.

198 To rotate a figure around a point,
select the figure, click on the desired point (the center of rotation) with the rotate tool, and drag the figure with the delta cursor into the desired rotated position.

205 Rotation to a precise angle
can be made using the optional dialog box accessed by holding down the Option key when you set the center of rotation. The box also shows the precise value of the most recent angle of rotation.

210 To reflect an object,
select the object to be reflected and use the reflect tool to set the line about which the reflection will take place (the axis of reflection).

217 To shear an object,
select the object to be sheared and use the shear tool to set the bottom point of the line along which the object will be sheared (the shear axis), then click the delta cursor to set the top of the shear axis and drag to create a shear of the selected object.

228 To create a shadow effect,
use a combination of shearing and nonuniform scaling to create the shadow image.

Chapter 5

TRANSFORMING GRAPHICS INTO NEW FORMS

Illustrator provides several tools that you can use to modify and transform an existing graphic object into some new form or shape. You have already used some of these tools in earlier exercises; rotating and scaling, for example, are both transformation operations. *Transformation*, as used here, means any process of bending, changing, or otherwise shaping an entire existing object into some new form. Illustrator has some powerful transformation capabilities that can produce spectacular results.

USING THE TRANSFORMATION TOOLS

The following five tranformation tools are provided in the Illustrator toolbox:

Blend tool	Transforms one object into another in a uniform series of steps
Scale tool	Reduces or enlarges selected objects in proportion
Rotate tool	Rotates a selected object around a defined center of rotation
Reflect tool	Reflects a selected object along a defined axis of reflection (which is a straight line)
Shear tool	Slants a selected object uniformly along a defined shear axis (which is a straight line)

Each of these tools can be used individually or together, one after another on the same object. The tool functions can also be invoked repeatedly to generate some very unusual effects.

Basically, to operate any of the transformation tools, you select the object to be transformed, set a control point or starting point for the operation, and then drag or click to move the selected object to the desired location.

SCALING IMAGES

As you've seen in earlier exercises, the scale tool produces larger or smaller versions of the selected object.

Before we start on the major examples using the scale tool, we'll undertake a few simple exercises to see how all the features work.

1. Open a fresh desktop and new artwork with no template.

2. Select the circle tool and create a circle on the left side of the desktop.

This circle will be the subject of our scaling exercises.

3. Select the scale tool and click the cursor on the right edge anchor point of the circle.

This sets the origin for the scaling operation, which means that all other points on the circle will be magnified or reduced according to their distance from the right anchor point. Now the cursor turns into a delta form, which you have seen before in earlier exercises.

4. Click on the left anchor point and drag the circle a small distance away from the original graphic (see Figure 5.1).

Notice that you can generate large movements of the circle with really small movements of the mouse. Now we'll return to the original artwork (circle) for our next scaling operation.

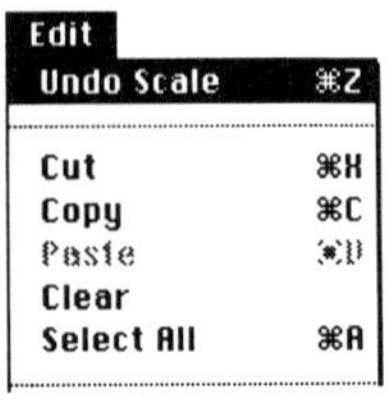

5. Choose Undo Scale from the Edit menu.

The cursor returns to the + form, indicating that it is once again ready to set a new origin for the scaling process.

6. **Click on the center anchor point of the circle to set the scale origin.**
7. **Position the delta cursor on the top anchor point and drag downward (see Figure 5.1).**

You'll notice that the right and left edges of the circle stay in place while the others move. They don't move because these two points lie along the x-axis of both the current figure and the scale origin, and you are moving the scale factor, represented by the delta cursor, at right angles to this axis. You can see, as you move the circle around, that the movements generated by the mouse are not as large as they were with the first scale origin.

8. **Again, return to the original circle by selecting Undo Scale from the Edit menu.**
9. **Click on the center anchor point to select it as the origin again.**
10. **Position the delta cursor on the upper-right edge of the circle, at about the 2 o'clock position, and drag inward.**

This time, the scaling operation works on both axes because the cursor is positioned at an angle to both the x- and y-coordinates. The result is shown in Figure 5.1.

11. **Select Undo Scale from the Edit menu.**
12. **Pull down the View menu and set the rulers on.**
13. **Set point (36, 40) as the origin for the scaling operation.**
14. **Move the delta cursor to point (24, 36), click, and drag toward the bottom-right corner of the desktop (see Figure 5.1).**

The flexibility to choose any points on the desktop in a scaling operation is tremendously powerful, but it is also the reason that you should be sure to select the correct object before you start clicking and dragging. If you select the wrong object, you may get some very unexpected results.

As you see from this example, it isn't necessary to choose points that lie on the selected graphic for either the origin or for the position that you are scaling. Wherever you choose, the selected graphic will be scaled accordingly.

Scaling Text

The scale tool can be used to create a variety of text effects. Our next exercise will demonstrate one of the many possibilities. We'll set what

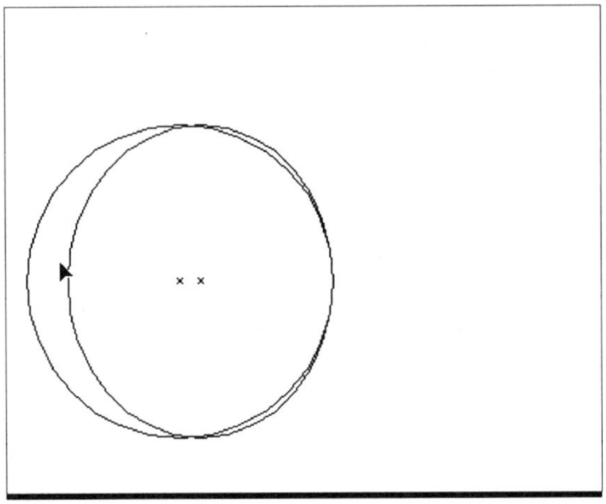

Step 4: *First scaling*

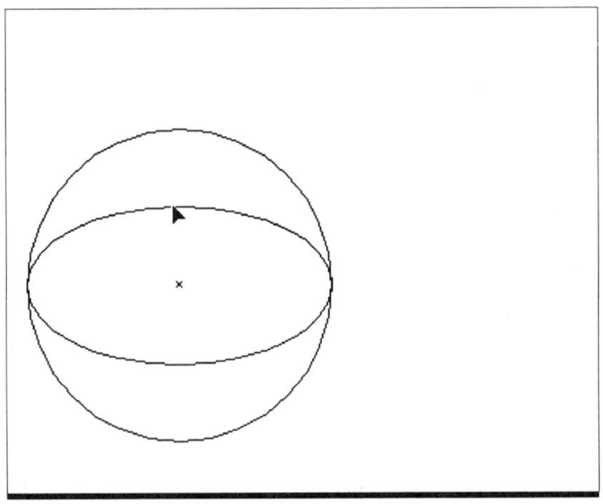

Step 7: *Second scaling*

Figure 5.1: *Scaling operations on a circle (continues)*

printers call a *drop cap* at the beginning of two lines of text. The actual text and selection of font, point size, and so on are not critical. Begin the exercise with a blank desktop.

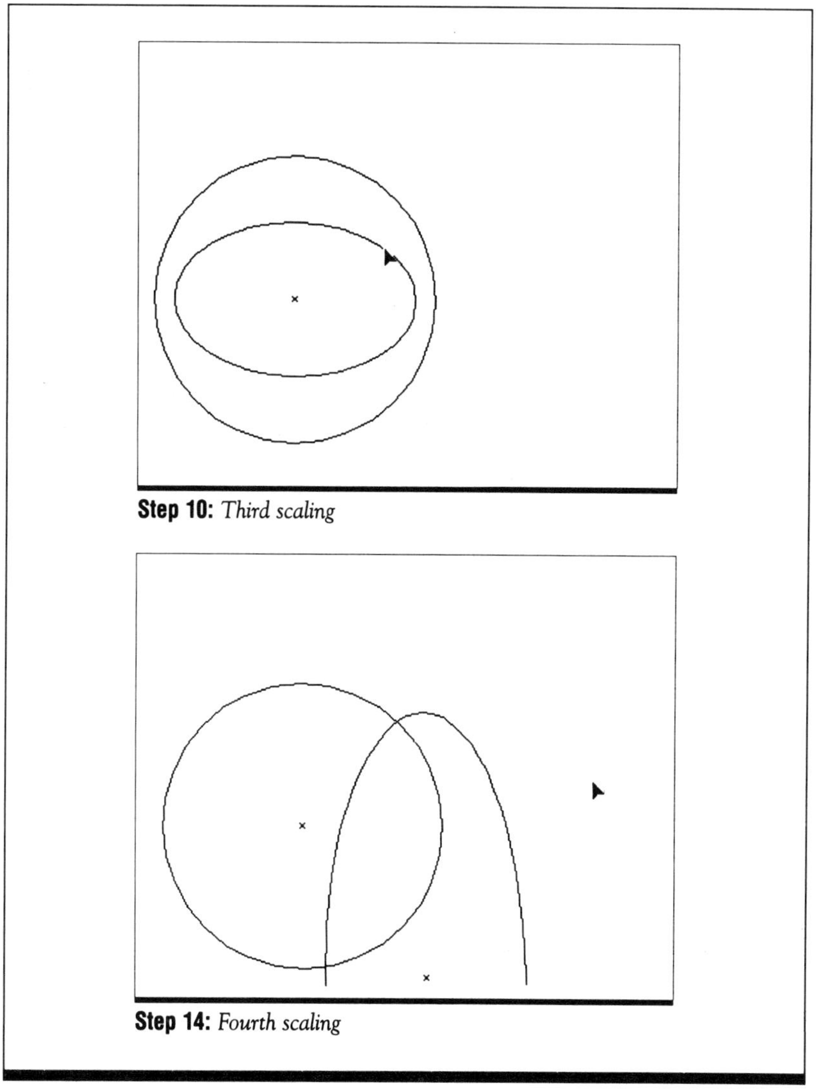

Step 10: *Third scaling*

Step 14: *Fourth scaling*

Figure 5.1: *Scaling operations on a circle (continued)*

1. **Select the text tool, move the text cursor to the left side of the desktop, and create a letter *R* in 36-point Times-Roman font, with a leading of 36 and left alignment.**
2. **Next to the R, enter, as a new block of text, *aised capitals*, press Return, and enter *can be very decorative*.**

The line return after the word *capitals* is necessary because, at 36 points, the entire line of text will not fit on the page. At this point, your screen should look something like the first screen in Figure 5.2.

3. Use the selection tool to move the R down to line up horizontally with the second line of the text: "can be very decorative."

4. Use the scale tool to expand the R to fill the space next to the two lines of text.

The easiest way to expand the *R* is by using the rulers and marking where the second line of text falls on them. Then maneuver the baseline for the *R* to match. When you scale the *R*, make the alignment point the scale origin.

5. Select the R and set Paint attributes of White Fill and 100% Black Stroke with a line weight of 1.

Figure 5.2 shows the resulting printout. This is another situation where the screen image does not do justice to the printed output.

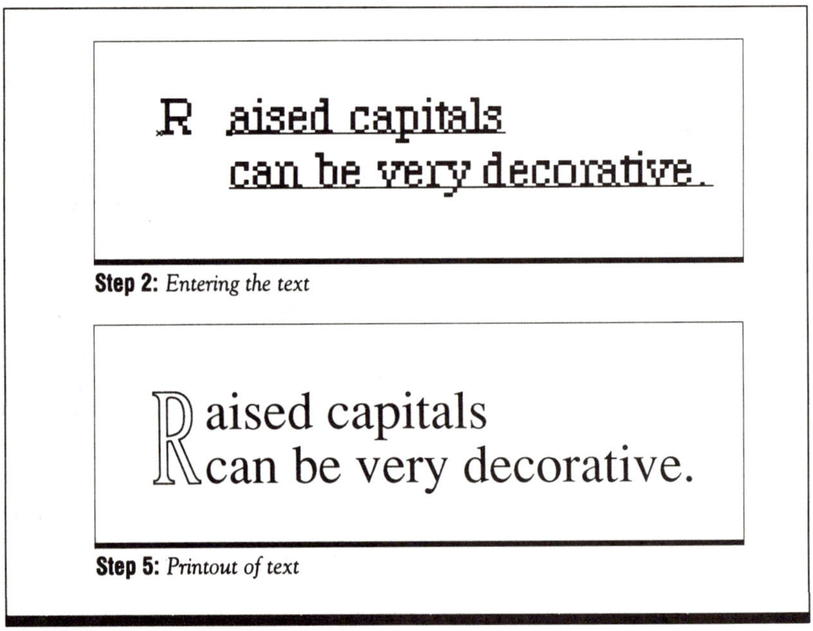

Step 2: *Entering the text*

Step 5: *Printout of text*

Figure 5.2: *Scaling and painting letters*

Let's continue with this example and see some of the alterations that you can make to text by using the Paint dialog screen options.

We'll create multiple copies of the letter R, one on top of the other, and change the painting characteristics of each version. Then we'll offset the final layer from the others to create a type of shaded outline.

6. **Select all the text you just created and copy it down below the original lines.**
7. **Select the first letter, the capital R, and set the Paint attributes of Fill to None and Stroke to 100% Black with a line weight of 2.**
8. **Choose Copy from the Edit menu, and then Paste In Front from the menu.**

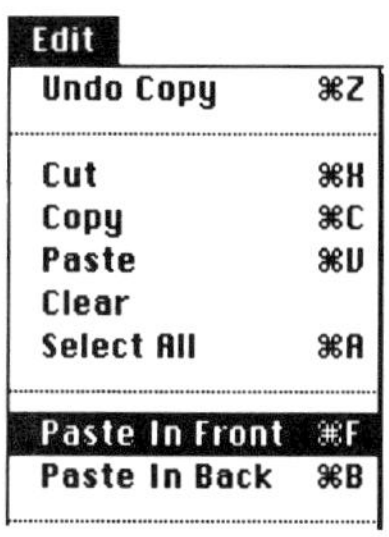

This pastes a second copy of the letter *R* in front of the first. We are going to change the Paint attributes of the front copy to produce a special, layered effect.

9. **Set the Paint attributes of Fill to None, Stroke to White, and a line weight of .8 point.**

This outlines the top letter in white, rather than black. Because the line weight of this copy is less than the preceding copy, the first copy of the letter will show behind the second as the difference in the line weights. So now you have one copy of the letter on top of the other; if you printed this now, you would see a letter that looks very much like the first, outlined *R*, but with a more chiseled effect. You may want to print this to see how it looks.

10. **Use the same technique to make another copy of the R and place it in front.**
11. **Set the Paint attributes of Fill to 100% Black and Stroke to None.**

This produces a final copy of the letter, not stroked but just filled. Now you need to move this letter just a little bit to the right and up to create the shading effect that we want. In this case, we need to use a new technique to move such a small amount.

12. **Hold down the Option key and click on the selection tool.**

You will see the Move dialog box (shown in Figure 5.3), which allows you to set distances for horizontal, vertical, and angled moves.

13. In the Move dialog box, set the move for the last copy with a Distance of 1 point and a Horizontal move. Then use the dialog box again to move the letter .25 point vertically.

In this way, you have offset the final, unstroked copy of the letter horizontally and vertically to create an outlined and shaded effect, as shown in Figure 5.4.

This exercise should give you some ideas for transforming text in interesting and imaginative ways. Remember that this is one area where the preview image on the screen is not a true indication of the printed output. The screen image is useful only for placement and providing some indication of what attributes you have set. For this reason, you may want to make a note of any specific combinations of font, size, scale, and movement that give particularly nice results.

Scaling Options

Each of the transformation tools has an accompanying optional dialog box. You used the optional Scale dialog box when we reduced the

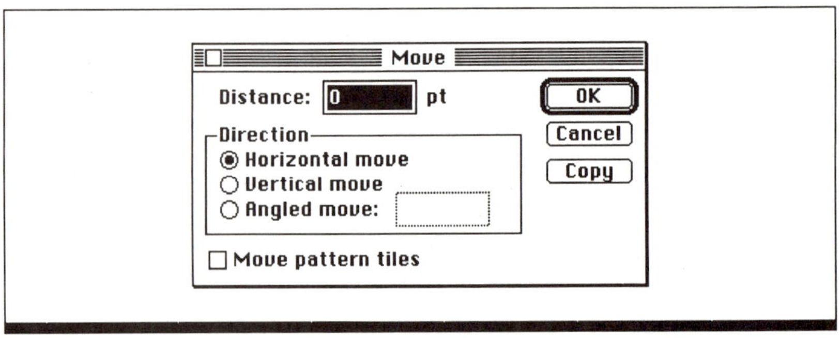

Figure 5.3: *Move dialog box*

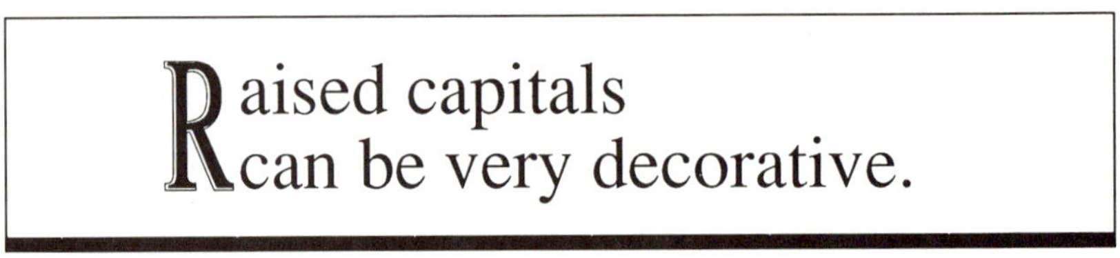

Figure 5.4: *Outlined and shaded letter R*

original logo for the letterhead exercise. Like all the optional dialog boxes, it is accessed by holding down the Option key while you set the fixed point—in this case, the scale origin.

The default options in the Scale dialog box (shown in Figure 5.5) are a Uniform scale of a 100%—in other words, no change—and Preserve line weights. Each of these has an alternative. You can choose to scale the line weights with the object, which is appropriate when you are scaling an outlined object (such as a letter) and want the line weight to change in proportion to the graphic image.

You can also choose to scale the object in a nonuniform way. You click on the Non-uniform scale button and then enter the percentage that you want to scale the object in both the horizontal and vertical directions. This type of scaling can be used to produce short, fat objects or long, thin objects out of regular graphics, and it is the key to producing isometric drawings, as you will learn in the next chapter.

BLENDING TO ADD CONTOURS

In concept, the blend tool works something like the scale tool. The blend tool transforms one artwork object into another in a series of regular steps. This is a very useful device and can be used to generate some spectacular effects. The most common use of the blend tool, however, is to add layers of gray or shades of color to produce the effect of a solid object. As a concrete example of this technique, we'll add contours, or dimensionality, to the apple artwork that you created before.

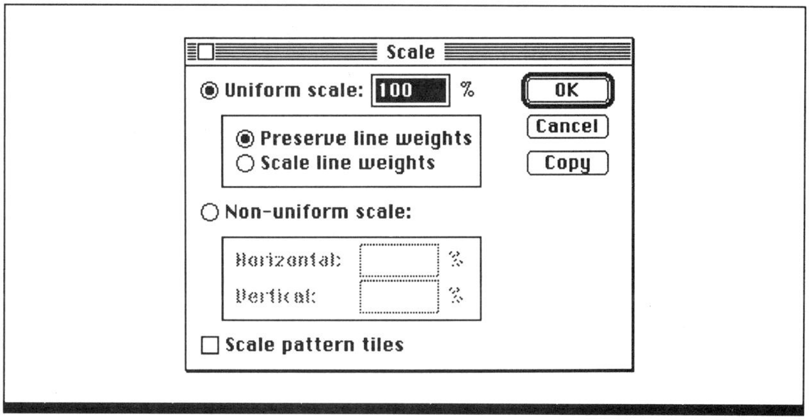

Figure 5.5: *Scale dialog box*

Although I used the latest version of the apple artwork (the one with two leaves on it), you may choose any version of the apple for this exercise. The major part of the exercise deals with the apple outline only, not the leaves and stem (however, they have to be taken into account).

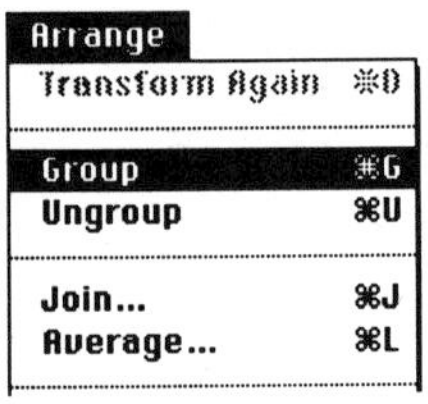

1. Open the Revised Apple art document.

We will start by grouping the leaf and stem artwork to make these elements easier to work with later.

2. Use the selection tool and the Option key to select the base of the stem, then use the same technique, with the addition of the Shift key, to add the stem artwork to the selection.

At this point, you will have both the stem and the base selected. Remember to add all the artwork pieces that make up the stem, including the small curve that forms part of the top of the stem.

3. Choose Group from the Arrange menu to make these objects one unit.

Now we're ready to begin working with the apple itself.

4. Use the selection tool and the Option key to select the entire outline of just the apple itself, not including the leaves and stem.

The apple should be positioned in the center of the screen and look something like the image shown in Figure 5.6.

5. Select the scale tool and position the cursor on the upper-right corner of the shoulder of the apple, indicated on the template by the slightly shaded area, to set the scale origin (see Figure 5.6).

6. Move the delta cursor down to the bottom of the apple and drag the outline up a substantial distance to form a highlighted area, as shown in Figure 5.6.

7. Hold down the Option key and release the mouse button to make a copy of the apple outline inside the original.

You could do all this through the Scale dialog box, setting the percentages of reduction and clicking on Copy. However, shadow and light effects are not really uniform, and so the more realistic effect produced by contouring by hand is worth the extra time.

While this new contour outline is still selected, you should set the final Paint attributes. We want to shade this section of the apple as a highlight, almost white without any stroke around the outside edge.

8. **Select Paint from the Style menu and set Fill to 5% Black and Stroke to None.**

Now we will use the blend tool to create a series of images between the outer apple outline and the inner copy that you just created. The blend tool will make a regular series of steps between the two images, while also changing the gray level for each step.

9. **Use the selection tool to select the anchor point on the upper-left corner of the apple highlight (see Figure 5.6).**
10. **Select the matching anchor point on the apple outline, using the Shift key so that both points remain selected, as shown in Figure 5.6.**

The blend tool works by making a series of steps between two selected anchor points. Be sure that both points are colored black; otherwise, you will see an error message.

11. **Select the blend tool from the toolbox.**
12. **Click the cursor on the selected anchor point on the apple outline. The cursor changes to the *sideways t* form to indicate that you are continuing a blend operation.**
13. **Click the transformed cursor on the selected anchor point on the inner apple highlight. You will see the Blend dialog box, as shown in Figure 5.7.**

This dialog box sets the number of steps between the two points and shows the transformation percentages that will be used to change from one gray level into the other. Obviously, the more steps you use, the finer the blend — up to the limits of the current device. However, more steps also take longer to calculate and display. So you want to choose a number of steps that will give the desired effect but still run reasonably quickly. In this case, we will use eight steps, which will provide a 5 percent change in the gray level at each step becuase we're starting at 50% Black at the apple outline and ending at 5% Black in the highlight.

14. **Enter 8 for the Number of steps and click on OK.**

Step 4: *Beginning the blending*

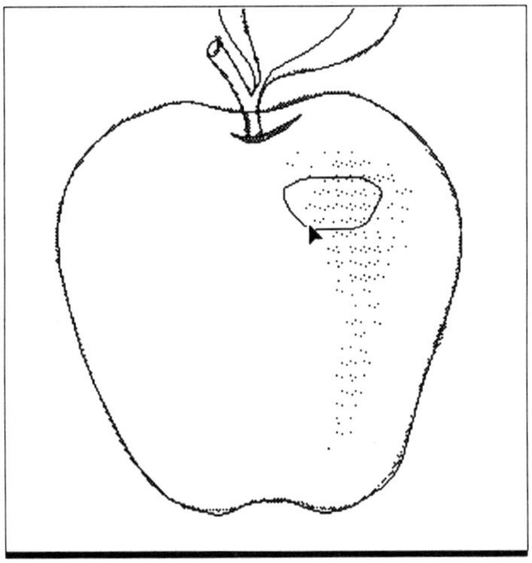

Step 5: *Setting the scale origin*

Figure 5.6: *Blending the apple artwork (continues)*

You will see the change in the blend percentage factors. Note that these are the percent of change in the existing gray level, not the calculated new values. In other words, eight steps always gives you the same percentages, whether the starting gray level is 50%, 100%, or any other

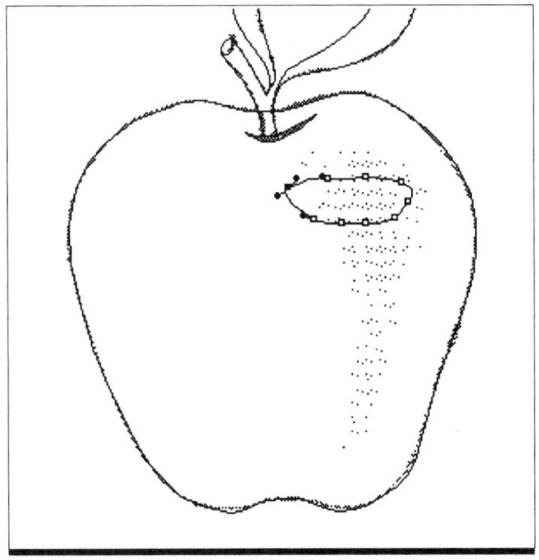

Step 6: *Dragging the outline*

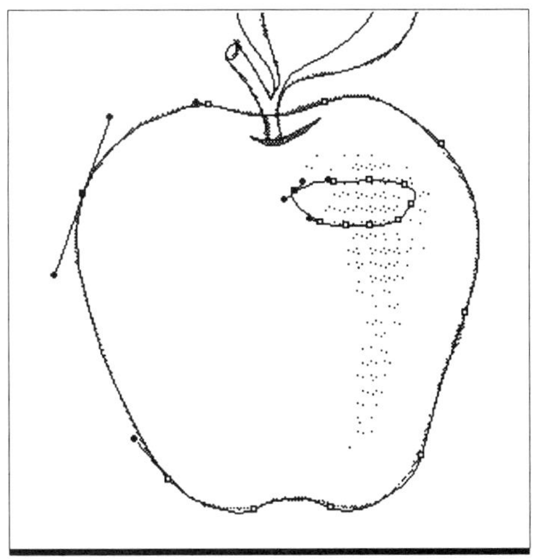

Step 10: *Selecting the anchor points*

Figure 5.6: *Blending the apple artwork (continued)*

value. The actual gray level of each step is calculated as the levels are produced.

After Illustrator calculates the necessary contours and gray levels, you will see the result on the screen, looking something like the image shown in Figure 5.8. You see that there are exactly eight new layers, and

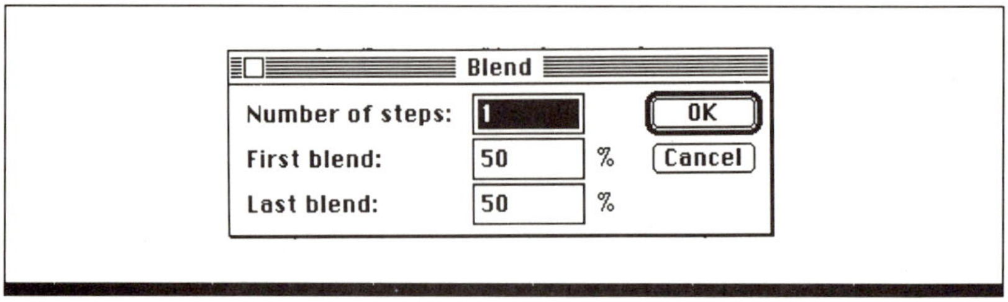

Figure 5.7: *Blend dialog box*

exactly eight points between the two anchor points that you used for the transformation. However, as you move around the apple outline, Illustrator has added points at some layers to make a smooth transition from the outline to the highlight. Also notice that the resulting layers are automatically grouped as a unit.

15. Choose Preview Illustration from the View menu to see how the apple looks.

> You should also be aware that the color levels shown on the screen are much more dramatic than the variations on the printed output. This is a good demonstration of the fact that WYSIWYG (What You See Is What You Get) can really be a misnomer. You can't accurately reproduce a high-resolution device on a low-resolution screen. You can get some information from the screen, but it's a good idea to stop and print a copy of your artwork once and awhile to be sure you're getting the proper effects.

As shown in Figure 5.8, not all the contours that you added show on the screen. This is because the LaserWriter and higher resolution devices will distinguish gray levels of 5 percent or less, but the screen display moves only in increments of approximately 10 percent. That is, if you want the Black Fill value to display as a distinct color on the screen, it must be at least 10 percent different from the previous level.

A 5 percent variation in the contour shadings shows on the screen only when the required gray threshold is crossed. In fact, the value displayed on the screen for 45% Black is identical to that for 40% Black, although the difference between 50% and 45% can be displayed on the screen. The net result is that you will not see any difference between the second contour and the third on the screen, but they will show as different shading levels on the page output.

In this first preview, however, you no longer can see the base of the stem because it now paints behind the apple contours. Actually, you could have foreseen that this was going to happen, knowing that the latest graphic on the drawing surface will always paint on top. Now we have to move the stem and base in front of the contour artwork.

16. Use the selection tool to select the grouped stem and base.

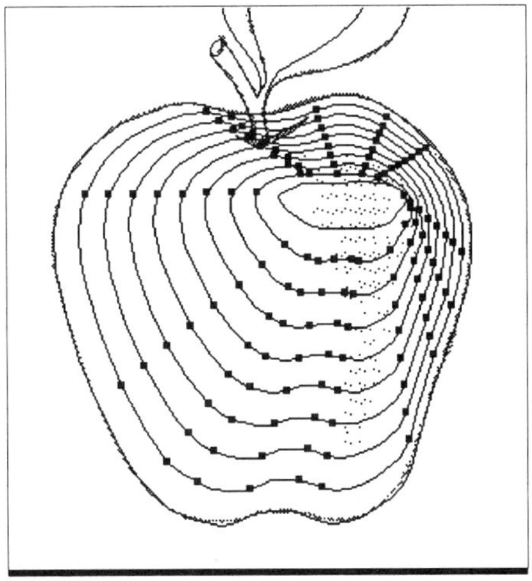

Step 14: *Blended apple*

Step 15: *Preview of blended apple*

Figure 5.8: *The shaded apple art*

Users of version 1.1 will have to use the standard cut and paste technique to move the artwork to the front.

17. Use Bring To Front from the Edit menu to move the selected artwork to the front of the contours.

As you see, grouping the stem and base earlier makes these related artwork elements much easier to work with now.

18. Save the artwork as *Shaded Apple art.*

Figure 5.9 shows both the screen preview image and the printed output of the apple with shading. You can see the substantial differences between the shadings on these two outputs, which clearly demonstrates the variation between the screen preview version of an artwork and the printed version.

ROTATING IMAGES

Rotation is another of the most common and useful Illustrator transformation techniques. As you have seen in earlier exercises, the rotate tool is probably the easiest of the transformation tools to use because you can visualize how the control origin and the tool work together.

In the case of rotation, the fixed point that you set is the center of rotation, and the selected object revolves around that point. You drag the object to rotate it, as we did to position the second leaf on our apple artwork, and to angle the ovals of the screw base on the light bulb artwork. Optionally, you can specify the angle of rotation in the Rotate dialog box, which is accessed by holding down the Option key while you set the center of rotation. Positive angle values represent counterclockwise motion, and negative values represent clockwise motion.

ROTATING TEXT

Our earlier exercises have given you a good grasp of the simple rotation of objects, so we will try a different rotation technique. As an example, we'll use the rotate tool to set circular text. This type of rotation is difficult to do with other drawing programs.

For our exercise, will set the name of a musical selection around a record label, with the composer's name inside it and the name of the orchestra outside the bottom of the circle. Start with a new desktop.

1. Use the circle tool to set a circle as a guide for the placement of the letters.

The circle should be about 16 ruler units (picas) wide. Draw the circle using the techniques that you have learned previously: hold down the

Preview of finished apple

Printout of finished apple

Figure 5.9: *The completed shaded apple art*

Shift key (to constrain the figure to a true circle) and the Option key (to draw the circle from the center). Center the circle in the approximate center of the desktop, allowing enough room for positioning a row of letters around the top.

2. **Move down to the lower-left corner of the visible desktop and set the words *LA CETRA, Opus* 9 as a text block in 16-point Helvetica Bold (see Figure 5.10).**

You will use this text as a guide to placement of the letters around the circle. You want to duplicate the natural spacing of the letters as closely as possible.

3. **Select the circle and make a note of the coordinates of the top anchor point so that you can return to it.**
4. **Select the text tool, move the text cursor directly over the top anchor point, and click.**
5. **Enter the first letter, *L*, setting the type as 16-point Helvetica Bold (the same settings you used before).**

6. **Select the rotate tool and click on the center of the circle to set it as the center of rotation.**
7. **Use the delta cursor to drag the letter about one-quarter of the circle (see Figure 5.10).**

The letter should rotate around the circle quite nicely, moving uniformly along the circumference.

This demonstrates the process that you use to set all the letters in the name on the label. We'll use a shortcut to speed this process up a bit.

8. **Set all the letters for the name individually in separate text blocks on the side of the circle. Enter each letter of the name *A CETRA, Opus* 9.**

You don't need the *L* because we have already positioned that letter.

9. **Select the rotate tool, hold down the Command key to access the selection tool, and select and drag the next letter to the top of the circle, to the coordinates of the anchor point. Then release the mouse button (see Figure 5.10).**

10. Move the rotation cursor down to the center of the circle and click to set the center of rotation.

11. Move the delta cursor back up to the letter and rotate it to the desired position.

Use the demonstration string in the corner as a guide to positioning; you will notice that the letters are probably closer together than you would expect.

Don't worry too much, at this point, about the position of the entire block around the circle. Worry about creating the correct spacing between the words and the letters. You will not be able to change that relationship after you have placed the individual letters. You can, however, adjust the set of letters around the circle.

Also, don't worry if your string overlaps the placement point for the rotation. Just continue to position the letters on the precise point, using the rulers as a guide, and then rotate right (if necessary) to position the character correctly. Figure 5.10 shows the result before the final adjustment.

12. Position the name so that it is correctly centered on the circle by selecting the entire block of text with a selection marquee and using the rotate tool to revolve the entire block, which will include the circle.

The final name placement should leave the screen looking something like Figure 5.10.

13. Create a smaller diameter circle, inside the first circle and with the same center.

This circle should have a width of about 12 units.

14. Use the same methods as before to set the composer's name, *VIVALDI*, in 12-point Helvetica Bold, around the outside of the smaller circle.

15. As a final edit, use Clear from the Edit menu to erase the two circles, leaving just the circular lettering.

You could use this same technique to set text around an arbitrary line.

The printed version of this is shown in Figure 5.10, which is a large improvement over the screen image.

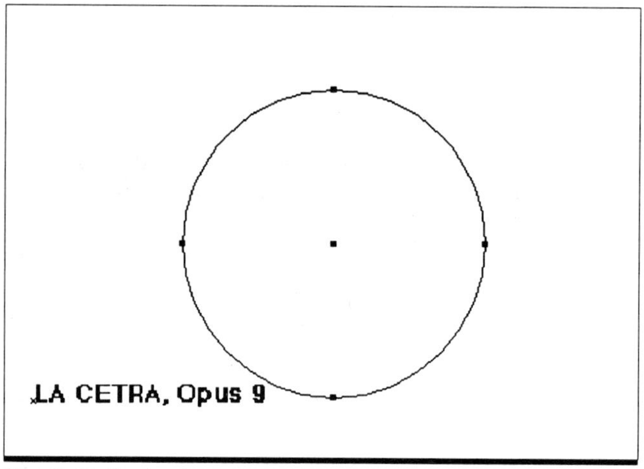

Step 2: *Guides for placement*

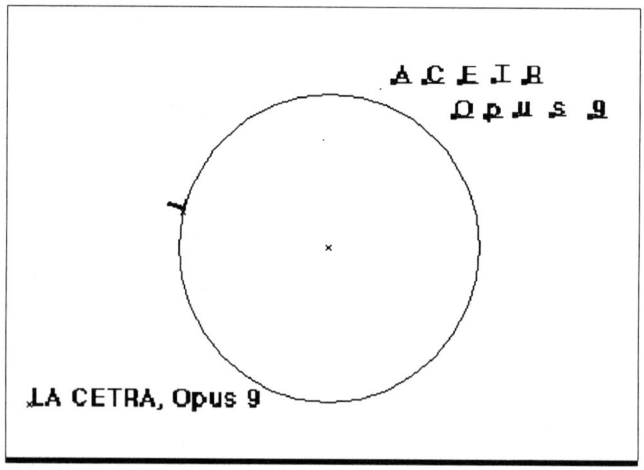

Step 7: *Placing the L*

Figure 5.10: *Creating circular text (continues)*

This is obviously a laborious process, and also subject to positioning errors if your hand is a bit unsteady. One way to avoid that problem, although at the expense of some fineness of interletter spacing, is to set the first letter, then copy it around the circle for as many times as there are letters in the caption. Then you can go back, click on each letter

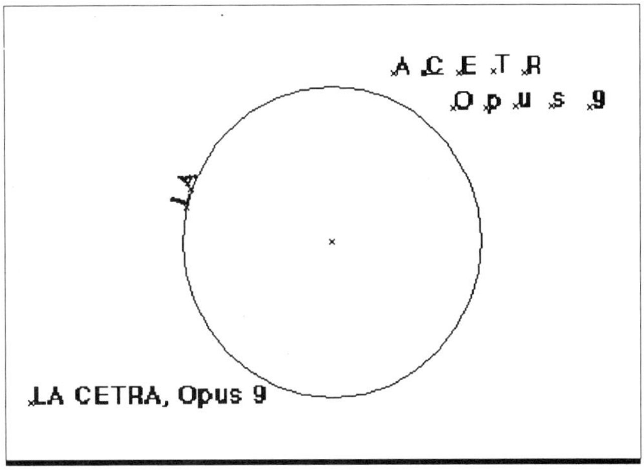

Step 9: *Placing the A*

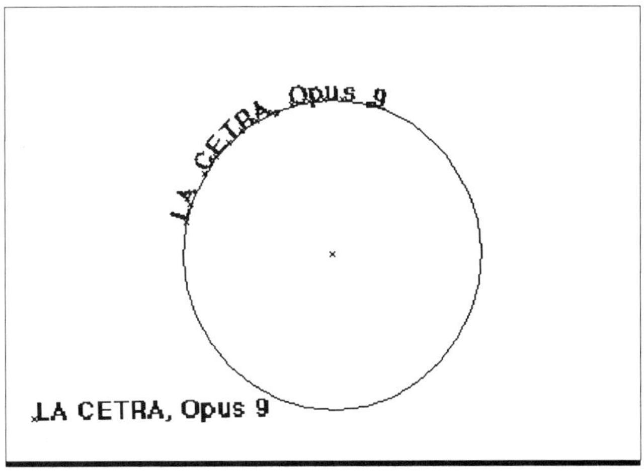

Step 11: *Placed text*

Figure 5.10: *Creating circular text (continues)*

individually, and change it to the correct one. The only problem is that when you position the letters around the circle, you won't see the real effect produced by the correct letter. Another alternative is to write a PostScript program that will precisely and perfectly position a string of text around a circle.

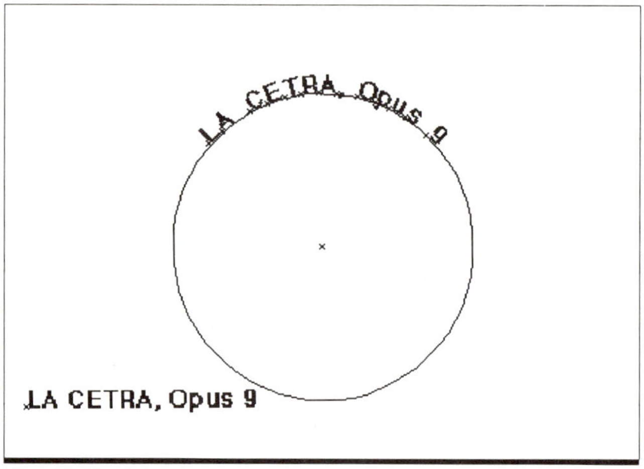

Step 12: *Final placement*

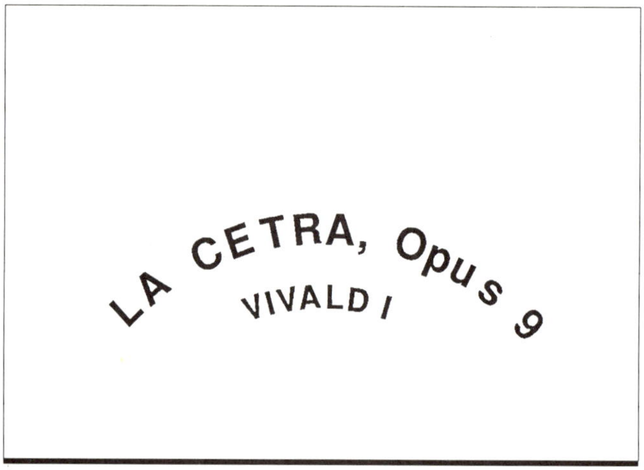

Step 15: *Printed version*

Figure 5.10: *Creating circular text (continued)*

USING ROTATING AND SCALING OPTIONS

The Rotate and Scale dialog box options are most useful when you are working with well-defined relationships. To demonstrate a practical application, we'll add some rays to the sun in our original logo artwork and then scale them.

ADDING ANGLED LINES FOR SUN RAYS

To begin, we will add four long rays at each of the principal directions of the sun, and smaller ones twice between each of the major rays; thus, the longer rays will be at 90° intervals and the smaller ones at 30° angles all around the circle.

1. **Open the Logo art document.**
2. **Move the graphic up on the screen until the sun is completely visible, with room for the rays to be added around it.**

Don't worry about going outside the border in this exercise. We'll adjust the lines later.

3. **Start the additional artwork by using the pen tool to draw a line extending from the right anchor point on the circle straight to the right, somewhat past the border line.**

Remember that you can constrain the line to be straight by holding down the Shift key as you click to construct the line.

4. **Set Paint attributes for the line of no Fill, 100% Black Stroke, and a line weight of 1 point.**
5. **Click on the rotate tool and set the center of rotation as the center of the circle, holding down the Option key as you click.**

You will see the Rotate dialog box, shown in Figure 5.11.

6. **Enter 90° as the rotation angle and click on Copy.**
7. **Use ⌘D or Transform Again from the the Arrange menu to create three more copies of the line around the circle.**

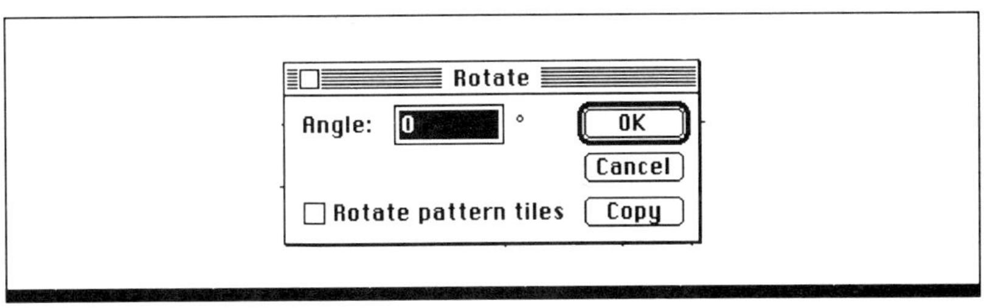

Figure 5.11: *Rotate dialog box*

Yes, *three* more. This produces one copy of the line that overlays the first line, which is now selected because it was the last one created. Your screen should look like Figure 5.12.

8. **Use the selection tool to move the anchor point at the end of the line furthest from the circle inward about one-third the total length of the first line.**
9. **Access the Rotate dialog box and rotate this new, shorter line by a 30° angle. Do not use Copy for this rotation.**

Remember to reselect the complete line (both anchor points) before you rotate it, or you will only move one end of the line.

10. **Use the Rotate dialog box again to make a copy of that line at another 30°.**
11. **Rotate the next copy of the line at a 60° angle (the longer line is already at the next 30° position).**
12. **Continue placing rays around the circle, alternating 30° and 60° increments for the copies until the lines are complete, as shown in Figure 5.12.**

This is just a simple example of how you can use the Rotate (or any other transformation tool) optional dialog box to aid in constructing and modifying graphics. As you can see, this technique requires precise numbers. When you know, or can easily figure out, the correct number or numbers to enter in the dialog box, then using the options is probably a good idea. When you don't know the angle (or axis or whatever the required numbers are), then you probably should "eyeball" the transformation by using the tool and the delta cursor (or whatever cursor is involved).

Calculating Transformation Values

There are, of course, some operations for which you might like to use a transformation tool dialog box but do not know and cannot easily calculate the necessary values. For example, you might need very much to scale line weights—an option that is only available through the dialog box. In these cases, you can use a tricky way to determine those necessary numbers.

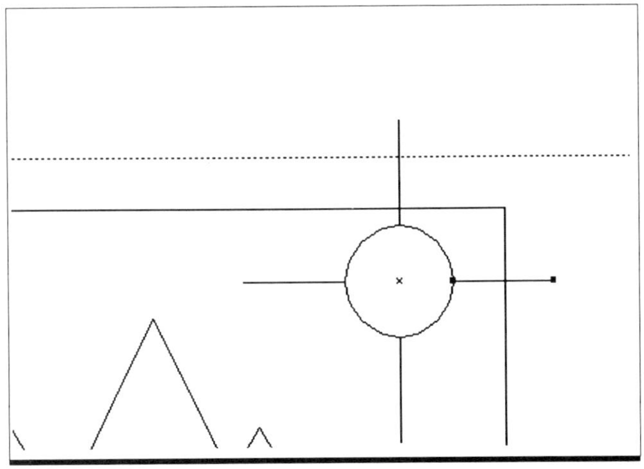

Step 7: *90° rotations*

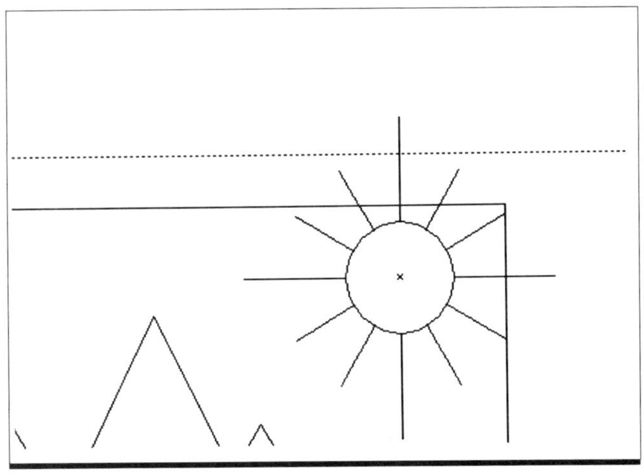

Step 12: *Completed rays*

Figure 5.12: *Sun with rotated rays*

This method involves performing the transformation once visually and then undoing it. Illustrator saves the coordinates for the transformation and displays them the next time you access the dialog box, if you do it right away. (Obviously, any subsequent access to the transformation or change of the desktop will lose the information.) This way, you can find out the exact numbers that you need to enter to effect a transformation through the dialog box, even if this is a nonuniform transformation.

SCALING THE SUN RAYS

As an example of the technique for getting Illustrator to calculate scaling values, we'll scale the sun, with the rays we just added, down to fit within the borders of the artwork. We don't know the scale factor and certainly cannot easily calculate it—yet we want to use the dialog box because it is important for the lines that make up the sun to be scaled in proportion to the graphic itself.

You should still have the logo art with sun rays on your screen.

1. **Select the circle and all the rays of the sun, being careful not to include the border.**
2. **Group these objects by choosing Group from the Arrange menu.**

Grouping will help you manipulate the graphic. This step is shown in Figure 5.13.

3. **Select the scale tool and set the scale origin as the center of the circle.**

As in the scaling exercise earlier in this chapter, you must scale from the center and, to get a uniform scale, work from about the 2 o'clock position. Use the Shift key to constrain the scale to maintain an exact circle.

4. **Scale the entire artwork until the longest ray on the top is just outside the border, then hold down the Option key to copy the original (see Figure 5.13).**

As always, the copy is automatically selected at the end of the transformation. It's rather difficult to tell precisely when you have scaled the lines to the correct point because the old and new copies are both showing on the screen. Close is good enough for this exercise.

5. **Choose Clear from the Edit menu to erase the unneeded copy.**
6. **Select the sun with rays artwork again, holding down the Command key to access the selection tool.**

7. Use the Option key while you set the scale origin once again as the center of the circle.

You will see the familiar Scale dialog box, but with a difference. Now the Uniform scale box has the value 56.0013% already filled in, rather than the usual default 0%. This is the value of the scale that you just completed on the copy a moment ago. Therefore, it is exactly the same size reduction that is required for the scaled artwork. Of course, you can still alter this number. In this case, for example, the top ray is still slightly outside the border, and you might want to compensate for that.

8. Change the line weight option to Scale line weights and click on OK.

9. Preview the scaled artwork (see Figure 5.13).

This is a handy little trick that can be used with any of the transformation tools. The basis of this technique is simply that Illustrator retains the information from a transformation for a short while so you can undo it, or redo it, or whatever; and that information is available to you through the optional dialog box.

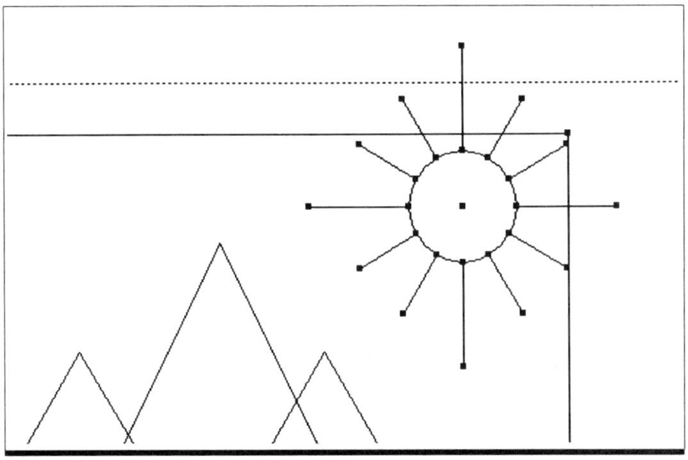

Step 2: *Grouping the sun*

Figure 5.13: *Scaling the sun and rays (continues)*

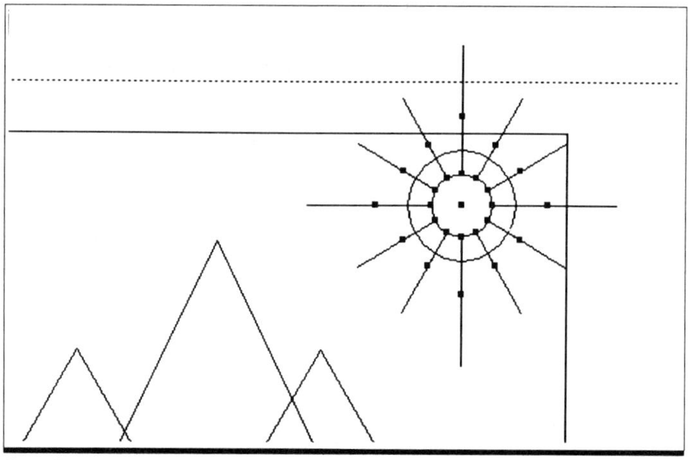

Step 4: *Copying the scaled rays*

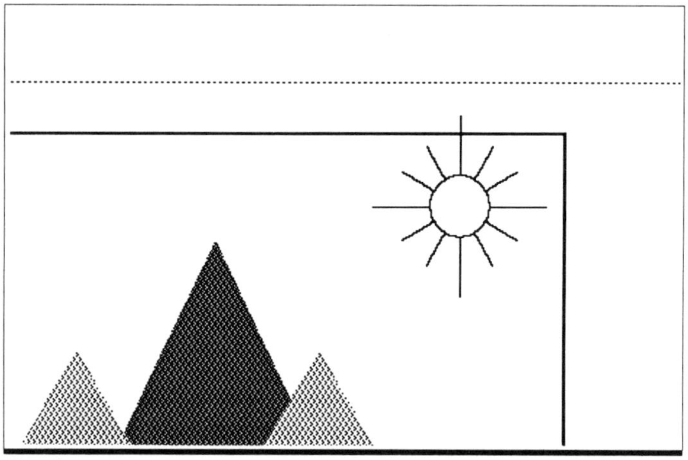

Step 9: *Preview of art*

Figure 5.13: *Scaling the sun and rays (continued)*

REFLECTING IMAGES

The reflect tool works like a mirror to move the selected object through a line of reflection to a matching position on the other side. Each selected point on one side of the line, called the *axis of reflection*, is moved a corresponding distance on the other side of the line. If you think of the line as the plane of a mirror, the concept is quite straightforward.

The reflect tool, unlike the other transformation tools, doesn't require any clicking and dragging to indicate how far you want to move. After you establish the line of reflection, all the selected points have exactly one matching mirror point; there is no other control necessary. For the reflect tool, the choice comes in establishing the *axis of reflection*, which is the line that makes up the mirror for the selected object. Figure 5.14 diagrams the important factors in the reflection process.

Illustrator allows you to reflect the selected objects along any axis that you want. First you click the reflect tool + cursor to set one end of the axis of reflection. Next you click on another point with the delta cursor to finish the axis of reflection as the straight line connecting the two points: the first point you clicked on and the last one. As always, you can constrain the axis by using the Shift key, as you will see shortly.

Optionally, you can access the Reflect dialog box, shown in Figure 5.15, by pressing the Option key as you set the axis of reflection. This allows you to reflect across a horizontal, a vertical, or an angled axis. If you select angled axis, you must specify the angle of the axis relative to

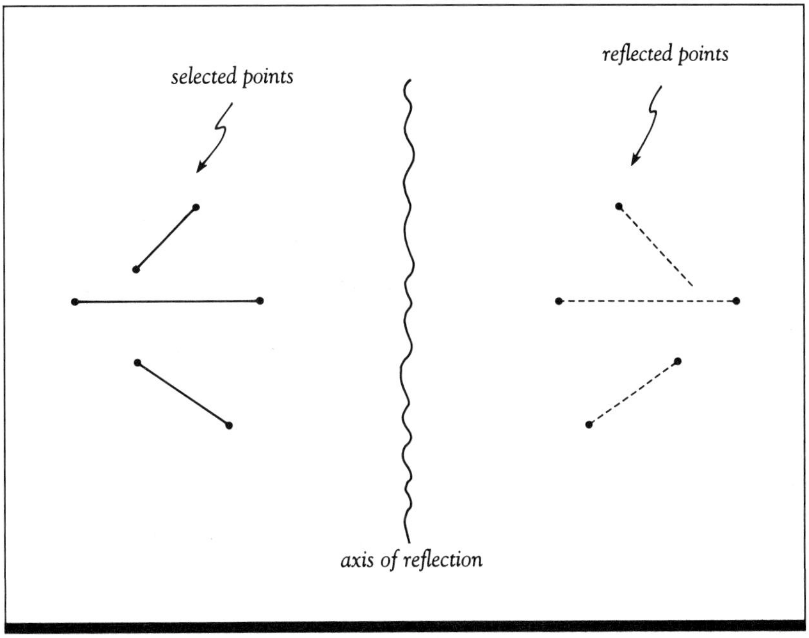

Figure 5.14: *Factors in reflection operations*

the horizontal axis. Again, the positive values reflect in a counterclockwise direction, and negative values reflect clockwise.

Reflection Concepts

Let's work through a simple set of exercises to demonstrate the reflection concepts. Begin with a fresh Illustrator desktop with no template.

1. **Use the square tool to draw a rectangle on the left side of the desktop (see Figure 5.16).**

2. **Select the reflect tool, place the cursor on the bottom-right corner of the rectangle, and click there to set the first point of the axis of reflection.**
3. **Move the delta cursor out at about a 45° angle to the long edge of the rectangle and up until it is about even with the top of the rectangle.**
4. **Hold down the Option key to create a copy and click here to set the axis of reflection.**

If you want an exact 45° angle, hold down the Shift key when you click on the second point. This constrains the axis to a multiple of 45°; the exact multiple chosen will be the one nearest the current cursor position. The result is shown in Figure 5.16.

5. **Leave the new copy of the rectangle selected, and click on the center of the first rectangle to set the next point for reflection.**
6. **Move the delta cursor directly right, in a straight line, past the end of the second rectangle; press the Shift key; and click to move the second rectangle from one side of the first to the other.**

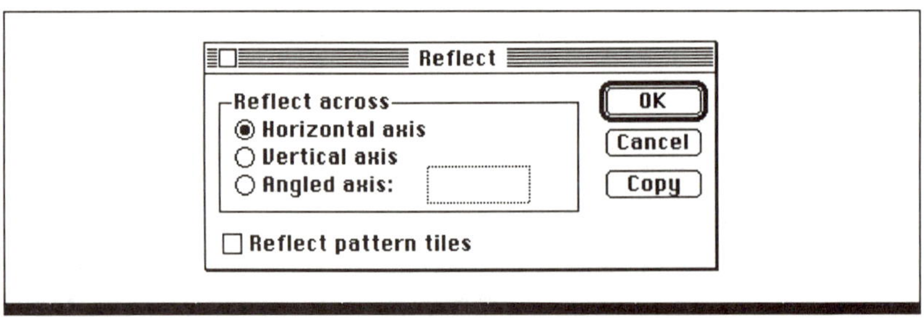

Figure 5.15: *Reflect dialog box*

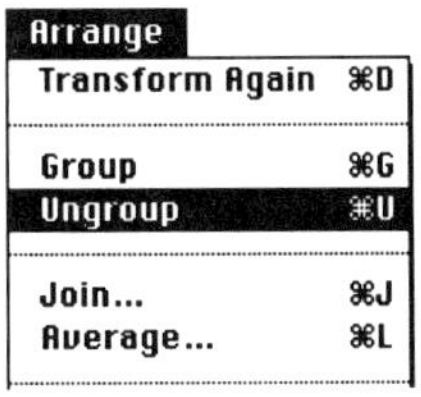

This gives an immediate and visible demonstration of the power of the reflect tool, as shown in Figure 5.16. Now let's see how the selection of the figure or points affects the reflection operation.

7. **Select Ungroup from the Arrange menu.**

This removes the group effect that created the rectangles and allows you to select anchor points individually.

8. **Use the selection tool to deselect the top rectangle; then use it again to select only the top two anchor points (see Figure 5.16).**
9. **Select the reflect tool again and set the axis of reflection from the center of the first rectangle in a straight line to the right, just as you did for the last reflection. Use both the Shift key, to constrain the axis to the horizontal, and the Option key, to create a copy.**

The result is shown in Figure 5.16. This may be a surprise to you. You may have expected to reflect the top rectangle down to the bottom. Instead, only the top two points were reflected because they were the only points selected on the figure. Remember that all the transformation tools work only on selected points. When you want to transform a complete graphic element, you need to be careful that the entire graphic is selected, not only a part of it. One way to ensure this is to first group all the elements before proceeding with the transformation operation.

REFLECTING TEXT

One practical use of reflection is to change text orientation. A short example will help you see how this works. In this exercise, we will create a label for a diskette (the same technique can be used for a cassette label). The diskette label will have the selections and associated information on one side and its other side will have two marks to show the locking status of the diskette.

Although the exact dimensions are not too important, you can use a rectangle 16 units wide by 18 units high for the basic label area. The height is divided into two sections: the larger one is 14 units and holds the names and other data; the second, smaller area is 4 units, shaded in grey (it would be colored on an actual label), and has the lock indicators set on it.

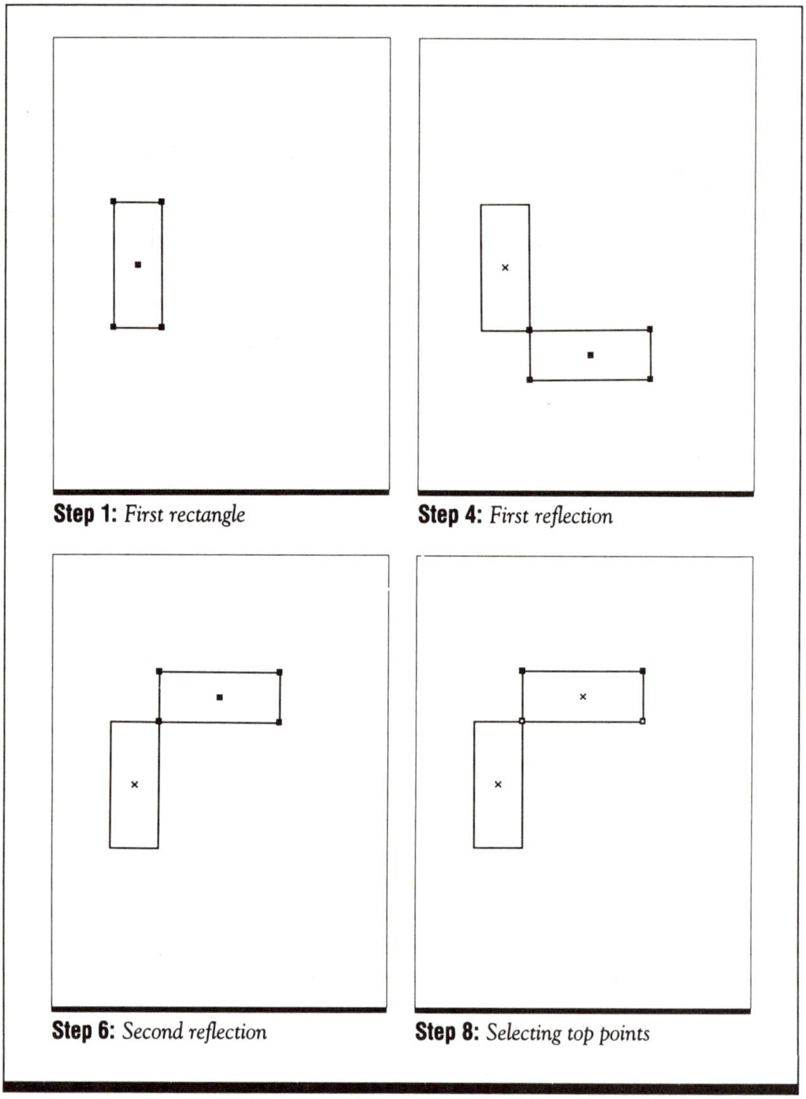

Figure 5.16: *Reflection exercise (continues)*

Begin with a fresh Illustrator desktop.

1. **Make an outline of the label with the dimensions given above, using the rulers.**

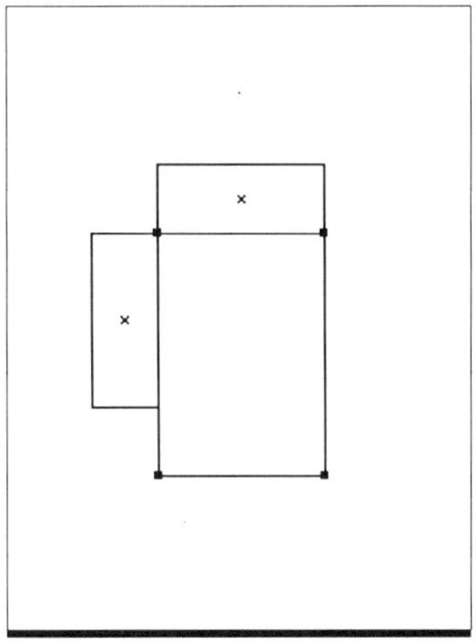

Step 9: *Third reflection*

Figure 5.16: *Reflection exercise (continued)*

This puts the four corners at points (12, 42), (28, 42), (28, 24), and (12, 24).

2. **Set the Paint attributes of Fill to None, Stroke to 100% Black, and a line weight of 2.**
3. **Create the top area of the label, which will fold over the top of the diskette and read on the reverse, by making a rectangle at points (12, 42), (28, 42), (28, 38) and (12, 38).**
4. **Set the Paint attributes of Fill to 30% Black and Stroke to None.**
5. **Select the smaller area and choose Send To Back from the Edit menu to place it behind the first part of the label so that the edge of the first will show correctly all around the figure.**

The preview of the result, up to this point, is shown in Figure 5.17. Next we'll make a set of thin lines across the label for entering the names of the items on the label. This label will be blank; it will be a template for data entry. The lines will be every 2 units from 26 to 34.

6. **Create the first line by using the pen tool and clicking to extend the line from one side of the label to the other.**

7. Set the Paint attributes of Fill to None, Stroke to 100% Black, and a line weight of .5.

After the first line is completed, you can copy the others very easily by using the Move dialog box.

8. Select the entire line (both anchor points) and then click on the selection tool while holding down the Option key.

You will see the same Move dialog box that appeared when we scaled text to create a raised letter. In this case, we know that we want to move 2 units, or 24 points, directly down the page.

9. Select Vertical move and enter – 24 as the distance to move in points. Click on the Copy button.

You have to enter the movement value as a negative number to move down the page because the coordinates decrease in that direction. Just remember that positive values move objects up the page and negative values move them down.

10. Use ⌘D (or Transform Again on the Edit menu) to duplicate the line on down to line 34.

11. Select the text tool and set the heading *CONTENTS:* at point (12.25, 36) (that's one division inside the 12 rule) in 9-point Helvetica.

This creates the front side of the label, ready for data entry.

12. Use the zoom tool to magnify the top-right edge of the label by one click, and create two small triangles.

The example triangles are ½ unit at the base (3 divisions) and 1 unit wide, with the base lying along line 26, as shown in Figure 5.17.

Now we come to the real subject of this exercise: placement of the status text next to the triangles. The problem here is that the text should run in reverse, so that it can be read while holding the diskette upright. We can do this by using the reflect tool.

13. Set two lines of type in 6-point Helvetica with 18-point leading, enter *WRITE PROTECT*, press Return, and enter *WRITE ENABLE*.

You can set this text anywhere off the label. In my example, I placed the lines off to the right side, opposite the heading on the label.

14. Select the reflect tool and set the axis of reflection as a straight line an appropriate distance above the two lines of text.

Remember that you can ensure that the axis of reflection is horizontal by using the Shift key, or you can use the optional Reflect dialog box. This operation inverts the two lines of text and makes them into "mirror writing."

15. Reflect the two lines of text again across the vertical axis towards the label.

Now they are upside down and no longer mirror writing; they are exactly in the orientation that we want them.

16. Move the lines of text over beside the triangles and position them at an appropriate distance (see Figure 5.17).

17. Choose Print from the File menu to see the printed version (shown in Figure 5.17).

18. Save this file as *Diskette Label art*.

SHEARING IMAGES

The easiest way to visualize the effect of the shear tool is to consider the effect of the wind blowing a tree. The tree, bending in the wind, is a classic example of a sheared object. In that case, the shear is called a *horizontal* shear because the wind is acting parallel to a horizontal surface, the ground. During an earthquake, the earth often moves in a *vertical* shear.

The important point here is that the shear motion occurs parallel to some plane, or line on the drawing surface, and the amount of shear is measured by the angle that the sheared object moves. Consider the tree

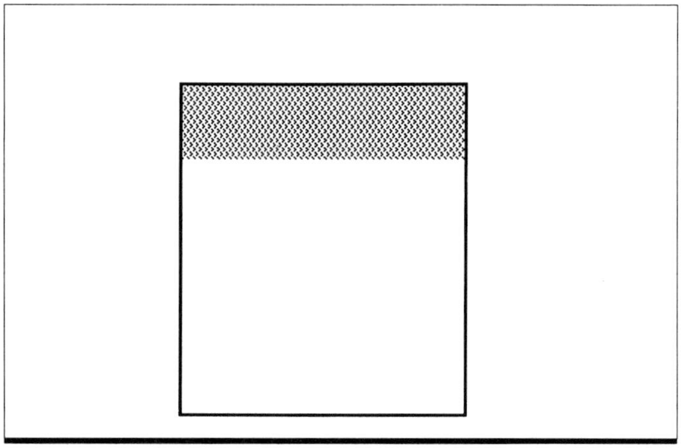

Step 5: *Preview of label*

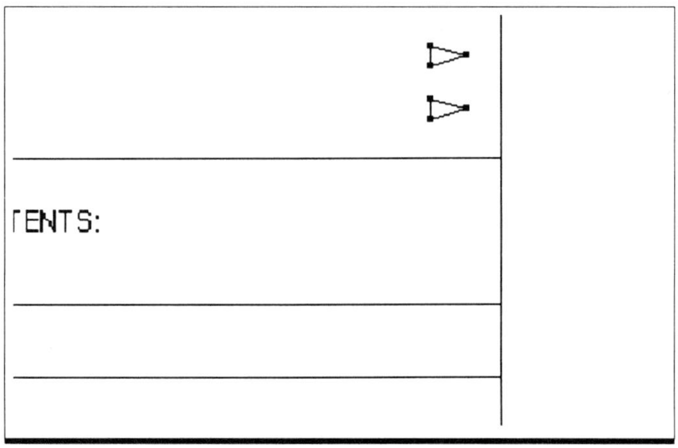

Step 12: *Drawing the triangles*

Figure 5.17: *Placing reflected text (continues)*

again; the harder the wind blows, the more the tree leans. One good measure of the strength of the wind is the angle that the tree trunk makes with the *vertical* position it normally maintains. In other words, a 30° shear would bend the tree 30° from a vertical position.

Illustrator works the same way. You set a shear axis, then you use the familiar delta cursor to shear the selected object perpendicularly to the axis defined by the starting point of the shear. The axis of the shear is

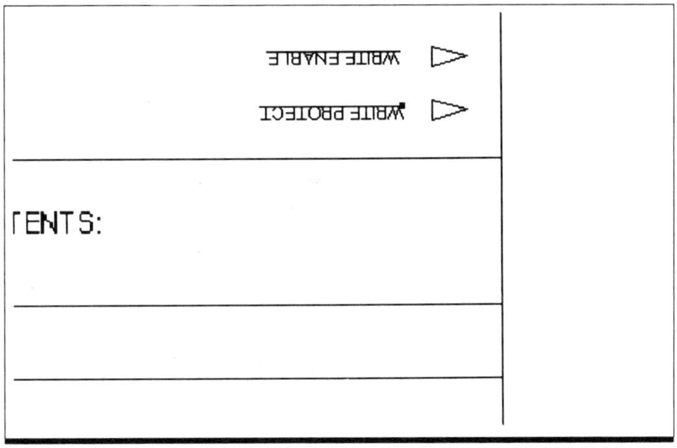

Step 16: *Positioning the text*

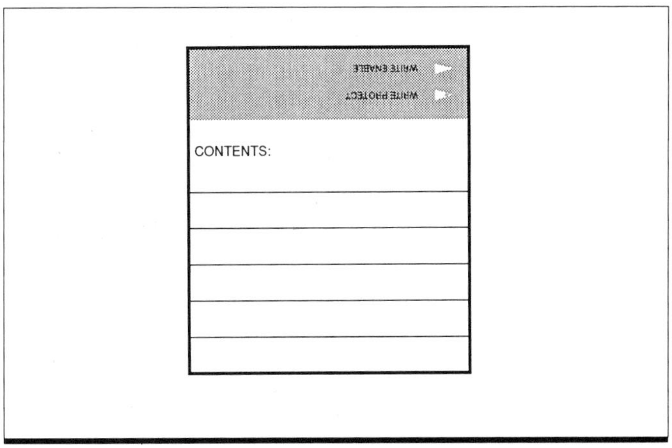

Step 17: *Printed version*

Figure 5.17: *Placing reflected text (continued)*

the line perpendicular to the line defined by the point that you click on with the delta cursor and the first point that you set. This may prompt you to recall your high-school geometry: through any point there exists one, and only one, line that will be perpendicular to a given line. In this case, the perpendicuar line extends between the first point that you set and the point that you began the shear motion from. Figure 5.18 shows you the essential components of the shear transformation.

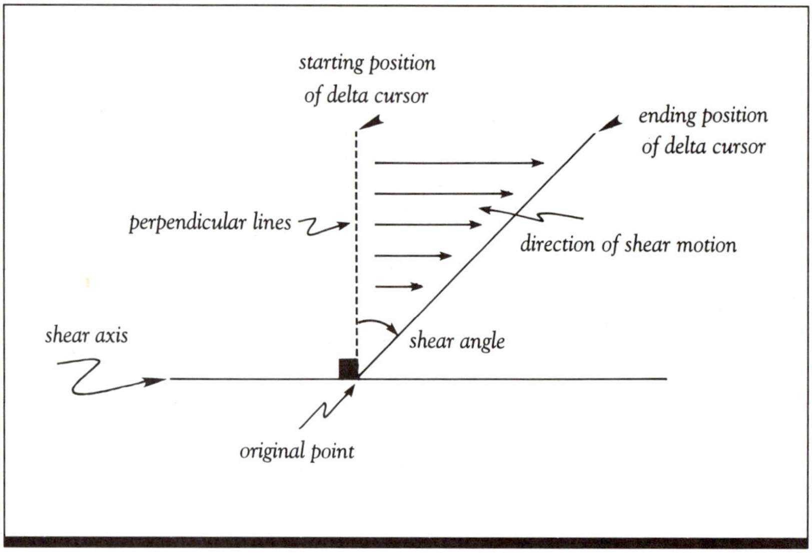

Figure 5.18: *Factors in a shearing operation*

You can see on the figure each of the components of the shear: the original point, which is the point you fix first with the + cursor, and the starting point for the delta, which defines the perpendicular line to the original point and hence defines the shear axis. And you also see the angle that measures the shear; the greater the value of the angle, the more pronounced the shear. In this case only, positive angles represent movement in a *clockwise* direction.

This applies to all angles in the shear; both the shear angle itself and the measurement of the angle of the shear axis to the horizontal axis. This is of most concern in using the Shear dialog box (shown in Figure 5.19), which is accessed by pressing the Option key while you set the first point. In this dialog box, the angle must be specified if you want to produce an angled shear. The angle of the axis is measured from the horizontal, or x-axis. Thus, for example, an angled shear with a setting of 90° is the equivalent of a vertical shear. Actually, in this case, the angle can be positive or negative and it will have no effect on the outcome; both axes are vertical. Similarly, angled shears of 180° or −180° are also identical in result, since both define the horizontal axis. However, for the angles in between, the sign makes a difference.

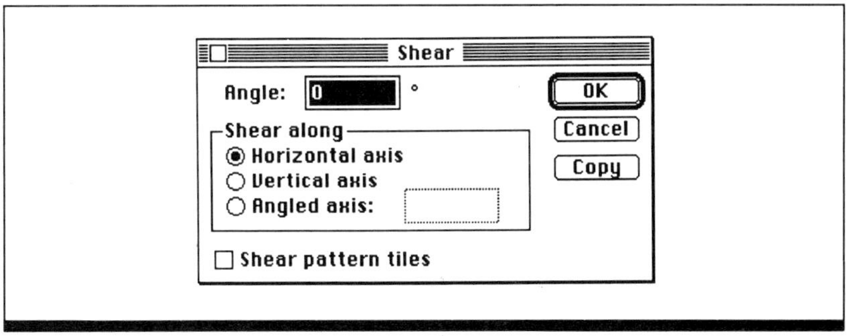

Figure 5.19: *Shear dialog box*

SHEARING LINES

Again, let's try some simple exercises. Begin, as usual, with a blank Illustrator desktop and no template.

1. **Use the pen tool to create two separate lines, one vertical and one, a reasonable distance away, horizontal.**
2. **Select both lines by pressing ⌘A (or choose Select All from the Edit menu), as shown in Figure 5.20.**

3. **Select the shear tool and position the first point at the base of the vertical line.**
4. **Move the delta cursor directly up over the line and click, then drag directly to the right in a straight line.**

5. **Use the Option key to make a copy (see Figure 5.20).**
6. **Select Undo Shear from the Edit menu to start again with just the two lines. Then reselect both lines.**
7. **Position the cursor in the same place, at the base of the vertical line, but move out directly to the right, past the end of the horizontal line, and click and drag straight up. Use the Option key to make a copy again (see Figure 5.20).**

Notice that the vertical line has not moved, since it lies entirely along the shear axis.

8. **Undo the shear again, select both lines, and set the shear origin point at the base of the vertical line.**

9. **Move the delta cursor to the right end of the horizontal line, then click and drag up and to the left, toward the top of the vertical line. Use the Option key to make this a copy (see Figure 5.20).**

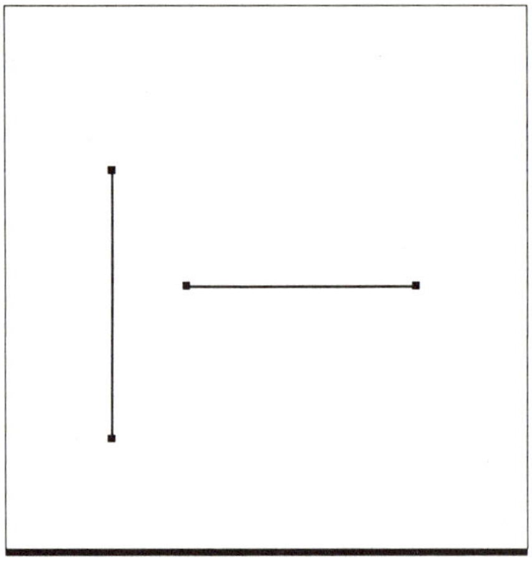

Step 2: *Selecting both lines*

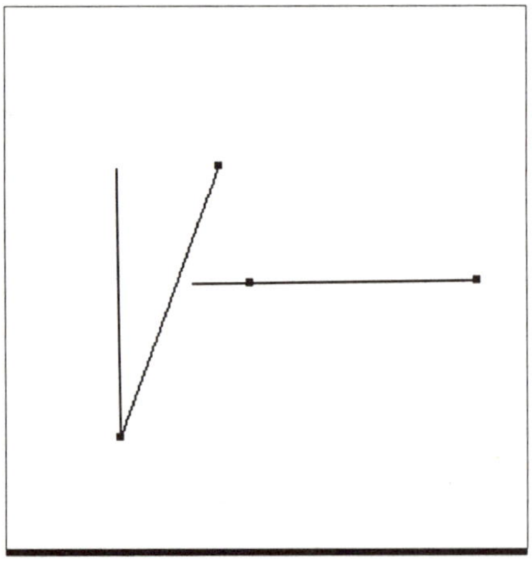

Step 5: *First shear*

Figure 5.20: *Shear examples (continues)*

Notice how both lines move this time, going in the direction of the shear and parallel to the shear axis that runs at right angles to the line formed by the bottom of the vertical line and the right end of the horizontal one.

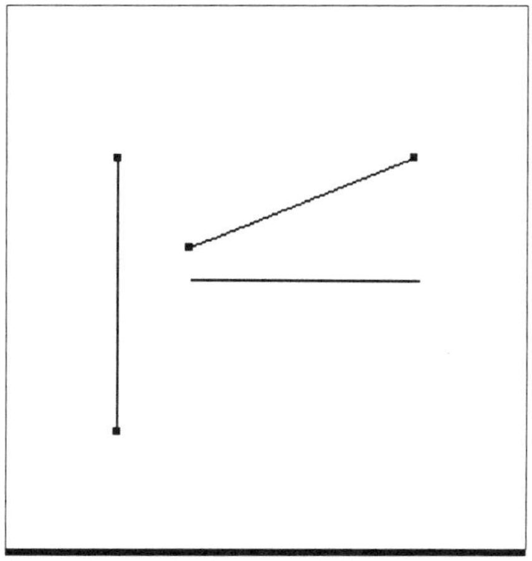

Step 7: *Second shear*

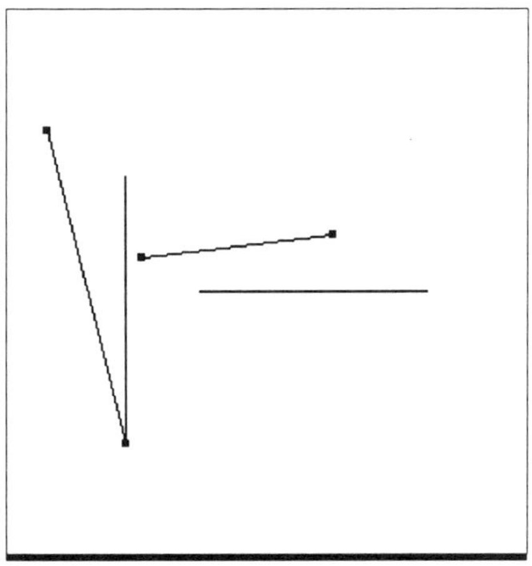

Step 9: *Third shear*

Figure 5.20: *Shear examples (continued)*

You may want to repeat these movements, using the optional Shear dialog box. The pair of lines, distinct and at right angles, makes it easier to visualize what the shear is doing.

Text Shearing for Shadowing

You saw earlier how you can use the scale tool to create certain shading effects with type. You can also use the shear tool to create shading and shadow effects. If you think about it, any shadow is just a sort of sheared image of the original.

We will use the letterhead artwork that you created earlier for this exercise.

1. **Open the Letterhead art document.**
2. **Scroll up so that you can see the letterhead name and address.**

We are going to change this from Helvetica Bold Oblique to a standard Helvetica Bold, and then add a shadow effect behind it, so that it looks like it is coming from the sun on the logo.

3. **Select the line of text *MOUNTAIN SPORTS, LTD.* and change the font to Helvetica Bold (see Figure 5.21).**
4. **Click once on the zoom tool to magnify the line of type for the name.**

This makes it easier to see what you are doing to the type.

5. **Make a copy of the original type on top of itself by choosing Copy from the Edit menu and then choosing Paste In Front.**

This gives you a new copy of the type to work with for the shadow effect.

6. **Paint that type 30% Black.**

If you previewed the artwork at this point, it would look like you had just changed the line of type from 100% Black to 30% Black; actually, there is still a line of black type behind the gray. This front copy of type is going to form the shadow effect for us.

7. **Select the shear tool and click on the type alignment point.**

For this line of type, that point is in the center of the type, under the first *S* in *SPORTS*, and is shown by a filled-in black square.

8. **Move the delta cursor directly up and then click and drag to the right by a reasonable angle, less than 30° (see Figure 5.21).**

Now you have to scale this type to make it look like a shadow. You do this by keeping the scale in the horizontal direction at 100 percent (since the base of the shadow will be unscaled), but changing the scale in the vertical direction. This is best done using the optional Scale dialog box.

9. **Set the scale origin on the alignment point of the text while holding down the Option key.**
10. **Set Non-uniform scale, with Horizontal as 100% and Vertical as 50% (see Figure 5.21).**

The only point that remains is to move the shadow to the back of the lettering. Right now, the shadow will paint in front of the letters because it was the last object created.

11. **Select Send To Back from the Edit menu.**

This gives a nice, shadowed effect to the text, as shown by the printed output in Figure 5.21.

Shadowing Objects

This same sequence of steps can be used to create shadow effects on graphics as well. Let's do a short exercise to see how this works. You can use the apple that you have worked on so often in the book; this time I chose the simplest version of the apple that we first prepared.

1. **Open the Simple Apple artwork and position the apple on the desktop.**
2. **Make a copy of the apple and paste it in front of the original artwork.**
3. **Paint it with 80% Black and set Stroke to None.**
4. **Shear this copy to the left, using the left-bottom curve on the base of the apple as the original point.**

Step 3: *Changing the font*

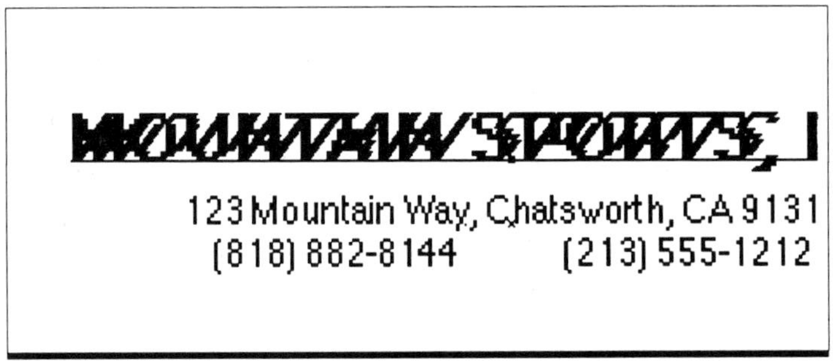

Step 8: *Shearing the text*

Step 10: *Scaling the shadow*

Figure 5.21: *Shearing text for a shadow effect (continues)*

You want to shear from a point that would be common to both the shadow and the object, naturally, and the bottom of the apple is the appropriate place. The result of the shear is shown in Figure 5.22.

Step 11: *Printed text*

Figure 5.21: *Shearing text for a shadow effect (continued)*

Notice the arrow at the bottom of the figure, which points to the original point for the shearing action, while the delta cursor was moved straight up until clear of the apple and then sheared to the left.

5. **Select the scale tool and, using the same point as a scale origin, set the scale through the optional dialog box with the values of 100% Horizontal and 40% Vertical scaling.**

This produces the result shown in Figure 5.22, which would, in and of itself, be quite sufficient. However, we will distort the shadow some more to improve the effect. You can do this by continuing the shearing process, but only shearing a portion of the shadow.

6. **Use the selection tool to deselect the entire shadow, then reselect the five points along the top of the shadow, as shown in Figure 5.22.**

You accomplish this by selecting each anchor point in turn while holding down the Shift key, which allows you to select multiple points.

7. **Select the shear tool again and set the same point of origin as before.**
8. **Move the delta cursor up to the top right of the shadow and pull and drag to the left to distort the shadow, as shown in Figure 5.22.**

This gives a more realistic shadow effect by elongating the shadow somewhat. Notice here that you have distorted the shadow by shearing only some of the points of the shadow artwork. This may remind you of the earlier discussion regarding transformations on portions of artwork; here is an excellent example of the deliberate use of the technique of transforming only a portion of the artwork to achieve a special effect.

9. Select the shadow and choose Send To Back to place it behind the apple artwork. Use the preview mode to ensure that the painting order is as you want it to be.

For this example, it's necessary to make small adjustments to the anchor points at the base of the shadow so that it looks correct. You can do this at a high magnification, so you can easily see and grab the individual anchor points without getting the other artwork inadvertently. A preview of the final result is shown in Figure 5.22.

10. Save this artwork as *Shadowed Apple art*.

To review, the steps for a shadow effect are as follows:

- Make a copy of the artwork that you want to shadow and paste it in front of itself.

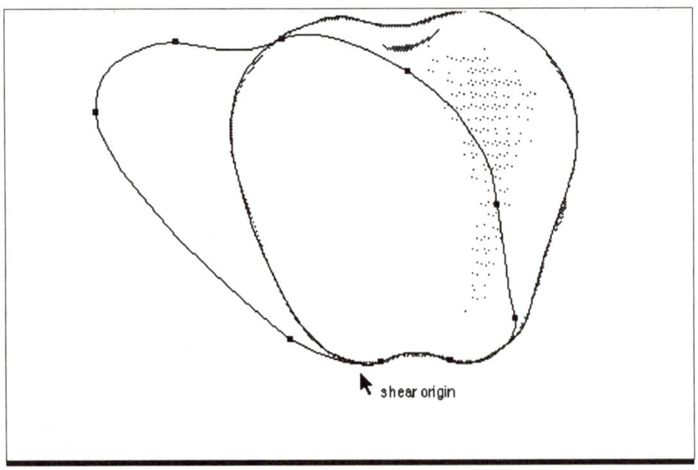

Step 4: *Shearing the copy*

Figure 5.22: *Shearing for shadows (continues)*

- Make the appropriate changes to the Paint characteristics.
- Shear the copy in the direction that you want the shadow to go.
- Scale the copy nonuniformly, with no scale on the horizontal axis (presuming that it represents the base of the shadow) and some appropriate value for the vertical axis.

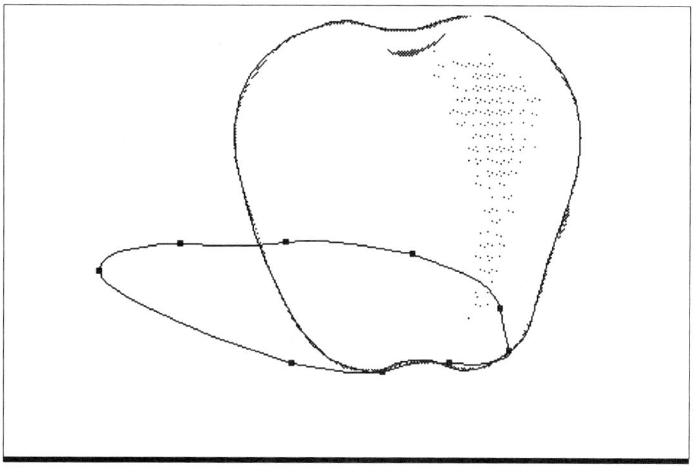

Step 5: *Scaling the copy*

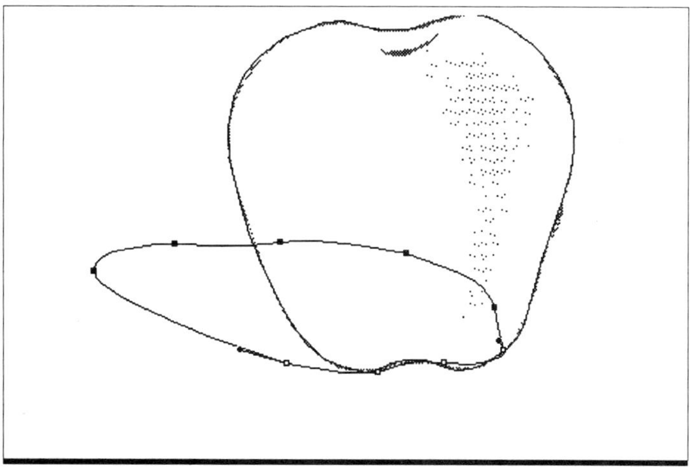

Step 6: *Selecting the top*

Figure 5.22: *Shearing for shadows (continues)*

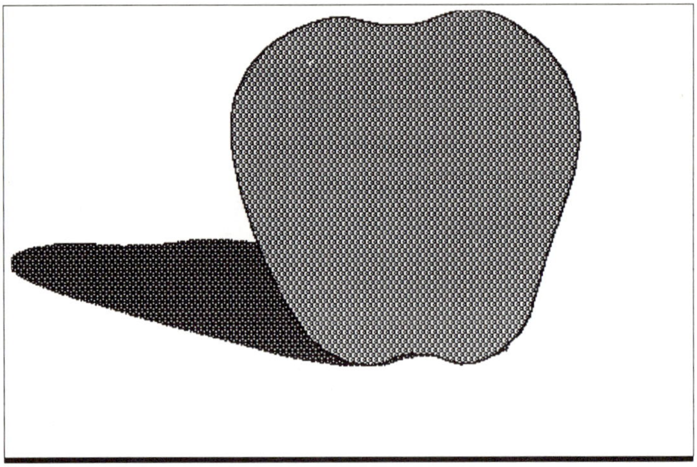

Step 8: *Distorting the shadow*

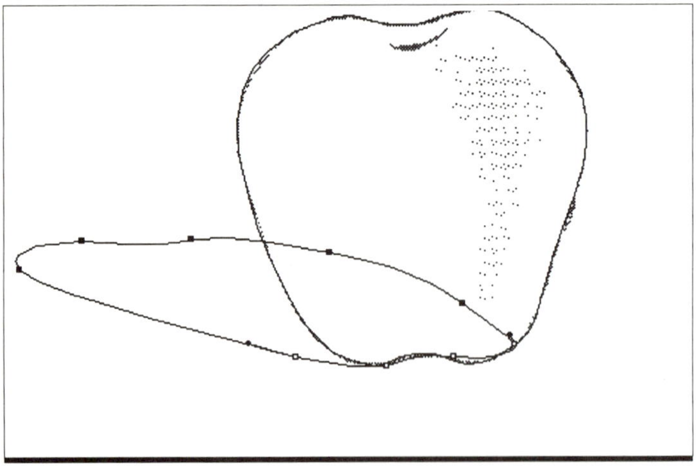

Step 9: *Preview of art*

Figure 5.22: *Shearing for shadows (continued)*

- Modify the final shadow as necessary to create the effect that you want.
- Place the shadow behind the original artwork so the shadow paints correctly.

We'll explore some more complex techniques and use other Illustrator tools in the next chapter.

Fast Track Chapter 6

239 To overlay two identical curves,
use the scissors tool to cut out the curve segment to be duplicated. Use Copy and Paste In Front from the Edit menu to overlay the two segments. Then you can work on the top segment, which is automatically selected.

241 To create a dashed line,
choose Dashed in the Dash pattern box of the Paint dialog screen and set the length of the dashes and the gaps, in points.

249 To move a section while keeping it connected
to the remainder of the artwork, select only the points to be moved and move them. The connecting lines will remain in place.

250 To create a strobe effect,
make copies of the artwork with lighter painting and stroking attributes. Move each copy into position to create the desired effect.

254 To create a template from Illustrator artwork,
preview the artwork and save the screen image. Then use MacPaint to clean up the result and generate the template that you want.

263 To constrain the axes to an arbitrary angle,
choose Preferences from the Edit menu (or press ⌘K) and use the Constrain angle option in the Preferences dialog box.

264 To determine the distance and angle between two points,
use the distance tool and click on each of the points.

265 To create an isometric drawing
with the plane at a given projection angle, scale the artwork nonuniformly in the vertical axis by the tangent of the angle, rotate the scaled artwork through the complement of the angle, and constrain the axes to the angle.

267 To mask parts
of Illustrator output, select the section of the artwork printing will be confined to (the clipping region), and click on the Mask button in the Paint dialog section.

Fast Track

271 **To autotrace an entire template,**
click the autotrace tool cursor once at any point on the template.

273 **To autotrace a specific portion of a template,**
click the autotrace tool cursor on the starting point, drag the cursor to the ending point that you want to trace, and release the mouse button. Autotrace works in a clockwise direction.

280 **To use the freehand tool,**
click and drag the freehand tool cursor to draw the line on the page.

286 **To use Illustrator output with other PostScript applications,**
choose either Macintosh or IBM PC in the Include preview for box portion of the Save dialog box when you save the artwork.

Chapter 6

ADVANCED MODIFICATION & TRANSFORMATION TECHNIQUES

The tools for transforming artwork are very powerful, as you have seen in the previous chapter. This power can be greatly extended by using the transformation tools in combinations, either with one another or with other Illustrator tools.

The power of tool combinations lies in the cumulative effect that they produce; the difficulty in using them is in defining what sequence of tools needs to be applied to generate the result that you want. A good example of this is the upside-down lettering we placed on the example diskette label in Chapter 5. You need to realize that reversed text is most easily and accurately positioned by using a double-reflection process, once through the horizontal and once through the vertical axis.

This chapter is primarily devoted to exercises that will show you some (but, of necessity, only some) of the ways that you can combine the tools to create interesting effects. It also introduces the tools we have not covered yet: the freehand and autotrace tools.

CREATING EXPLODED VIEWS

Exploded, or cutaway, views are easy to create with Illustrator. To create them, cut out the portion you want to expose with the scissors tool, and modify the artwork as necessary. You can use the basic tools in combination to make a complex graphic image.

CUTTING AN APPLE SLICE

As an exercise, we'll use the apple artwork—which you are, by now, intimately familiar with—and cut out a segment from the apple to make the traditional cutaway view of an object. Then we will label some elements.

1. **Open the Revised Apple art document and position the artwork so that the body of the apple is a bit to the right of the center of the screen (see Figure 6.1).**

Because there is no template that closely matches the work we will be doing, I would recommend working in the Artwork Only view for these changes.

2. **Use the scissors tool to cut the apple outline at the anchor point that is on the top-left shoulder of the apple and at the anchor point that is at the bottom-left curve.**

3. **Select the cut segment and move it away from the apple outline (see Figure 6.1).**

This segment will form the basis of the slice of the apple.

4. **Use the pen tool to connect the top and bottom anchor points with a curved line that approximates the shape of the apple segment.**

You can do this by eye; I would recommend that you use one additional anchor point along the curve to define the shoulder of the apple. The result is shown in Figure 6.1. Notice that the middle anchor point is a mild form of a curved corner. You don't need to set any Paint attributes here because this segment inherits the characteristics of the apple outline, which is what we want.

5. **Finish off the segment by drawing a line from the top anchor point to the bottom one.**

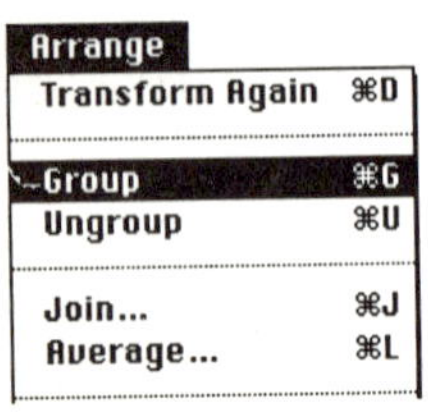

6. **Set the Paint attributes of 80% Black Fill and a line weight of .5.**
7. **Select both parts of the cutaway segment and group them by using Group from the Arrange menu (or press ⌘G).**

These attributes will make the line light but visible. Now we need to complete the apple outline with the missing segment.

8. **Select the apple outline in its entirety, so you can see the anchor points.**
9. **Form a new curved line, beginning at the depression in the center of the apple and extending down to the base of the apple to represent one side of the cut (see Figure 6.1).**

The curve arcs up from the center to cross over the top anchor point of the apple, then moves rather sharply downward to reflect the missing segment and joins the apple outline at the base anchor point.

10. **Continue with the inner portion of the cut by making a corner anchor point at the bottom, moving back up toward the top of the apple, and finishing by rejoining the beginning point (see Figure 6.1).**

Step 1: *Positioning the apple*

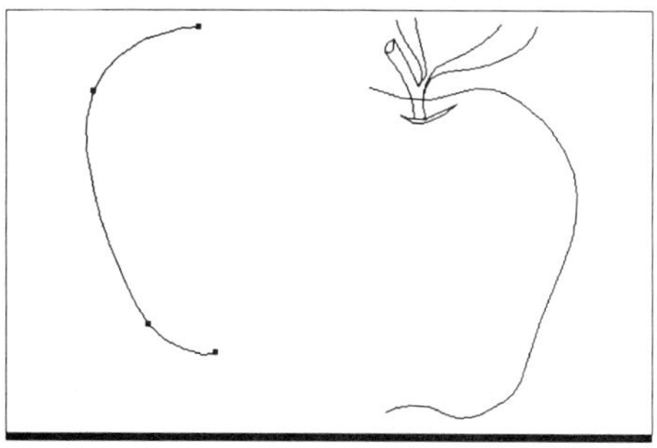

Step 3: *Moving a segment*

Figure 6.1: *Cutting out the apple slice (continues)*

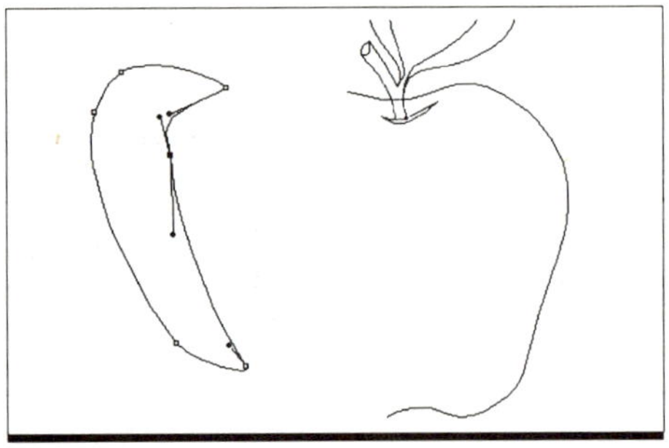

Step 4: *Connecting the points*

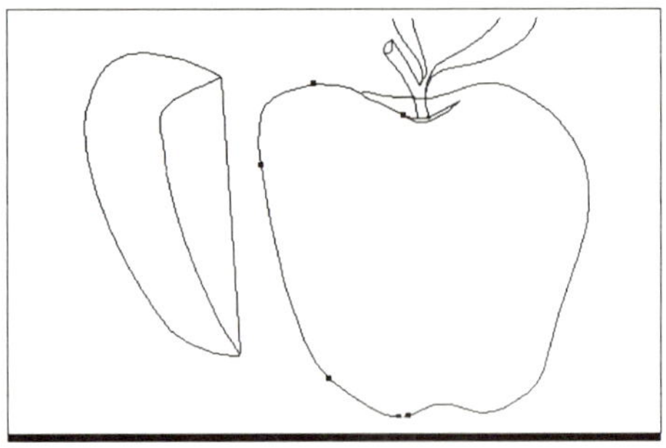

Step 9: *A side of the cut*

Step 10: *The completed slice*

Figure 6.1: *Cutting out the apple slice (continued)*

This would be excellent, except that the two curves that make up the outline of the apple and the cut surface are partially distinct and partially joined. If you previewed the artwork now, you would see that the cut portion of the apple paints gray and the inner surface of the cut paints white, but the colors don't join correctly. The outer surface of the apple is not closed, and so the paint just stops along the straight line that goes from the top of the apple to the bottom. We want the color to follow the shape of the inner cut. All the pieces are in place, as you can see. How do we make it paint correctly?

Adjusting the Apple Cutaway

To adjust the painting characteristics, we need to create two outlines: one for the outside of the apple and another for the inner cut surface. The solution is to make two paths that share the one common line that forms the inner edge of the cut, and color one side white and the other with the current shade of gray. As always, there is an easy way to do this with Illustrator.

1. **Start by selecting the scissors tool and cutting the apple outline at the anchor point at the base of the apple that is the common point to both surfaces.**

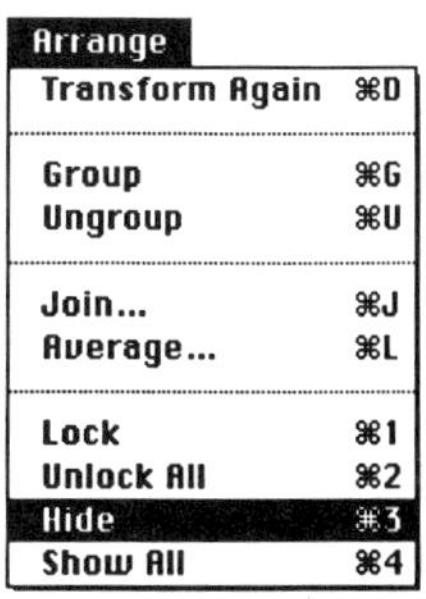

2. **To remove the cutaway segment from view, select it, and then choose Hide from the Arrange menu (or press ⌘3).**

This leaves the selected artwork (the cutaway segment) in place but prevents it from displaying on the screen in any mode. As in this case, removing a portion of an artwork from view sometimes makes it easier to work with its other elements.

3. **Select the outer portion of the apple and move it slightly away from the rest of the apple (see Figure 6.2).**

You could do the remainder of the exercise with the cut portion in place, but it's easier and faster to move the cut segment slightly out of the way and then continue the work.

4. **Add a new anchor point to the revised apple segment at the top, where it would meet the outer segment, by clicking on the curve with the scissors tool while holding down the Option key (see the placement of the cursor in Figure 6.2).**

When you hold down the Option key, the scissors tool creates a new anchor point on an existing curve rather than actually cutting the curve.

5. Select the inner anchor points, as shown in Figure 6.2.

Notice that the two end points (the one under the cursor and the one at the bottom of the segment) are not selected.

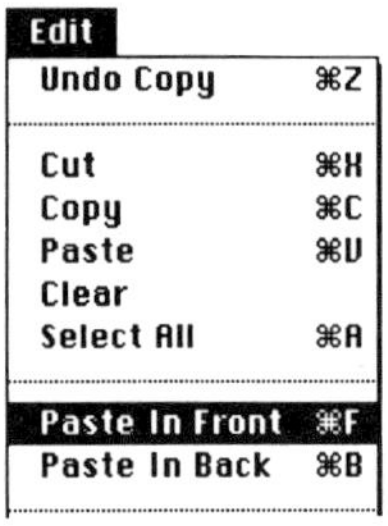

6. Use Copy and Paste In Front from the Edit menu to make a copy of this line segment and paste it in front of the other artwork.

7. Move this segment in to match up with the parts of the outer apple outline (see Figure 6.2).

This forms one piece of the common border. We still have to close up the two paths that make up the outer part of the apple so that it forms one continuous outline. The two outlines are quite separate, even though their endpoints are exactly on top of one another.

8. Use the selection marquee to select both points at the top of the apple.

All the endpoints should be selected, as shown in Figure 6.2.

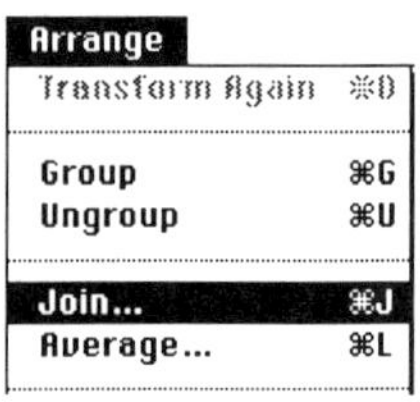

9. Choose Join from the Arrange menu.

You have selected two matching and overlapping endpoints; Join tells Illustrator to make them into one point and join the two curves that they represent. When you do that, the multiple direction points disappear, leaving only one anchor point and two direction points.

10. Perform the same function on the two bottom endpoints to achieve the same results.

11. Select the entire outer apple outline to see the completed line adjustment, as shown in Figure 6.2.

12. Move the cut segment of the apple back into its original position, which will match the curve of the outer portion precisely.

13. Set the Fill to White and the Stroke to the same value as the outer segment: .2 line weight and 100% Black.

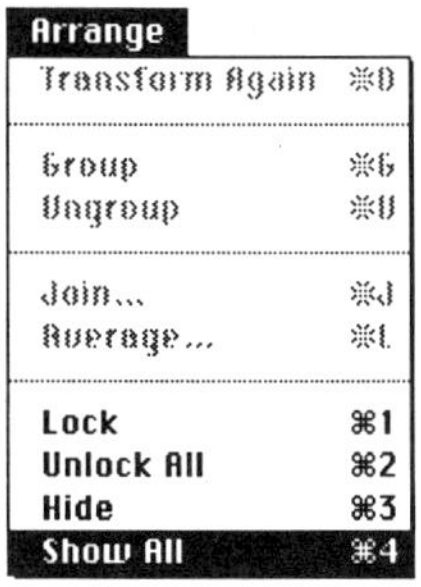

Now you can adjust any features of the artwork. I moved the top of the cut to the top of the depression to give a more realistic effect and made some changes to the cutaway segment to match the cutout more closely.

14. **Choose Show All from the Arrange menu to display the hidden segment again.**
15. **Preview the artwork.**

The preview of my version at this point is shown in Figure 6.2.

Creating Dotted Lines

We'll continue by adding two dotted lines that connect the cutaway segment and the cut portion of the apple.

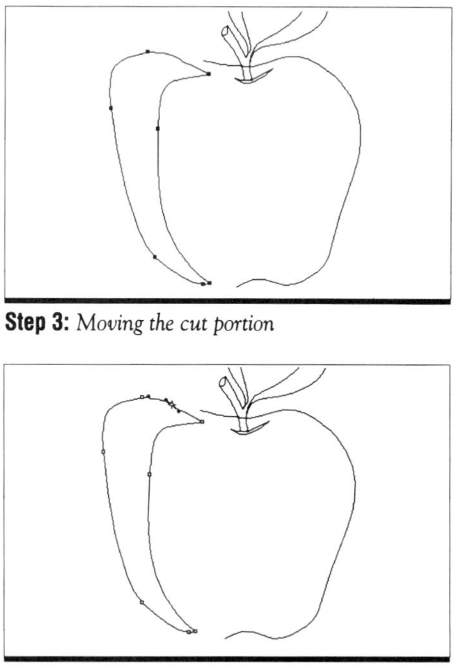

Step 3: *Moving the cut portion*

Step 4: *Adding an anchor point*

Figure 6.2: *Adjusting the cutaway (continues)*

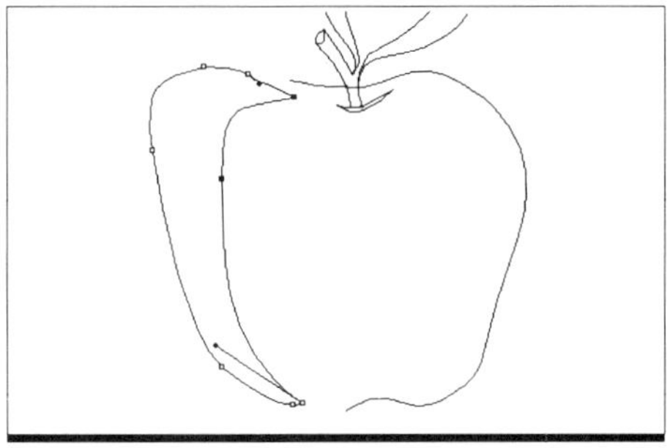

Step 5: *Selecting the inner points*

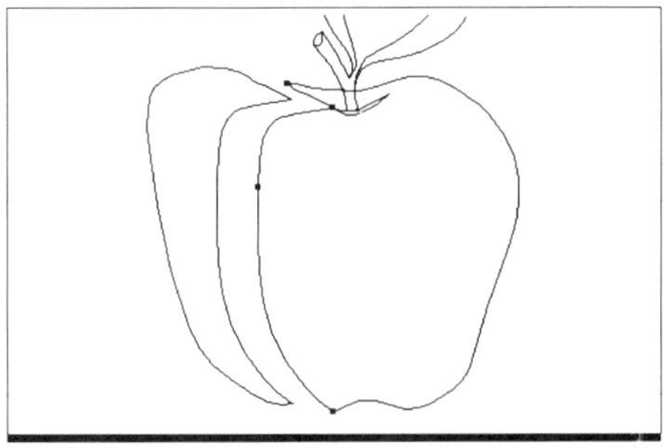

Step 7: *Moving the segment in*

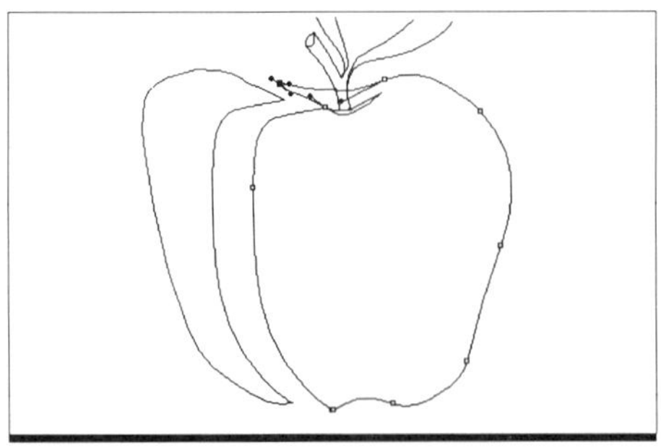

Step 8: *Selecting the endpoints*

Figure 6.2: *Adjusting the cutaway (continues)*

1. Use the pen tool to draw a line from the top of the cutaway segment to the top of the apple.
2. Set the Paint attributes as shown in Figure 6.3.

Step 11: *Completed adjustment*

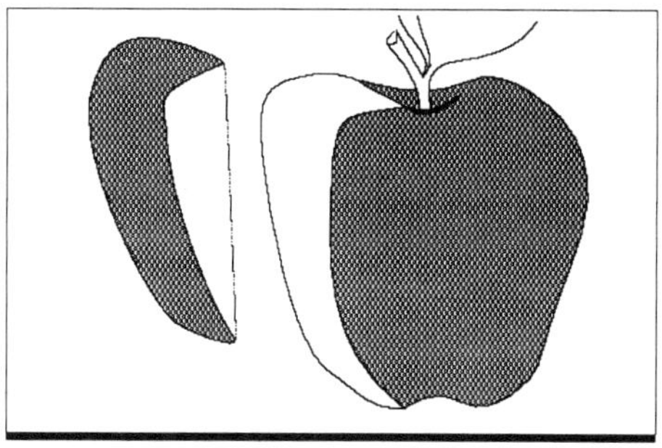

Step 15: *Preview of art*

Figure 6.2: *Adjusting the cutaway (continued)*

As shown in Figure 6.3, choose the Dashed option under Dash pattern (at the bottom of the box) and set the length of the dashes as 2 points and the gap between them as 5 points. You must specify both the length of the dash and the length of the gap between the dashes.

The Dashed option allows up to six alternating specifications for dashes and gaps. These boxes come in pairs: the first box specifies the length of the first dash in points, and the second box specifies the length of the subsequent gap in points. The next pair of boxes governs the lengths of the next dash and gap, and so on. Illustrator repeats the specified dash and gap pattern for the length of the entire line. By entering values in multiple boxes, you can vary the dotted line. However, generally, you will want your dashed lines to use uniform gaps and dashes; furthermore, to create a real dashed effect, the gap has to be longer than the dash by some visible amount.

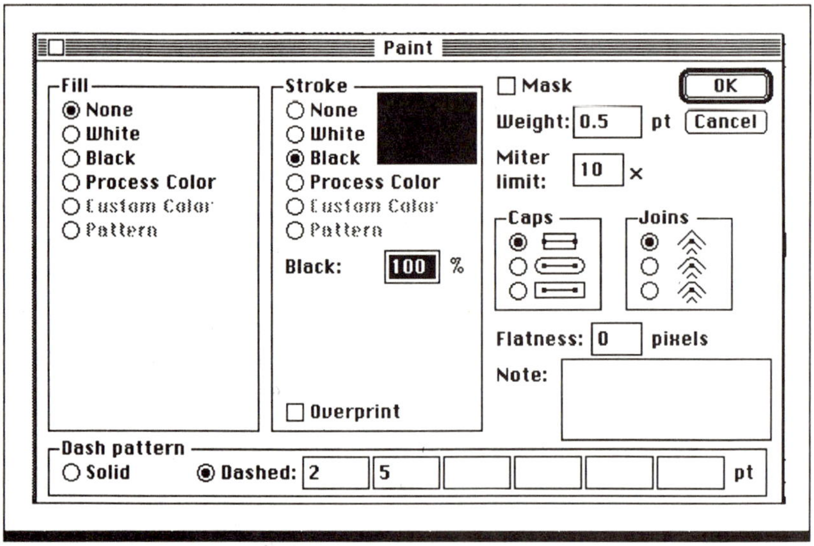

Figure 6.3: *Paint attributes for dashed line*

3. **After you create the line, check to be sure that it has not automatically been joined to the line that defines the front of the cutaway segment by using the selection tool with the Option key.**

If this shows more than just the line you created, disconnect the two lines by cutting them apart at the common point with the scissors tool.

4. **Create the bottom dotted line in the same way and with the same attributes and precautions.**

The preview of the final result should look something like the one shown in Figure 6.4.

Adding a Core

We can finish off the apple cutaway by adding a small circular core section and a few seeds.

1. **Draw the core section, which is just a curve set onto the cutaway segment, as shown in Figure 6.5.**
2. **Set the Paint attributes to a solid line, 100% Black, and a .5 line weight.**

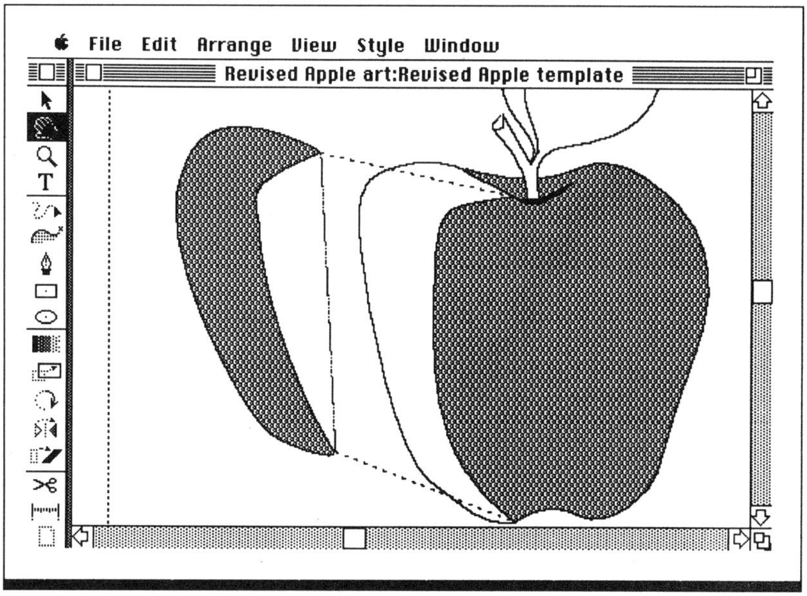

Figure 6.4: *Preview of apple cutaway with dotted lines*

3. Add the seeds by using the circle tool in the core area.

Magnify the area so you can make small ovals for the seeds, and place several of them at random intervals over the core.

4. Paint these with a Fill of 100% Black and no Stroke.

5. Preview the artwork (see Figure 6.5).

6. Save this artwork as *Cutaway Apple art*.

Now we'll add labels to the artwork and see how to move the exploded segment.

ADDING LABELS TO THE APPLE SEGMENTS

You have already merged text with graphic images in earlier exercises. This example shows some more ways to place and handle text and how to move a graphic for text placement.

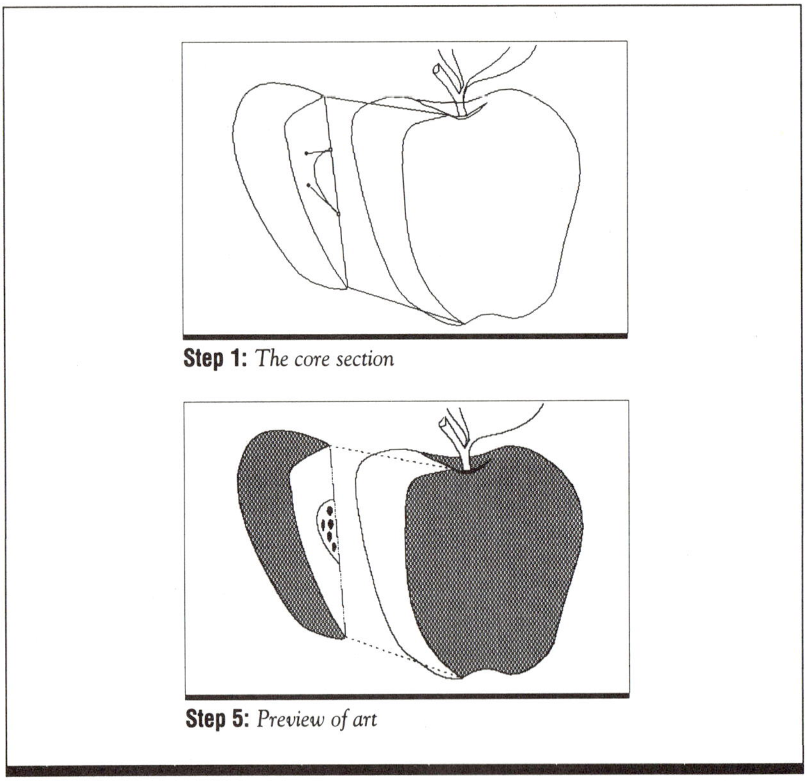

Figure 6.5: *Adding the apple core*

Deleting the Template Association

We'll start by deleting the association of the Cutaway Apple art with the template, which has become mostly irrelevant and a distraction at this point.

1. **Temporarily rename the template.**
2. **Open the Cutaway Apple art and and choose None when Illustrator asks you to select a template to associate with the artwork.**

Your starting screen should look like the one shown in Figure 6.6. Now, when you save the artwork, there will no longer be any template associated with it, even when you restore the template's original name.

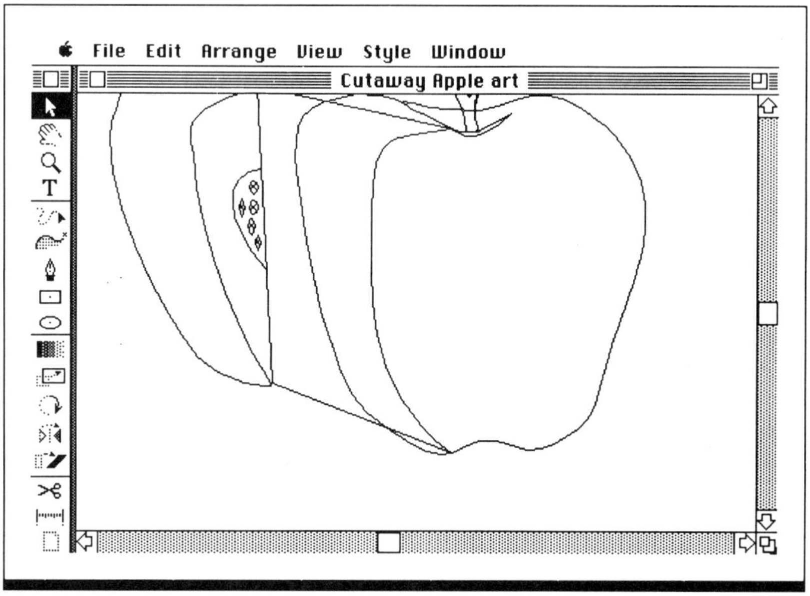

Figure 6.6: *Cutaway Apple art without the template*

Creating the Arrow

We will use arrows to indicate the apple elements identified by labels. First, we will create a large version of the arrow, which we will scale down later. This allows us to keep the arrow in constant proportion to the text size, while also maintaining the correct shape.

1. **Use the pen tool to draw an arrow that has the dimensions given in Figure 6.7, in the upper-left corner of the page, using 1 unit on the rulers for each unit on the plan.**

You may find this easier to do if you magnify the area by one click before drawing the arrow.

2. **Copy the arrow to an area some distance away.**

3. **Make a scaled copy of the arrow. Using the scale tool and Option key combination, set the scale origin at the nose of the arrow (so that the scale is completely symmetrical). Reduce the arrow by 25%, and scale the line weights, too.**
4. **Set the Paint attributes for the arrow to no Fill and 100% Black, with a line weight of 1 point.**

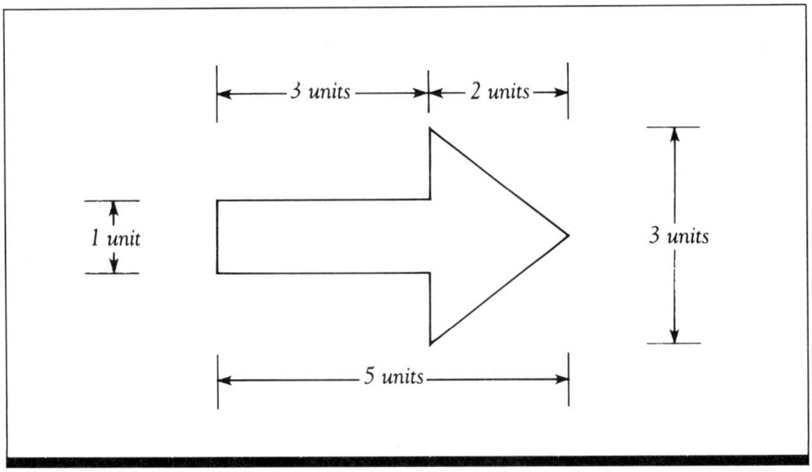

Figure 6.7: *Dimensions for the arrow*

The result is shown in Figure 6.8. (The image is enlarged in the figure to make it clearer, and I've added some type to show the arrow's relative size.)

This small arrow is scaled so that the width of the arrowhead is about the size of 10-point type. You can check that, if you want to scale it by hand, by typing some characters and measuring the arrowhead against them.

5. **With the small arrow still selected, pull down the Arrange menu and select Group.**

Now you can move and rotate the arrow without worrying about accidentally selecting only a part of it.

Placing the Labels

Now we are ready to add the labels to the cutaway apple.

1. **Use the text tool to set the figure labels *stem, leaf,* and *segment* in 10-point Times-Roman.**
2. **At the bottom, set the caption *The Apple* in 15-point Helvetica Bold.**

3. **Place an arrow next to each caption, using the rotate tool to position it in the correct orientation (see Figure 6.9). Rotate the arrows by the bottom point on their tails.**

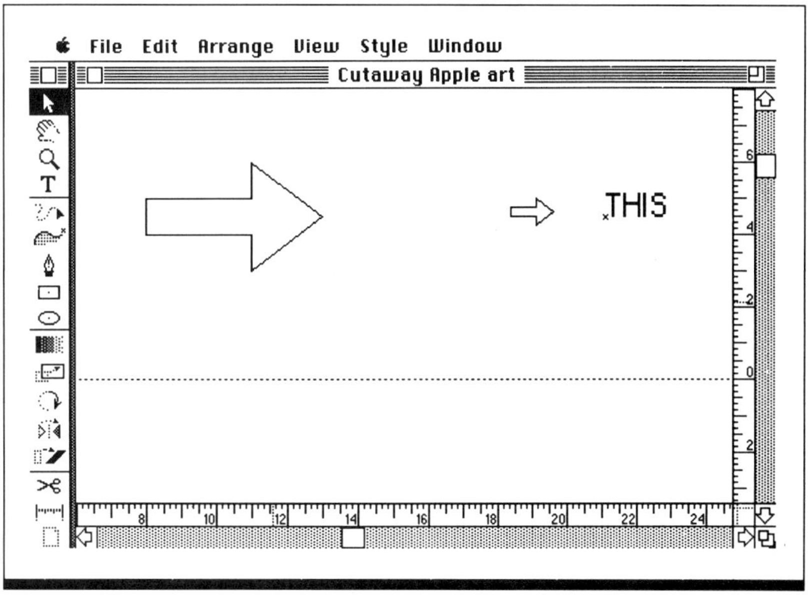

Figure 6.8: *Large arrow and reduced arrow*

We still need to label the seeds; however, there isn't room between the cutaway segment and the main body of the apple. The trick here is to move the segment out enough to make space for the label. We can do this by moving the segment as a unit. We want to move the associated label and arrow with the segment.

4. **Use the selection marquee to select the entire section of the page, as shown in Figure 6.9.**

You might be tempted to group the results to ensure that they will move together, but don't. Making a group out of this segment would add the endpoints of the two dotted lines to the figure, which, you will notice, are not currently included in the selected points. We particularly want to exclude these points because we want to move only one end of the dotted lines, not both. The ends at the apple need to stay fixed.

5. **Use the zoom tool to reduce the artwork by one click.**
6. **Use the selection tool to move the selected graphics up and to the left, as shown in Figure 6.9.**

You can place this segment anywhere that you want, and the dotted lines will follow the motion because one end of the lines is moving while the other end is fixed at the apple. Position the cutaway segment so that there is enough room to place the label next to the seeds.

7. **Enter the label *seeds* in 10-point Times Roman and position it as indicated in the preview version shown in Figure 6.9.**

We still have one small problem: the moved slice now spills over onto another page. We need to move it to the right. You could choose Select All from the Edit menu and physically move the entire graphic as one unit to a better position on the page, but this approach has some drawbacks. First, it's hard to position such a large graphic accurately because all the lines tend to overlap, making a confusing image for placement. Second, moving so many points is a slow process. As an alternative, we'll use the page tool to reset the page to fit the graphic rather than the other way around.

8. **Select Fit In Window from the View menu (or press ⌘M) to see the entire artwork and its placement on the page.**

9. **Click on the page tool and center the new page around the existing graphic, as shown in Figure 6.9.**

The printed version of the final cutaway apple art is shown in Figure 6.10.

MAKING MULTIPLE COPIES FOR REPEATING ELEMENTS

Some graphics are formed by creating multiple copies of the same or similar images; repeating elements are very common in artwork. In this section, we will use repetition for two different purposes: to create a strobe effect, where the same image is repeated in slightly different orientations (to mimic motion), and to simplify drawing a figure with a large number of repeated elements.

CREATING A STROBE EFFECT

In our first exercise, we will draw a falling tomahawk. There is no template for this, so open a new desktop without a template.

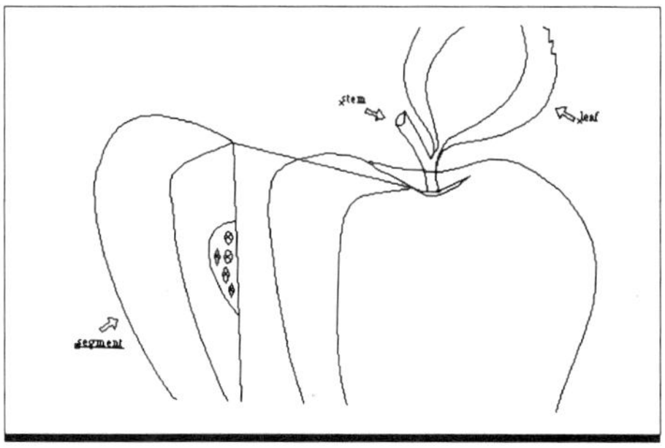

Step 3: *Labels and arrows*

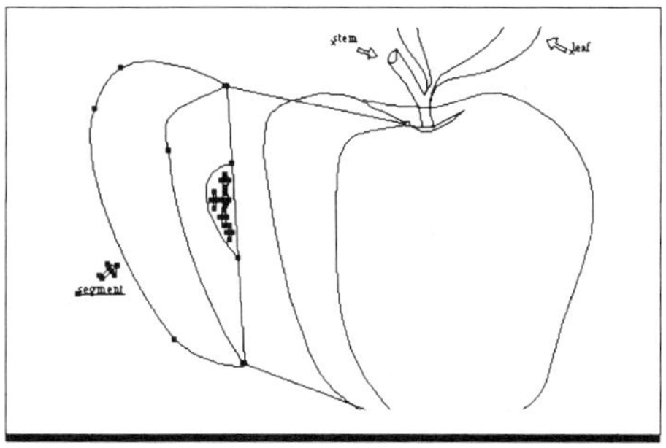

Step 4: *Selecting the section*

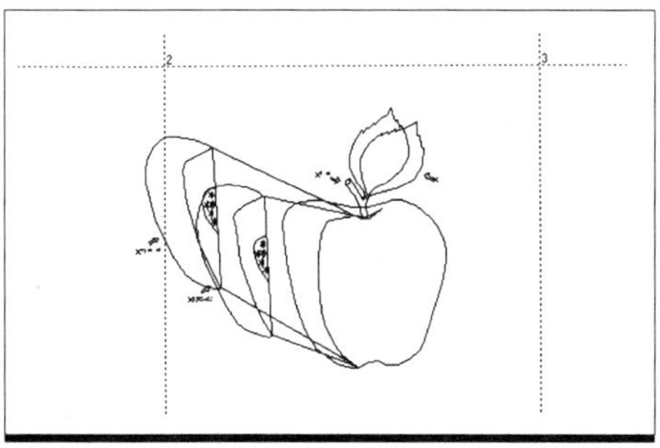

Step 6: *Moving the section*

Figure 6.9: *Adding the labels to the cutaway apple (continues)*

1. **Start by using the pen tool to draw the head of the tomahawk in the center of the desktop, as shown in Figure 6.11.**
2. **Paint the head with White Fill and a Stroke of 100% Black, with a line weight of 1 point.**

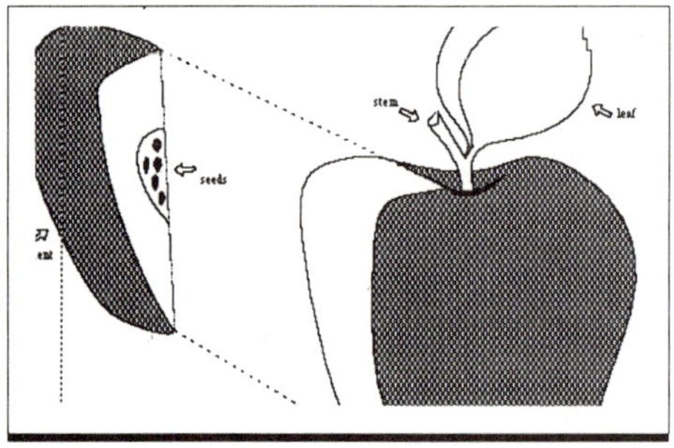

Step 7: *Preview of labeled art*

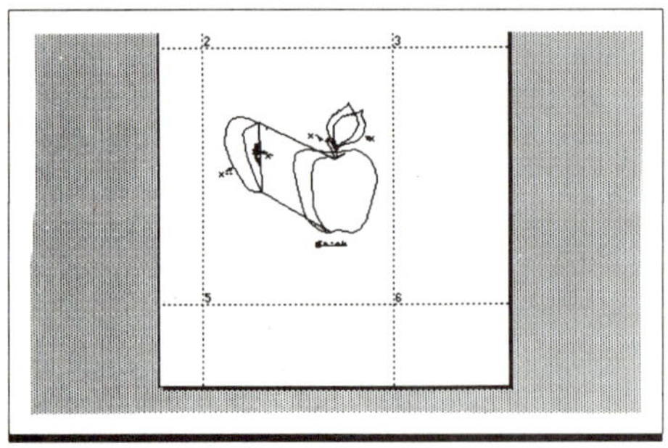

Step 9: *Resetting the page*

Figure 6.9: *Adding the labels to the cutaway apple (continued)*

3. **Add a handle, which is most easily done by using the square tool.**
4. **Paint the handle with 50% Black Fill and a Stroke of 100% Black, with a .5 line weight.**

As a final touch, we'll add two crossed thongs that hold the head onto the handle. There is a fast way to do this.

5. **Draw one thong across the head and handle as a straight line.**
6. **Paint the thong with no Fill and a Stroke of 100% Black, with a line weight of 3 points.**
7. **Select the entire line (both endpoints), as shown in Figure 6.11.**

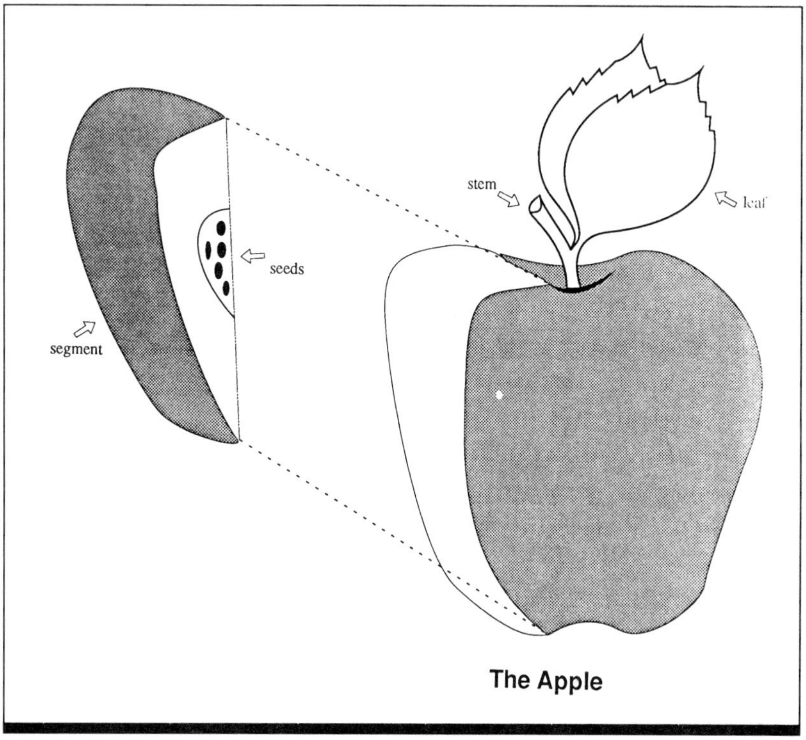

Figure 6.10: *Page output from cutaway apple with labels*

8. **Position the reflect tool at the center of the thong, where the second thong should cross.**
9. **Use the Option key to access the optional Reflect dialog box, choose reflection across the Horizontal axis, and click on Copy.**

This creates a perfect second thong. You want to use horizontal rather than vertical reflection because the head, and therefore the thong, are not symmetrical vertically; the front is larger than the back.

10. **Group the entire tomahawk (see Figure 6.11).**
11. **Use the rotate tool to rotate a copy of the entire image 20°.**

I used a center of rotation about 4 units below the bottom of the handle; you can use whatever distance looks best to you. After the rotation, the entire copy of the artwork is still selected. Now we want to make the copy much lighter and less "real" than the top version of the object. We can do this by setting the Paint attributes in a global fashion.

12. Select Paint from the Style menu.

You will see that most of the information in the Paint dialog screen is blank. This happens whenever you have selected objects with differing attributes; Illustrator can't show them all, so it doesn't show any. We will override these individual settings by creating global values.

13. Set Fill to None, Stroke to 80% Black, and the line weight to .5 points.

14. Do two more rotations, using angles of 30° and 40°, respectively.

The result is shown in Figure 6.11, which has the graphics reduced to allow you to see the entire image in preview mode.

Repeating Shapes to Form a Graphic

Next we will use repeated shapes to create a drawing of a dinosaur with a row of spines down its back. This exercise uses a template, made from a series of curves, lines, and ovals in Illustrator itself. This is a very useful technique that you may want to use.

Creating a "Sketch" in Illustrator

The template, shown in Figure 6.12, is a rough outline of the image that we want. This is very much like creating a pencil sketch before you draw a final version over it. In this case, the dinosaur was drawn using ovals, simple lines, and curves that clearly are not suitable for the final figure, but which give some guidance for the final artwork.

1. **Use the Illustrator tools to prepare the dinosaur sketch shown in Figure 6.12.**
2. **Preview the outline.**
3. **Save the screen in a MacPaint format.**
4. **Edit the screen to remove the extraneous elements, such as the Illustrator borders.**

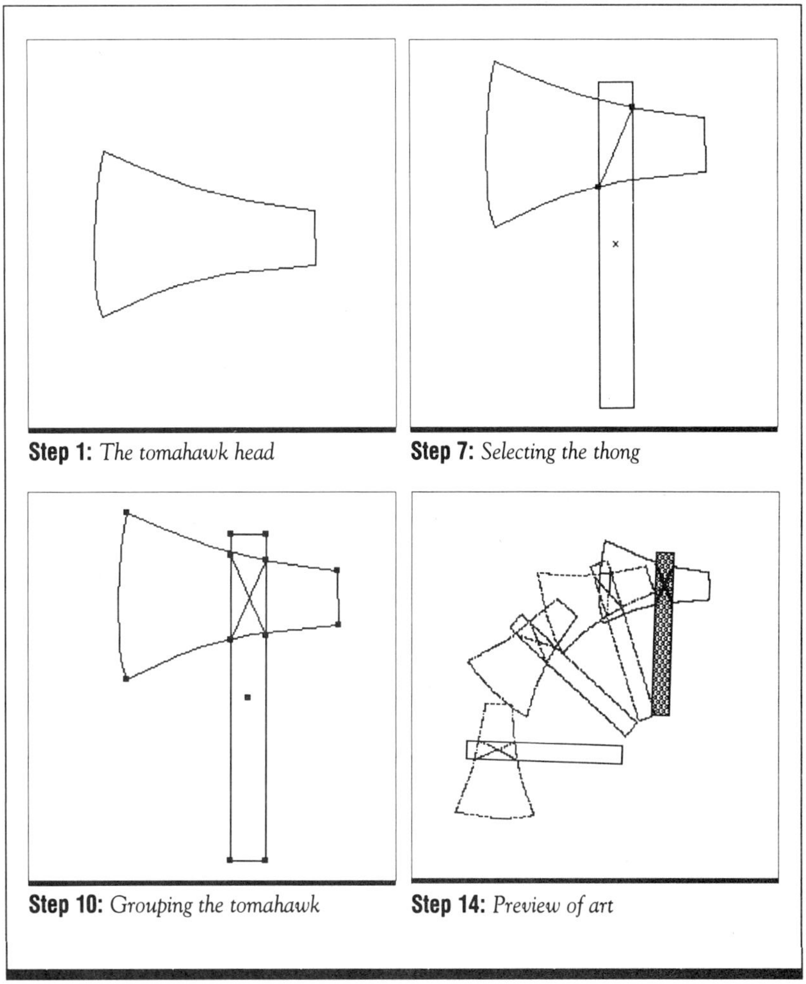

Figure 6.11: *Creating a falling tomahawk*

The sketch is now available as a template. Part of the advantage of making a template in this way is that you can always go back, modify the artwork, and create a new version of the template relatively painlessly.

Drawing the Body

We'll start by drawing the body of the dinosaur.

1. **Open a new desktop with the dinosaur template.**
2. **Outline the body (see Figure 6.13).**

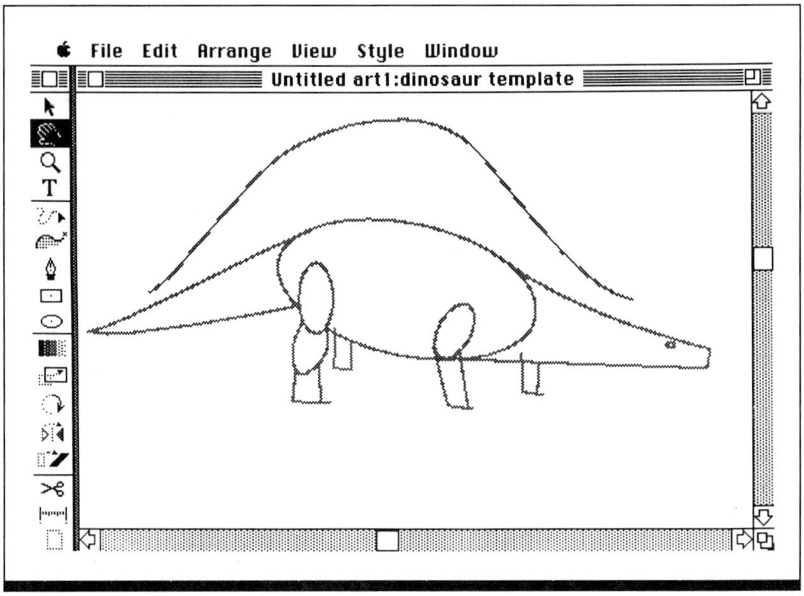

Figure 6.12: *Template for dinosaur art*

The nose should not be quite so straight and flat as the template shows; make it more pointed. Remember to form corners where required.

3. **Fill the body with 50% Black, Stroke it with 100% Black, and set a line weight of 1.**
4. **Next add the dinosaur's legs.**

Although the template shows the thighs and legs as ovals, you should draw them as open figures.

5. **Set the same Paint attributes for the legs as you did for the body.**
6. **Draw two curves along the front of each thigh, to give some contour to the body.**
7. **Add a single line with a weight of 1.5 for the mouth.**

The artwork at this stage is shown in Figure 6.13. Now we want the two far legs, on the other side of the body, to paint behind the body, not in front of it.

8. **Select each rear leg and choose Send To Back from the Edit menu.**
9. **Preview the dinosaur body (see Figure 6.13).**

Adding the Spines

Now we need to add the spines down the dinosaur's back. The height and relative scale of the spikes is shown by the continuous curve that runs along the top of the dinosaur template. Also, the spines run in two rows, so the effect should be of alternating front and back spines. For the correct painting order, we need to draw the back spines first.

1. **Draw the first spine at about the shoulder and up to the curve in height (see Figure 6.14).**

The spines have a vaguely diamond shape, so you will have to make corners at the edges and top.

2. **Change the Paint attributes to a Fill of 30% Black to make the spines slightly lighter than the rest of the body.**
3. **Select the spine and move it forward, making a copy of it with a space between the two spines of about one-third to one-half the width of the first one.**

Remember that we are going to come back and place another row of spines over this one.

4. **Using the scale tool, set the scale origin under the front anchor point of the spine and pull the top point down until it reaches the curved template line (see Figure 6.14).**

At this point, you could modify the spine form a little if you want, just as you did to the leaf tip copy earlier.

5. **Use this same process to complete the first row of spines, rotating the spines as well as enlarging them as you go over the top of the back (see Figure 6.14).**

As you move toward the back, you will get better scaling results if you set the scale origin at the back anchor point rather than the front (the point that doesn't move is the one lower down the figure).

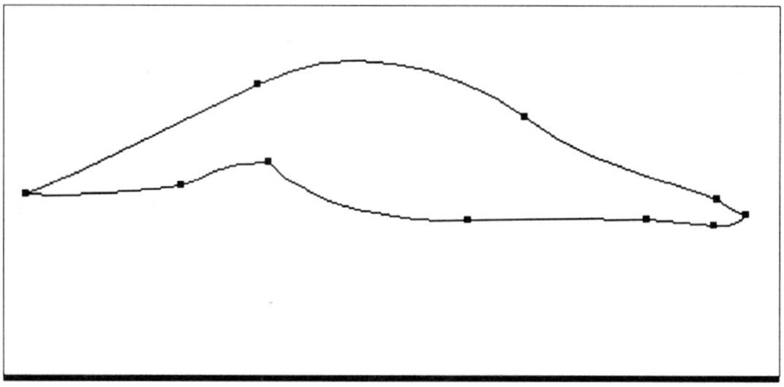

Step 2: *Outlining the body*

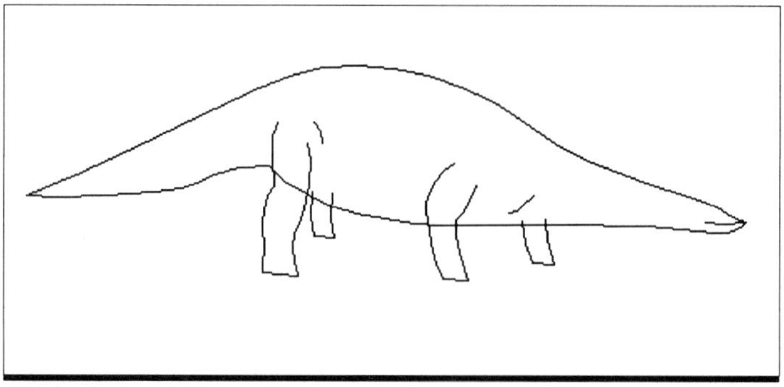

Step 7: *Adding the legs and mouth*

Step 9: *Preview of the body*

Figure 6.13: *Drawing the dinosaur body*

Now we need to form the next row of spines, which overlaps and paints in front of the previous row.

6. **Move each existing scale forward or backward as necessary to create a matching overlapping scale. Preview the art periodically to make sure that the spines are going in order.**

The real caution here is to remember that whenever you move a spine, it automatically paints in front of the previous objects; therefore, if you want to move or adjust any of the spines in the back row, do it before you create the overlapping front spines. If you do get out of sequence, use the Send To Back or Bring To Front option on the Edit menu to place the spines in their proper order again.

7. **Use the zoom tool at the back and front ends to help place the spines.**
8. **Adjust the spines as necessary to create the desired effect (see Figure 6.14).**
9. **Now take a moment to add the eye, using the circle tool. Use the zoom tool to help position the circle accurately.**
10. **Paint the eye with White Fill and 100% Black Stroke, with a line weight of .5 points.**
11. **Preview the result (see Figure 6.14).**

Finishing the Dinosaur

The dinosaur art still needs some finishing touches. First, the dinosaur outline should paint in front of the spines. Now you can't just use Bring To Front here; if you do, the legs will not be in the proper painting order. You need to use the Group function to make the body and the legs one unit. This maintains the painting order within the group, which is what you want, while allowing you to paste the entire group in front of all the spines. To make this group, you need to select all the components of the body, including the legs, eye, and mouth. You cannot use the selection marquee to pick all the points because, if you try, you will include some of the spines, which you don't want. You can, of course, use the selection tool and the Shift key to select each piece individually, but there is a faster way.

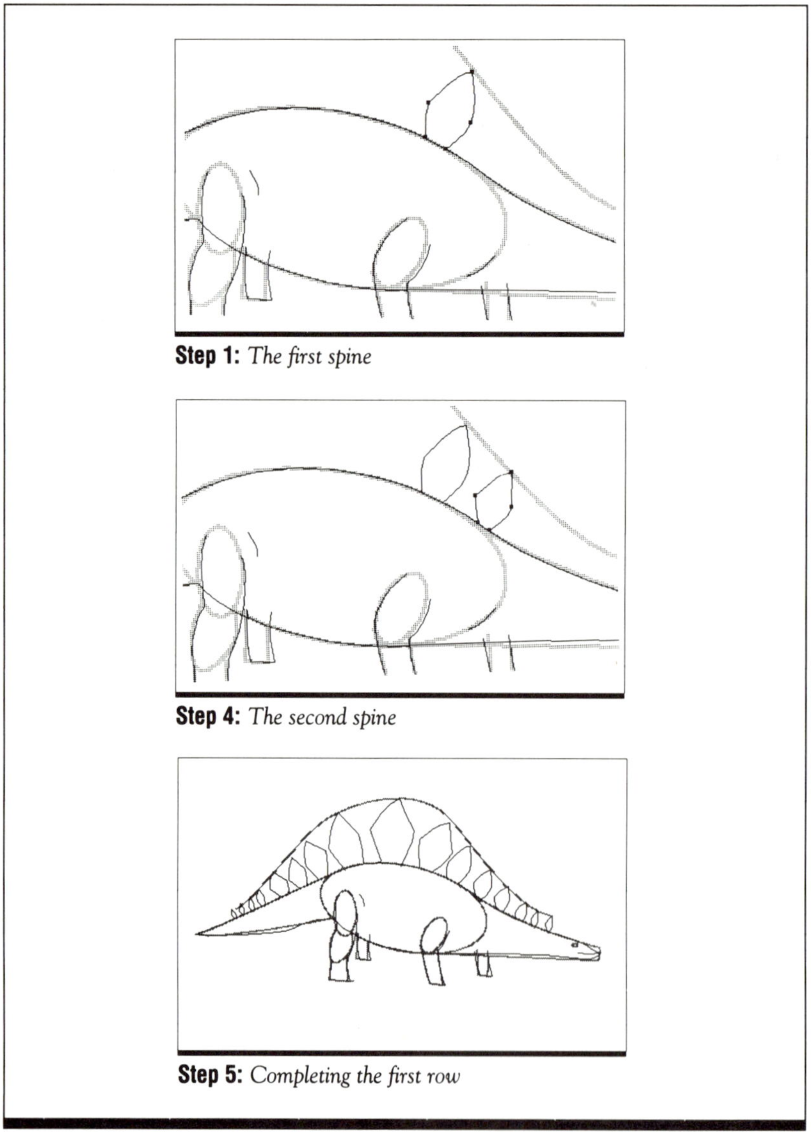

Step 1: *The first spine*

Step 4: *The second spine*

Step 5: *Completing the first row*

Figure 6.14: *Adding the spines (continues)*

1. Use the selection marquee to select part of the work, then choose Group from the Arrange menu.
2. Use the selection marquee to select another part and group that, and then repeat this process.

Step 8: *Completed spines*

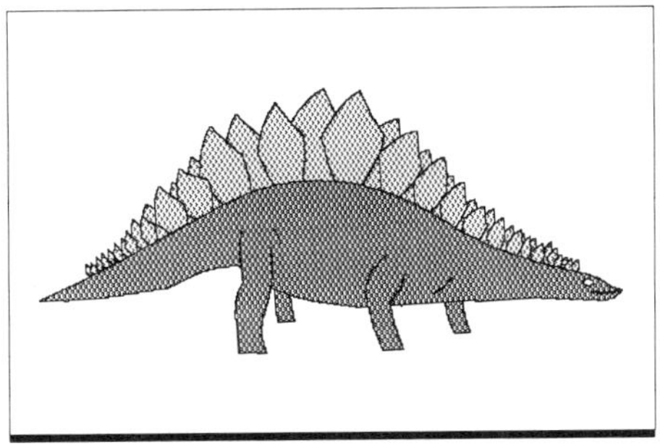

Step 11: *Preview of art*

Figure 6.14: *Adding the spines (continued)*

You should be able to get the entire range of artwork grouped in about three steps.

3. **Use Bring To Front to paint the entire group in front of the spines.**

The legs, eye, and so on will still paint in the original order, giving the effect we want.

4. **Check that you have been successful by previewing the artwork.**

There is one further item to add to this dinosaur. It should have a set of four spikes at the end of its tail.

5. **Draw two tall, thin triangles on the tail.**

Don't close the triangles at the bottom; like the legs, these should blend into the body. There are two sets because the spikes are in two rows, just like the spines.

6. **Copy the set of triangles over themselves to make the next, overlapping set, using the same techniques you used for the overlapping spines.**

Now we want to set the same Paint attributes for these spikes as you have for the body. There is a quick way to do this.

7. **Select the body, choose Paint from the Style menu, and immediately click on OK.**

This sets the Paint attributes for the next object to the same as those for the body. The preview of the final result is shown in Figure 6.15.

These exercises should give you some idea of the various uses that you can make of repeated shapes. Both of these forms of repetition can be very useful as you work with Illustrator. As you have seen, using

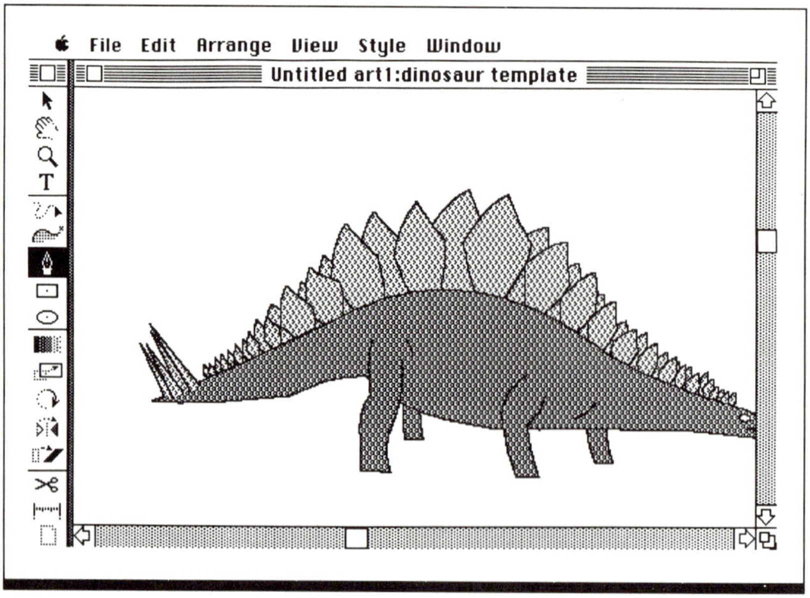

Figure 6.15: *Preview of final dinosaur art*

repetition in combination with other Illustrator tools can produce striking results.

CONSTRAINING TECHNIQUES: CHANGING THE AXES

You have already used the most simple form of constraint—to keep lines straight, and circles round—in many exercises. Actually, in all these cases, the Shift key does not constrain the figure to horizontal and vertical lines; it constrains the figures according to the current x- and y-axes. These axes are normally horizontal and vertical, parallel to the sides of the desktop, and that is how we have used constraints so far. It is possible, however, to rotate these axes to any arbitrary angle. This flexibility can be very useful, as you shall see.

SETTING CONSTRAINTS ON THE AXES

To constrain the axes, you effectively rotate the x-axis to some defined angle relative to the horizontal. This is accomplished by choosing Preferences from the Edit menu, which displays the dialog box shown in Figure 6.16.

In Illustrator 1.1, you access the axes-constraining options by choosing Constrain from the Arrange menu. In the Constrain dialog box, set the Angled axes option.

In the Constrain angle box, you can set an angle for your axes, such as 30°, by entering a value in degrees. This sets the x-axis at the given angle to the horizontal axis, with positive angles being, as usual, counterclockwise. The y-axis is always at 90° to the x-axis; so, in a sense, the y-axis is also rotated from the vertical position by the same number of

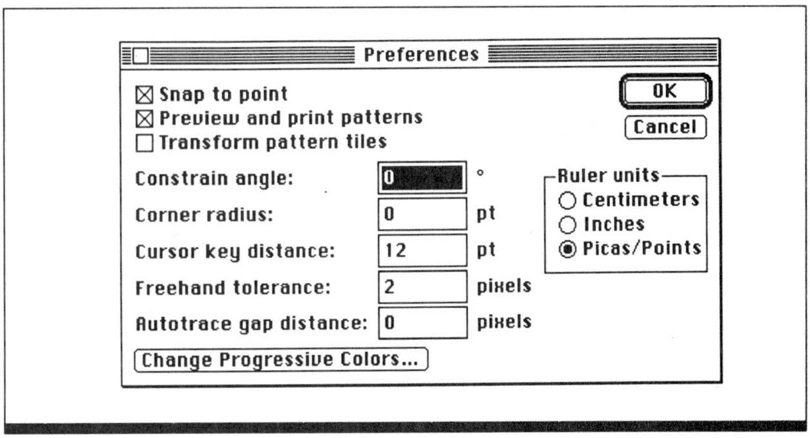

Figure 6.16: *Preferences dialog box*

degrees. You can always reset your axes to the default by entering 0° as the Constrain angle.

When you use the Constrain angle option to set constraints on the axes, it affects all the Shift functions that you use thereafter. Of course, a square is still a square and a circle is a circle, but the sides of the square will be at the defined angle, and the anchor points on the circle will also be at the defined angle. Any type that you set will run along the new x-axis, just as it ran horizontally before. This obviously makes setting captions or other type on an angle very easy indeed. In the same way, the constraint on squares and circles means that you can apply all the techniques that you have previously learned to any arbitrary angled perspective. For example, you can make precisely angled half-circles by ungrouping a circle, as we did earlier.

You can use the Constrain angle box and the distance tool together to set axes at any angle.

1. **Select the distance tool from the toolbox.**
2. **Click on any two points on the Illustrator desktop.**

This provides a precise measurement of the angle and distance and the horizontal and vertical displacement between the two points. The information is presented in the Measure dialog box, as shown in Figure 6.17.

3. **Note the value shown next to Angle and click on OK.**
4. **Choose the Preferences option from the Edit menu (or press ⌘K).**
5. **Enter the value that was shown next to Angle in the Measure dialog box as the Constrain angle and click on OK.**

This sets the new constrained axes to the given angle.

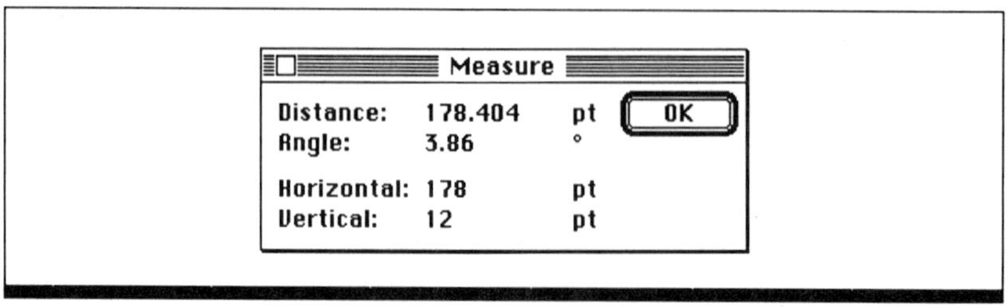

Figure 6.17: *Measure dialog box*

MATCHING "OFF-AXIS" TEMPLATES

You will find this capability to set new constrained axes really helpful, indeed, possibly essential, for matching templates exactly. If you use scanned images with any regularity, you will soon discover that they are often scanned in off-axis. This is quite annoying because you can't alter the template with Illustrator. Furthermore, scanned images usually are presented in MacPaint format, and MacPaint can only rotate by multiples of 90° because of the limitations of bit-mapped graphics. What to do?

You could, of course, repeatedly scan the document until you get the scanned image exactly horizontally and vertically aligned, but that's tedious and time-consuming. Instead, you should constrain the artwork that you create to the axes of the template. To do this, trace any straight line of the template in Illustrator, select two end points of the line and use the distance tool and the Preferences option to set the new constraint values. Now you can trace all the template with an exact match, and rotate the final artwork back to true horizontal and vertical when you're done. This is an elegant solution to a vexing problem.

CREATING ISOMETRIC DRAWINGS

Since it would be excessively optimistic, not to say unreasonable, to expect that you had a slightly skewed template around to practice on, we'll practice using the constraint mechanism in another typical fashion. This is the process of creating isometric drawings, which are quite common in engineering and architectural work. In isometric drawings, the axis or axes of some figure are at a constant angle to the page (sound familiar?).

The following are the four basic steps for creating isometric drawings (using an angle of 30° as an example):

- Draw the basic object full face on the desktop.
- Scale the object in the vertical dimension only, leaving the horizontal dimension alone. The scaling value of the vertical dimension is exactly the tangent of the angle of the isometric axes; in this case, .57735.
- Rotate the figure clockwise through the complementary angle (that is, 90° minus the desired angle); in this case, 60°.
- Constrain the axes to the desired angle; in this case, 30°.

These steps will produce a drawing with the isometric axes at 30° from the plane of the drawing surface.

As an exercise, we will create a simple ring and shaft arrangement that is angled to the page to provide an exploded, three-dimensional effect. We'll use an angle of 25°. The tangent of 25° (as you can easily determine from a table of trignometric functions or your trusty calculator, if it has trig functions) is .46631. This means we will scale the figure by 46.631 percent vertically and 100 percent horizontally. The complement of 25° is (90 − 25), or 65°. So the work proceeds as follows.

1. **Start with a new desktop with no template. In the center, draw three concentric circles, as shown in Figure 6.18.**
2. **As the Paint attributes for all the circles, set Fill to None, Stroke to 100% Black, and a line weight of 1.**
3. **Choose Select All from the Edit menu (or press ⌘A), then group all the points to simplify the operations.**
4. **Use the scale tool and Option key to set the scale origin under the bottom point of the outermost circle and a nonuniform scale with 100% horizontal scaling and 46.631% vertical scaling (as we discussed above).**

We have completed the second basic step in creating an isometric drawing, as shown in Figure 6.18. Now we need to move the circles into position for the isometric view. To do this, we must rotate them clockwise through the complement of the angle of the axes. You subtract the angle from 90° to get the complementary angle. For 25°, the complement is 65°.

5. **Using the rotate tool and Option key, set the center of the rotation at the bottom of the circles and enter −65 in the Rotate dialog box.**

Remember that positive angles in Illustrator move counterclockwise. The result is shown in Figure 6.18. You can see how the circles rotated clockwise to the right, angling the line of the centers of the circles up to the right at 25°. This completes the third step of the process.

6. **Deselect all the artwork by clicking anywhere outside it with the selection tool.**
7. **Choose Preferences from the Edit menu (or press ⌘K) and set the Constrain angle to 25°.**

This sets the artwork for the rest of the isometric exercise and completes the four basic steps. Let's see how you can add to the artwork.

8. **With the pen tool, draw a line up and to the right from the "top" point of the center circle, using the Shift key to constrain the lines along the new axes (see Figure 6.18).**

This will be the axle from the disc, which will be represented by two versions of the circles we drew earlier.

9. **Draw another line the same way from the "bottom" anchor point of the inner circle; make it about the same length as the first line.**
10. **Use the selection tool with both the Shift and Option keys to move a copy of the circles up a small distance to show the other side of the disc.**
11. **Ungroup one set of circles and copy the small, inner circle out to the end of the axle (see Figure 6.18).**
12. **Preview the finished isometric drawing (see Figure 6.18).**

I'm sure that you can find many more advanced examples of isometric drawings if you work with them. You can use the basic constraining techniques discussed here, along with the other advanced techniques that you have learned, to produce very complex drawings.

MASKING PARTS OF ILLUSTRATOR OUTPUT

A new Illustrator 88 feature is the capability to confine the printing of artwork to a defined section of a page. This section of the page is called a *clipping* region and is defined by using the Mask setting in the Paint dialog screen. A clipping region's function is similar to a stencil's: only marks made inside of the area show on the page.

As a simple example, we'll define a clipping region, draw some ovals, and preview the result.

1. **Open a blank Illustrator desktop without a template.**
2. **Use the square tool to create a large rectangle on the desktop, as shown in Figure 6.19.**

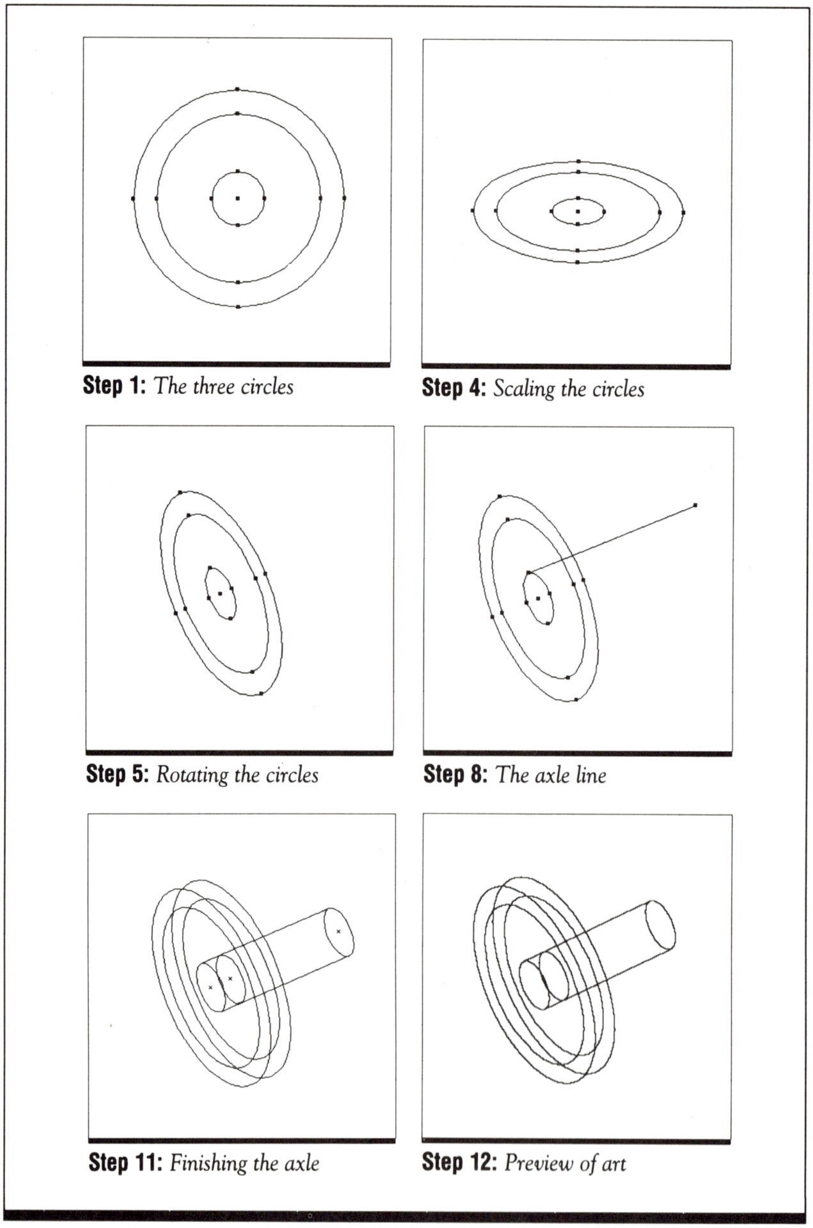

Step 1: *The three circles*

Step 4: *Scaling the circles*

Step 5: *Rotating the circles*

Step 8: *The axle line*

Step 11: *Finishing the axle*

Step 12: *Preview of art*

Figure 6.18: *Creating isometric art*

This rectangle will define the clipping region that we will use to mask off other artwork.

3. **With the rectangle selected, choose Ungroup from the Arrange menu.**
4. **Use the selection tool to select only the center point and delete it.**

It is essential that the clipping region be an ungrouped, closed figure in order for the Mask setting to function correctly. And, while we're at it, we might as well delete the extraneous center point as well.

5. **Select the remaining portion of the figure (see Figure 6.19).**
6. **Choose Paint from the Style menu; set Fill to None, Stroke to 100% Black, and a line weight of .1 and then click on the Mask button. These settings are shown in Figure 6.20.**

The Mask option sets the rectangle as a clipping region. We have also stroked the rectangle so it will show the outline of the selected area. Now we will create some circles and ovals inside and outside the rectangle.

7. **Create a series of circles and ovals both inside and outside the rectangle, as shown in Figure 6.21.**
8. **Choose Preview Illustration from the View menu to see the results of the mask operation (see Figure 6.21).**

Like a stencil cutout, the clipping region rectangle allowed only those portions of the other artwork that lie within it to show on the output. This is a simple example of the mask feature in operation.

Illustrator does not display any error messages regarding the masking facility. If you choose the Mask option for a grouped object, or you paint the mask last instead of first on the page, you will simply not get a clipped result; you will not be notified of any error.

Besides being careful to use an ungrouped, closed figure as a clipping region, you must also be sure that it paints on the page before any objects that you want confined to that area. So, if you paint some of your artwork before you paint the clipping region, those figures will run over the mask's boundaries. If you would like to see this for yourself, follow this short exercise.

1. **Select one of the ovals that overlaps the rectangle that you drew (see Figure 6.22).**

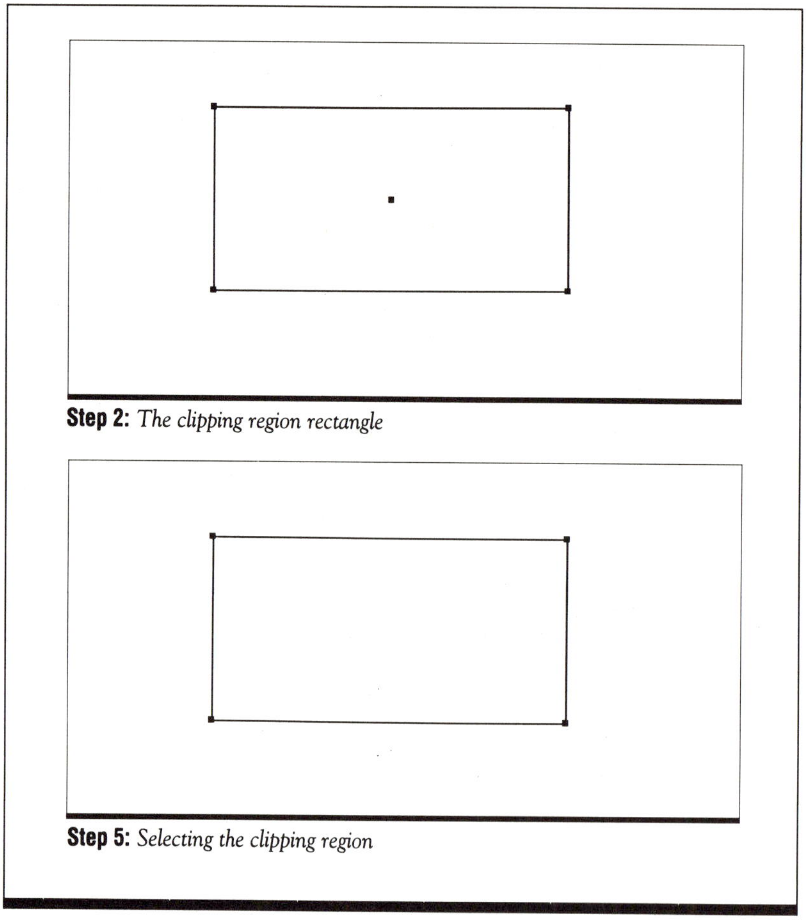

Step 2: *The clipping region rectangle*

Step 5: *Selecting the clipping region*

Figure 6.19: *Setting up a clipping region*

2. **Choose Send To Back from the Edit menu.**

This forces the oval to paint before the rectangle, while the others paint after, since they were created in that order.

3. **Choose Preview Illustration from the View menu to see the result, as shown in Figure 6.22.**

As you expect, the oval that you forced to paint early is no longer confined to the clipping region.

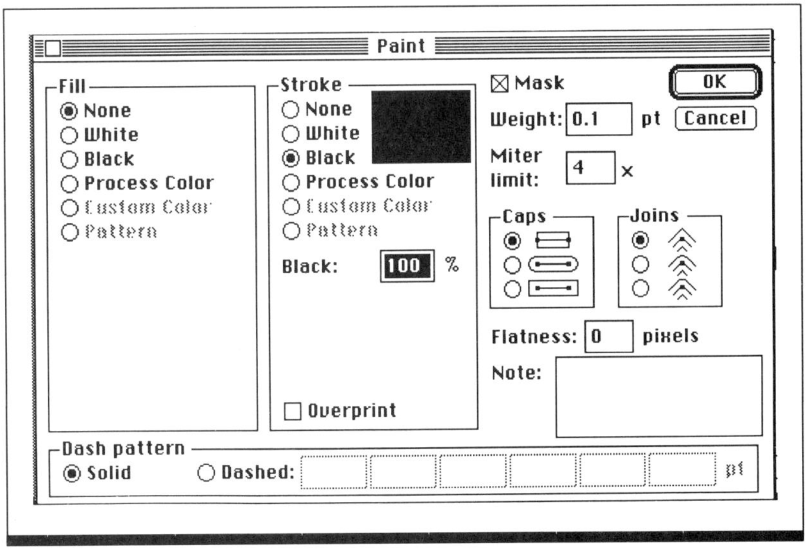

Figure 6.20: *Paint dialog screen for defining a clipping region*

AUTOMATICALLY GENERATING ARTWORK

We have now covered all the basic Illustrator tools and techniques. However, Illustrator 88 has two additional tools that can make your work in generating artwork, particularly from templates, even easier. These are the autotrace and freehand tools.

Before you use the freehand and autotrace tools, you should have a clear understanding of how Illustrator works. It is important that you know what these tools are doing and how to do the work by hand if you are going to use them efficiently and effectively. Like a pilot whose airplane is equipped with an autopilot, you don't want to rely on the automatic functions to do something you couldn't do yourself and don't fully understand.

Neither of these tools does anything that can't be done with the pen tool. They just simplify or automate difficult or time-consuming processes. In the next sections, we'll discuss each tool in detail and practice using them.

USING THE AUTOTRACE TOOL

The autotrace tool provides a marvelous, fast way to generate artwork from a template. This tool will produce a curve around any template that you click it on. The advantages of such a quick method of generating artwork are obvious; however, there are some drawbacks. One of the problems is that the autotrace tool follows a simple and predictable, but fallible, routine for following the guiding template. As you will see in the next exercise, this can be a nuisance. In addition, it often generates more anchor points than you might use if you were working with the pen tool.

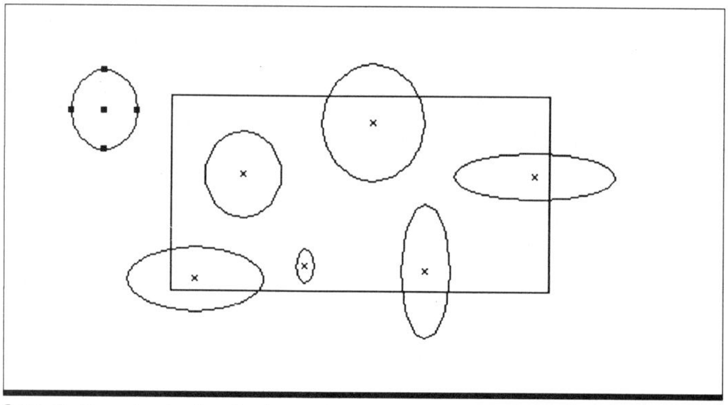

Step 7: *Drawing in the clipping region*

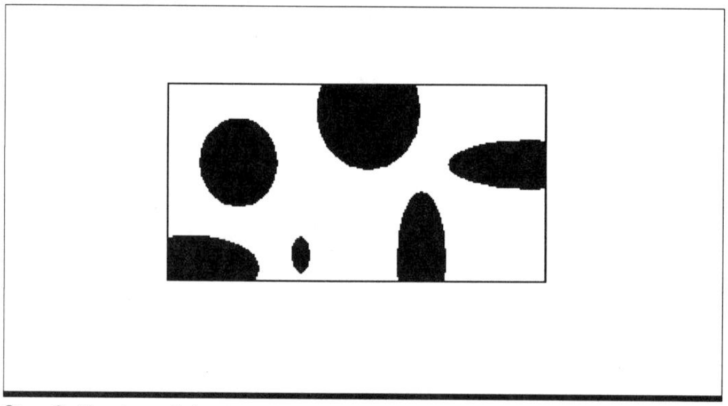

Step 8: *Preview of clipping region*

Figure 6.21: *Using a clipping region*

For our autotrace tool exercise, we will finish the Somba Man art we began in Chapter 4.

Adding the Flame

First we will use the autotrace tool to add the flame to the torch in the Somba Man art.

1. **Open the Somba Man art and template and position it on the desktop, as shown in Figure 6.23.**

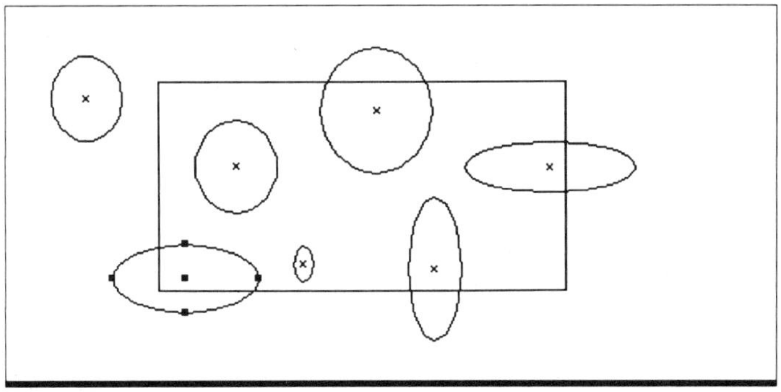

Step 1: *Selecting an oval*

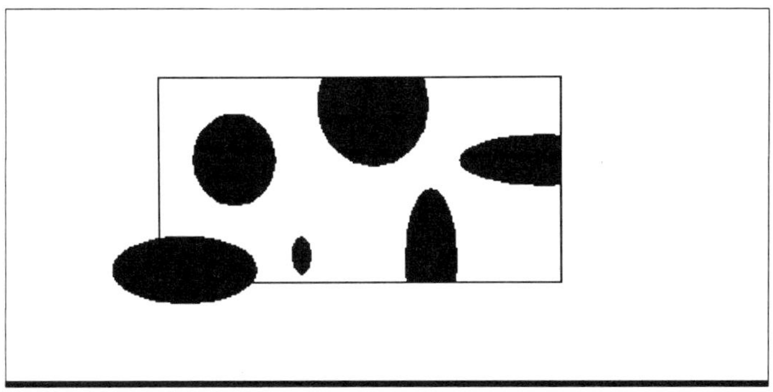

Step 3: *Preview of clipping region*

Figure 6.22: *Painting order for masking operations*

2. **Click on the autotrace tool and position the x cursor on the bottom half of the flame, at a point where you might ordinarily place an anchor point.**

The place that you click on will have an anchor point, so you want to select it with some care, just as you would if you were beginning to trace the template with the pen tool.

3. **Click once.**

You will see the clock icon for a short time (more or less time depending on the complexity of the template). Then you will see anchor points on the path around the curve, as shown in Figure 6.23. The point where you clicked becomes the starting and ending anchor point for the figure. Now let's use the autotrace tool again to trace the top half of the flame.

4. **Position the autotrace cursor at the very bottom tip of the top half of the flame and click once.**

You see that the autotrace tool generates a very poor approximation of the curve of the template. In addition, it has generated an anchor point along the top of the curve. Using the pen tool, you could form this curve with only two anchor points, one at each tip (like the curve at the base of the stem on the apple). However, if you want the convenience of automatic tracing, you will have to resign yourself to having a few extra anchor points.

5. **Delete the autotrace outline by pressing the Delete or Backspace key twice.**
6. **Position the autotrace tool cursor on the initial point along the top of the curve, about where the tool added the anchor point on the previous attempt, and click once.**

This time the curve match is quite good (as shown in Figure 6.23), although at the expense of having an extra anchor point. Not really a bad job unless you are pressed for space or have other reasons to be concerned about the length of your Illustrator file. However, there are some times when the autotrace tool is completely inappropriate. Let's look at an example.

7. **With the autotrace tool still selected, move down to the last lightning stroke, closest to the figure's head, and click once.**

Figure 6.23 shows what the autotrace tool has done. Because the stroke of the lightning is quite heavy, the tool has outlined the template. This is reasonable but incorrect, and results in an excessive penalty in terms of number of anchor points—eight in this case, instead of the necessary four.

8. **Delete the autotrace outline by pressing the Delete or Backspace key twice.**
9. **Trace the lightning line with the pen tool, using four anchor points.**
10. **Set the Paint attributes of Fill to None and Stroke to 100% Black, with a line weight of 4 points.**

By using a heavy line weight, we can create a line that has substantial thickness without outlining.

11. **Continue to create the lightning around the flame, using the pen tool.**
12. **Set the Stroke line weight for the remaining three lightning lines along the underside of the flame to 3 points.**
13. **Set the Stroke line weight for the lightning around the top of the flame to 2.5 points.**

At this point, your artwork should look like the last figure in Figure 6.23.

Step 1: *Positioning the art*

Figure 6.23: *Adding the flame and lightning (continues)*

Step 3: *Bottom half of flame*

Step 6: *Top half of flame*

Figure 6.23: *Adding the flame and lightning (continues)*

Outlining the Hand

Now we will use the autotrace and pen tools to outline the hand holding the torch. Most of this section of the artwork is straight, thick lines which, as you have already seen, aren't reproduced well by the autotrace tool. However, there is one place where the autotrace tool will speed up our work: the thumb outline.

Step 7: *Incorrect lightning*

Step 13: *Completed flame and lightning*

Figure 6.23: *Adding the flame and lightning (continued)*

1. Use the zoom tool to magnify the artwork and template to show the thumb and torch.
2. Select the autotrace tool and position the cursor at the base of the thumb.
3. Click and drag the cursor, which has changed to a delta shape, up to the top of the thumb, and then release.

You must be careful to click and drag, not just click. If you just click, the autotrace tool will attempt to trace the entire arm and torch. If it does, it is likely to run out of memory and you will get an error message. Even if you have extra memory and the autotrace tool completes its work, it will give you a very incorrect version of the artwork.

What we have done here is to constrain the autotrace tool to the template segment between the two points indicated. The tracing will start at the first point that you clicked on and continue in a clockwise direction to the point that you release on, as shown in Figure 6.24. Sometimes the autotrace tool will be fooled by the complexity of a template; in those cases, you may see it follow an interior line, or add some other part of the template into its figure. Notice here how we started and finished the line slightly inside and away from the lines that form the edge of the torch. Remember that the autotrace has no idea of what it's following; if there is a template line in its way, it will try to follow that all the way back to the ending point.

4. **Set the Paint attributes of Fill to None, Stroke to 100% Black, and a line weight of 4 points.**
5. **Use the pen tool to outline the torch and the outside of the hand and wrist in straight lines.**
6. **Set these with line weight of 3 points to make them slightly less heavy than the thumb.**
7. **Go back and extend the thumb lines, using the selection and pen tools, to meet the line that forms the edge of the torch (see Figure 6.24).**

You have to extend the thumb into the torch line by hand because the autotrace tool would have been confused and traced too much of the figure.

8. **Use the pen tool again to fill in the fingers with straight lines. These have a line weight of 4 points.**
9. **Trace the inner sleeve and shoulder of the figure with the pen tool. This line has the same characteristics as the preceding ones.**
10. **Finish the outer sleeve of the jacket with a single straight line with a weight of 5 points, and then preview the artwork (see Figure 6.24).**

The preview of the hand and torch shows that the thumb is quite pointed and looks a little unrealistic. If you had used the pen tool originally, you might have foreseen this problem and made it a curve initially. You could correct the autotrace work by using the scissors to

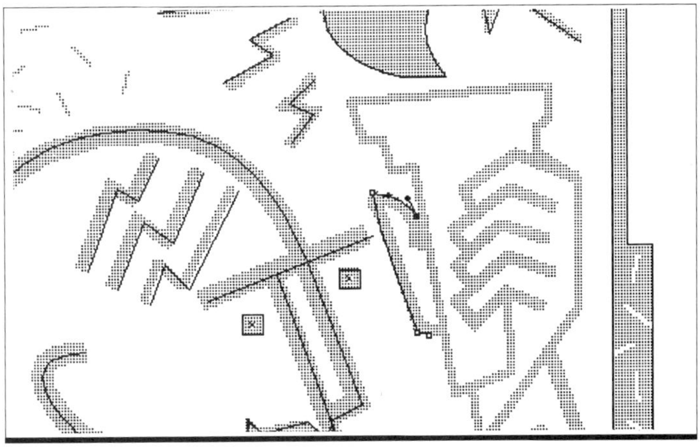

Step 3: *Tracing the thumb*

Step 7: *Outlining the hand*

Figure 6.24: *Adding detail to the arm and torch (continues)*

change this part of the artwork into a curve. However, in this case, there is an easier way to make the correction.

11. Return to the artwork and select the anchor point at the end of the thumb.

Step 10: *Preview of art*

Figure 6.24: *Adding detail to the arm and torch (continued)*

12. Select Paint from the Style menu, and you will see the Paint dialog screen, as shown in Figure 6.25.

13. Click on the bottom button under Joins (as shown in Figure 6.25) and then click on OK.

This selection changes the shape of the corner from a pointed join, shown next to the top button, to a rounded join, as shown next to the button you clicked.

14. Select Preview Illustration from the View menu again and see how Join rounded the thumb (see Figure 6.26).

15. Finally, use the circle tool to draw the two sleeve buttons.

16. Fill the buttons with 100% Black, no Stroke.

A preview of the artwork at this point, reduced one click so you can see more of it, is shown in Figure 6.26.

Using the Freehand Tool

As you might expect, the freehand tool provides freehand drawing capabilities. Unlike the pen tool, you can use it simply to trace the line

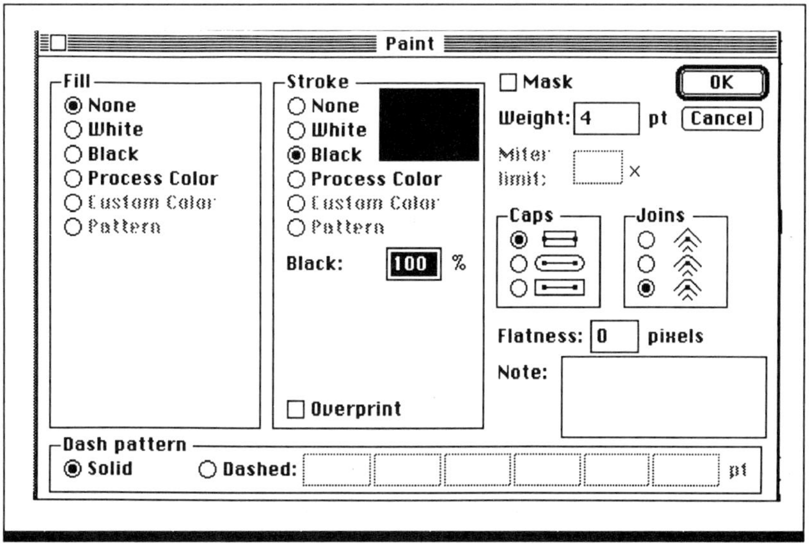

Figure 6.25: *Paint dialog screen with Joins*

you want to follow. Then Illustrator will turn that line into straight or curved line segments, with the appropriate direction points. The advantage of this is that you can use the tool as you might use a pencil, to make a drawing or sketch and turn it into PostScript code. The disadvantage, which is more subtle but equally real, is that the freehand tool, like the autotrace tool, usually generates more anchor points than you would using the pen tool, and the lines may be less precise.

To practice using the freehand tool, we will continue working on the Somba Man artwork.

Adding Background Strokes

Adding the background strokes that give definition to the Somba Man figure can be done most easily and effectively with the freehand tool.

1. **Expand the artwork in the top-left corner of the figure so you can see the background strokes (see Figure 6.27).**

2. **Select the freehand tool from the toolbox.**

The freehand tool is very easy to use and works just as you would expect. The freehand cursor, a small x, shows where you are working. When you click and drag, the cursor changes to a delta shape as you trace a line. When you release the mouse button, the line is finished, and Illustrator converts it into a PostScript line or curve.

3. **Use the freehand cursor to trace the line at the top left of the background. Click at the beginning of the line and drag the cursor to the end to create the line.**

Step 14: *Rounding the thumb*

Step 16: *Preview of art*

Figure 6.26: *Revised Somba Man artwork*

4. Select Paint from the Style menu and set the Paint attributes of Fill to None, Stroke to 100% Black, and a line weight of 1 point. Make sure that the Joins parameter is back to its default position (the top).

This generates a line, as shown in Figure 6.27, which is the exact equivalent of a quick pen or pencil stroke.

Step 1: *Expanding the background*

Step 4: *First freehand line*

Figure 6.27: *Adding texture to the background*

5. **Continue using the freehand tool to create the background strokes over the figure's head.**
6. **Move down and around to finish all the background strokes that are inside the border.**

As you do this exercise, you can see how sensitive the freehand tool is to your movements. I find it the hardest tool to control accurately and precisely. In this case, however, precision and accuracy are not essential.

You'll probably notice how long it is taking to preview the image now. As images become more complex, the display time increases proportionately.

7. **After finishing the background, choose Preview Illustration from the View menu. Your figure should look something like Figure 6.27.**

Now we need to add the texturing to the border region itself. We will use the freehand tool again, but with different Paint attributes. Because this work will be easier if the present border isn't visible, we'll "hide" it for a while.

8. **Select both the box that forms the top border and the line on the side, using the selection tool, the Option key, and the Shift key.**
9. **Choose Hide from the Arrange menu to hide these artwork lines (see Figure 6.27).**

This is a good example of when to use Hide; we are working on a complex figure and don't want to be distracted by the artwork we have already completed. Another use for the Hide function is to protect artwork that you don't need as you are working, to ensure it doesn't get selected accidentally, for example.

10. **Select the freehand tool again.**
11. **Draw the texture lines in the top border, with a Stroke of White instead of Black.**

Remember to set the Paint attributes after you have drawn the first line, so that they will also apply to the remaining lines.

12. **Choose Show All from the Arrange menu to restore the border that you hid earlier.**

13. Preview the top border (see Figure 6.27).
14. Continue using the same techniques to texture the bottom and side borders.
15. Save the final version of the artwork.

Step 7: *Preview of art*

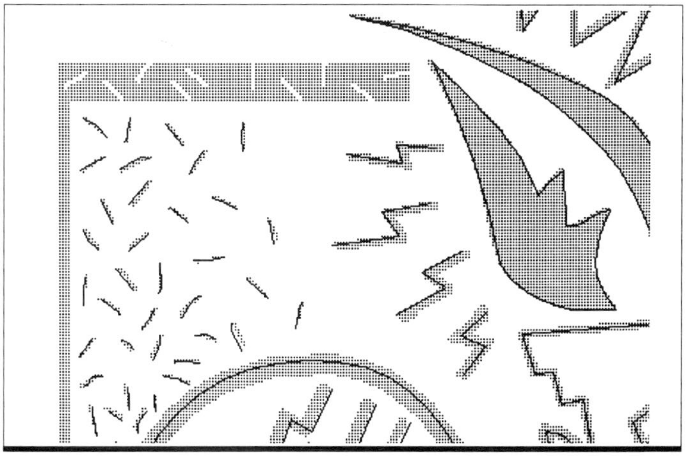

Step 9: *Hiding the border*

Figure 6.27: *Adding texture to the background (continues)*

Step 13: *Preview of top border*

Figure 6.27: *Adding texture to the background (continued)*

This is an interesting and instructive graphic. It shows that by using a few simple elements, basically straight lines of varying weights, you can quickly create complex images. In addition, because you prepared this image in Illustrator (and therefore in PostScript), it is transferable and transportable to a wide variety of environments and can be reused or modified as you want. The final printed version of the artwork is shown in Figure 6.28.

USING ILLUSTRATOR OUTPUT WITH OTHER APPLICATIONS

Both applications (Illustrator and the other) must generate PostScript, so the output code is completely compatible.

Illustrator produces a special structure of PostScript output that can be used directly by other PostScript applications. This means that you can create a graphic in Illustrator, import it into another application that generates PostScript, such as Aldus' PageMaker, and have the same high-quality output for your graphic that you will get for the text. You can even import such files back into Illustrator itself.

To have Illustrator generate output in a form that can be used by another PostScript application, you must save your artwork in a special code form, called *Encapsulated PostScript*. We will discuss the use of Encapsulated PostScript in this section. In addition, you will see how to

Figure 6.28: *Printed Somba Man output*

use the Illustrator utility DrawOver to quickly generate artwork from MacDraw PICT files.

Saving Output in Encapsulated PostScript

Up to now, you have saved all your Illustrator output in the default format of None, in the box labeled "Include preview for" in the Save dialog box, as shown in Figure 6.29. This is a perfectly acceptable option, and very likely the one you will want to use most of the time. The default option saves the file as a simple text file of PostScript language commands, which can be read or modified by any text editor. In this format, the file can be shipped to any other computer system; it is a simple text file with no ASCII characters above ASCII 128. This means that the file will not conflict with any file transmission protocols and can be handled, modified, and printed in the ordinary way.

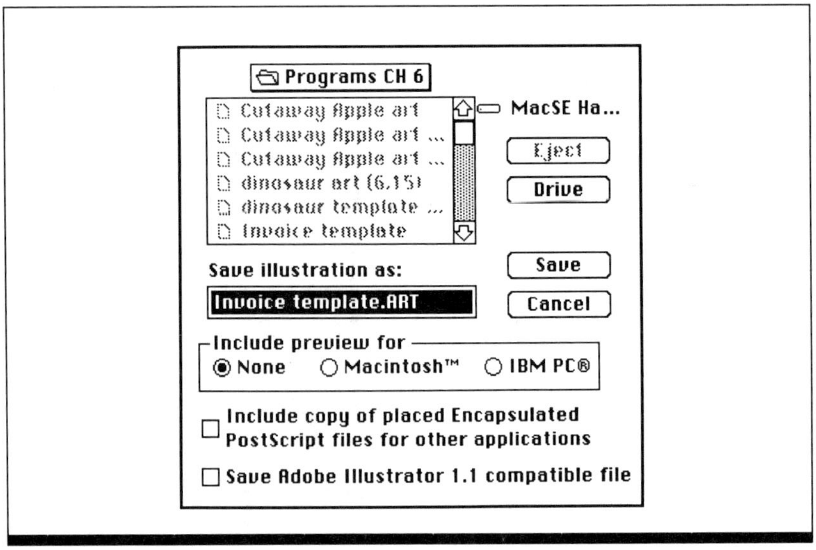

Figure 6.29: *The Save dialog box with save options*

The Save dialog box also presents two other choices: Macintosh and IBM PC. Each of these two alternatives represents saving your code in Encapsulated PostScript. This is a PostScript file that has a special structure, which is designed to allow other programs, most notably application programs that produce PostScript output, to view a PostScript graphic and manipulate it in certain limited ways. Encapsulated PostScript files are generally called EPSF files, and I will use that abbreviation here.

Forms of EPSF Files

The EPSF file format consists of two distinct parts. The first contains the PostScript program created by the *source* (the creator of the file) that will generate the desired image on the output device, and the second part contains a bit-mapped image of the resulting graphic itself. The bit-mapped image can be used by the *destination* application (the one that uses the file) for display purposes. The PostScript program follows a rigid structure that also allows the destination application to translate, rotate, and scale the image as required for the new output.

The destination application cannot change the image internally; it can't, for example, change the original apple graphic to add leaves. It can, however, take the apple, which currently fills a large part of a page, and scale it to fit into a defined space. The requirement here is that the space used must retain the same elements that the graphic already has. Generally, the destination application uses information provided in the structure of the EPSF file to determine the proportions of the graphic and fits the available space to that. You will see an example of this later in the chapter.

There are two forms of EPSF files because of this requirement for a bit-mapped image. Because the IBM and the Macintosh have quite different approaches to screen graphics, source applications must provide two separate file types to generate the required screen graphic and link it correctly to the PostScript output.

IBM PC® EPSF

The IBM format of EPSF files uses the Aldus/Microsoft TIFF graphic format to store the image, and any destination application that you want to display the image must be able to read that format. This is an important distinction that you should note carefully: when you choose the IBM format, you are not creating a file that can be read directly by an IBM PC or compatible computer. The file still requires the usual conversion from Macintosh format to IBM format. After conversion, however, it can be read and used by a destination application on an IBM system.

The IBM file should be transmitted to an MS-DOS file system and stored with a file extension of .EPS. The MS-DOS file must contain a header record in a specific format, which specifies the location and length of both the PostScript portion of the file and the screen bit-map portion. This header is provided by Illustrator when you save the file and include the preview for the IBM PC.

Macintosh™ EPSF

The Macintosh version of an EPSF file contains a standard Macintosh QuickDraw PICT format graphic as the screen display portion of the file. If you create an EPSF file yourself, or have one created by some other application, it may have a file type TEXT as an alternative. In any case, the file must follow all the relevant structural conventions, including providing a PICT resource that contains the screen representation of the graphic described by the PostScript file.

In both formats of EPSF files, the bit-mapped images are produced at a resolution of 72 dpi, and the image will correspond exactly to what you have seen in Illustrator preview mode. These bit-maps are not for final output; they are provided as an aid for page makeup and graphic placement within destination applications that cannot display PostScript code directly. The intention is that the final output will use the

PostScript definitions of the graphic, and the bit-mapped image will be ignored.

As the name implies, EPSF files are intended to be used as separate "capsules" of graphics, and not interact in most ways with the rest of the destination application's output. The significant deviations from this are the ability of the destination application to position the graphic on a page at any point, and to transform (scale, slant, rotate, and so on) the graphic as required for correct placement and viewing on the output page. It is the destination application's responsibility to create the necessary changes in the output environment to ensure that this occurs correctly, and to restore the original environment when it's done.

Generally, EPSF files cannot be edited with a simple text editor the way that PostScript-only files can be because they have the graphic image embedded within them. However, applications that understand the EPSF format can edit the PostScript portion of the EPSF file with standard text editing techniques, while ignoring the bit-mapped images.

Saving the Letterhead Art in EPSF Format

As an example, we will save an artwork that you have already prepared in an EPSF format. Later, we will use this output in another exercise.

1. **Open the Letterhead art that you created earlier.**
2. **Choose Save As from the File menu to display the Save dialog box.**
3. **Click on the button next to the Macintosh option under the Include preview for box.**
4. **Name the file *Letterhead art EPSF*.**
5. **Click on Save to save the file.**

You have now saved the file with the appropriate graphic information included in it. If you imported this file into another application that understands the EPSF format, such as Aldus' PageMaker, you would see the letterhead image displayed just like any other imported graphic, and you would be able to shrink or expand the image using the tools provided by the application.

One application that understands EPSF files and formats is Illustrator itself. Any version of Illustrator can read the EPSF files it created, just as it reads its own PostScript-only files. If you open an EPSF file with Illustrator, you can work with the image just like ordinary Illustrator artwork.

Illustrator 88 provides an additional option that allows you to load files as EPSF files. This is the Place option on the File menu. It displays a dialog box from which you can select an EPSF file for placement, as shown in Figure 6.30.

When you place an EPSF file with Illustrator, you can no longer modify the graphic elements of the file, as you could before, but you can still position and transform the graphic as described above. This can be a very useful technique, as we shall investigate next.

USING THE ILLUSTRATOR DRAWOVER UTILITY

Illustrator 88 comes with a new DrawOver utility that you can use to speed up the process of creating artwork from Macintosh files in MacDraw PICT format. This utility converts a PICT format file into PostScript automatically. It is a sort of super autotrace for PICT output. This section presents a quick way to create the identical invoice form that you produced earlier (in Chapter 3), but with almost no work.

1. Load the DrawOver utility program.

This is the single exception in the book to the statement in the Introduction that you don't need anything but Illustrator to do the exercises. Here, you either have to have MacDraw or have a copy of the MacDraw template to work with. If you don't have one, just follow along mentally. You'll still see how the process works quite clearly.

This displays the selection dialog box, as shown in Figure 6.31.

2. Select the Invoice template that you used earlier.

If you remember, this template was prepared in MacDraw PICT format.

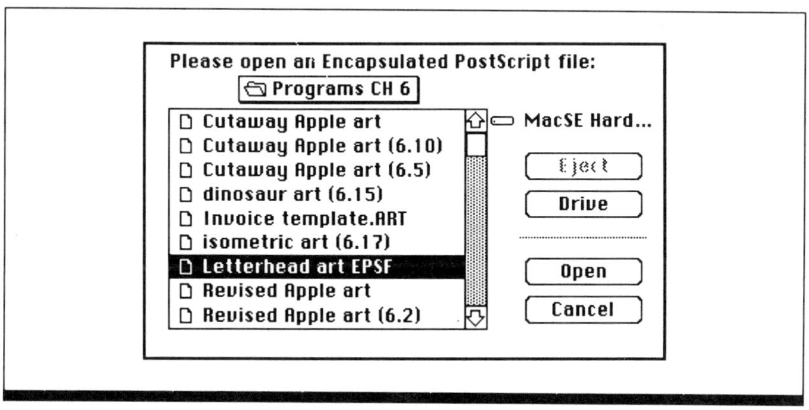

Figure 6.30: *Place dialog box*

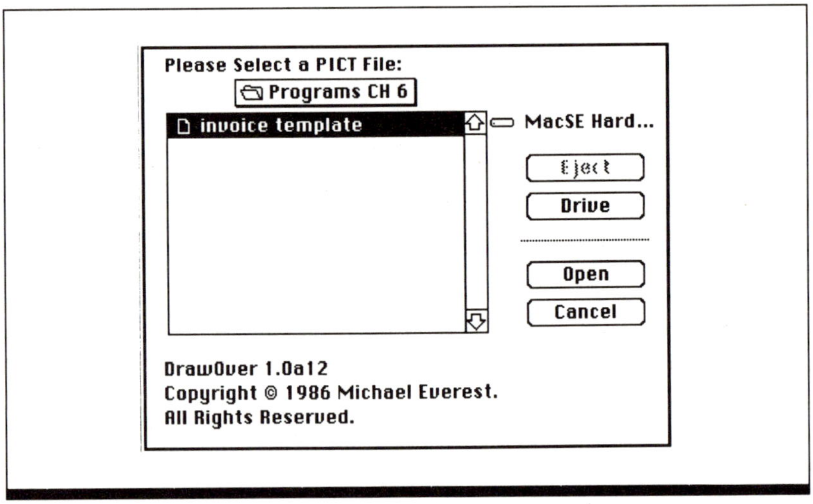

Figure 6.31: *DrawOver selection dialog box*

3. Click on OK.

DrawOver next shows you a preview of what the artwork will look like, as shown in Figure 6.32. This is a perfect copy of the template, including the text.

Next you will see a standard selection box that allows you to choose a name for the PostScript output.

4. Save the file as the default, *Invoice template.ART.*

Finally, you will see an informational dialog box that tells you the size of the file. After it is finished with the conversion, DrawOver returns to the template selection dialog box (Figure 6.31).

5. Click on Cancel to exit DrawOver.

Unfortunately, DrawOver doesn't follow the Macintosh standards for menus and presentation; nevertheless, it performs its job very creditably. Of course, the fine adjustments that you made to the column headings and their precise placement can only be done by hand. You could, however, easily make these changes in the PostScript output, as we did earlier. Because that would be redundant for the purposes of this exercise, we won't repeat the work here.

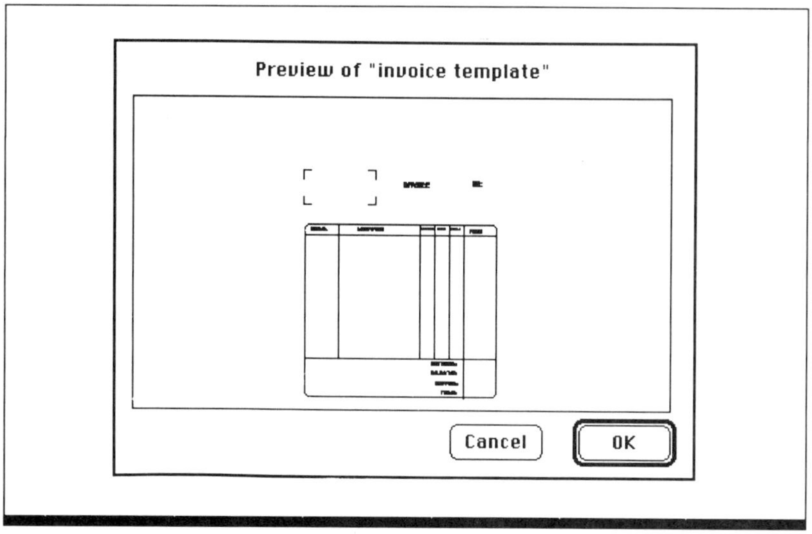

Figure 6.32: *DrawOver preview*

6. **Open the Invoice template.ART. When you see the standard template selection dialog box, select the Invoice template and click on Open.**
7. **Choose Fit In Window from the View menu to see the entire page. It will look something like Figure 6.33.**

Notice that the DrawOver output is centered on the desktop, but the page setup is not standard. This is a function of the header information in the file, and is easily corrected by using the page tool.

8. **Select the page tool from the toolbox and reset the page so that the artwork is positioned correctly on the output page, as shown in Figure 6.33.**

This positioning leaves sufficient room at the top of the page for our letterhead.

9. **Choose Place from the File menu.**

This command allows you to pick up a file in EPSF format and position it on the page as a unit. This is exactly analagous to the use of EPSF in other applications, such as PageMaker.

10. When you see the selection dialog box that allows you to choose an Encapsulated PostScript file for placement, select the Letterhead art EPSF file that you saved earlier and click on Open.

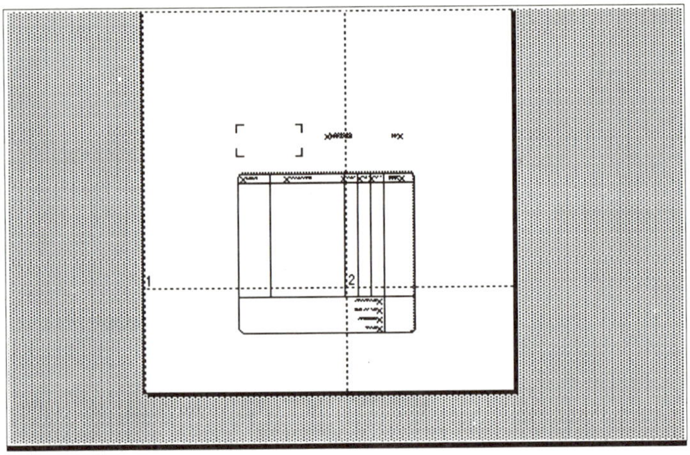

Step 7: *Fit In Window view*

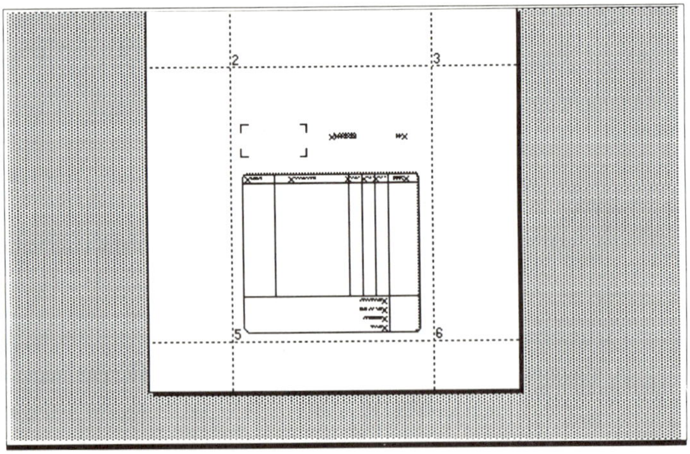

Step 8: *Positioning the page*

Figure 6.33: *Adding the letterhead art to the invoice artwork (continues)*

This displays a box, with the dimensions of the EPSF graphic, placed in the center of the desktop and selected; the result is very similar to pasting an artwork from the clipboard.

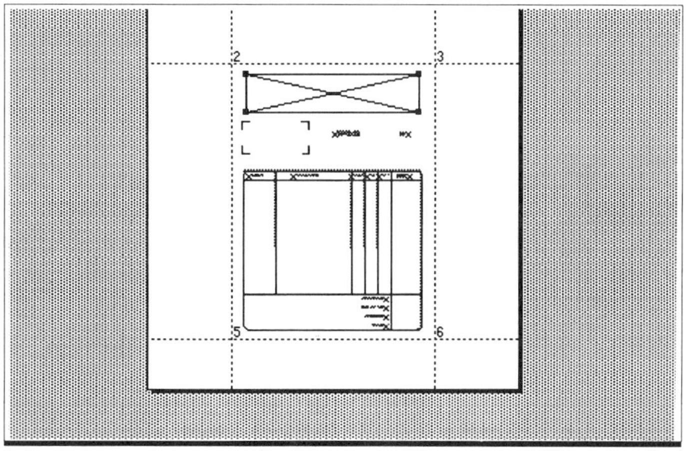

Step 11: *Positioning the letterhead*

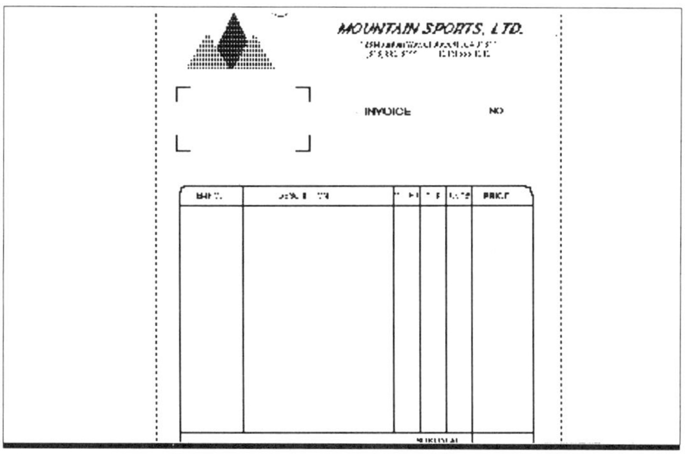

Step 12: *Preview of the form*

Figure 6.33: *Adding the letterhead art to the invoice artwork (continued)*

11. Use the selection tool to position the box (which contains the letterhead artwork) at the top of the page (see Figure 6.33).

You have now recreated, in 11 steps and with much less time and effort, the invoice artwork that we produced earlier.

12. Magnify the artwork one click and preview it to see the completed form, which is shown in Figure 6.33.

You can use any of the transformation tools on the EPSF file. That means that you can scale, rotate, or otherwise adjust the graphic to fit into a predetermined space on the page. Again, that is what other applications can do with EPSF format graphics. This provides great freedom in handling and combining graphic elements to make up a page of output.

There is one more point to mention before we finish this discussion of EPSF files. The Save dialog box also provides an option to include copies of EPSF files that have been placed into the artwork. Normally, Illustrator does not save an EPSF file with the artwork that it is placed in because the file is independent and saving it would be redundant and wasteful of disk space. However, that means that the artwork is not complete as stored; and, if you moved it to another system or disk, you would have to move the associated EPSF file with it in order to print the artwork correctly. To save you the trouble, Illustrator offers the copy option instead. If you check this box, the file as saved will include the EPSF files as well, and will be complete and ready to print.

Appendix

A

ILLUSTRATOR INSTALLATION

Like most Macintosh applications, Illustrator is quite easy to install. How and where you install your copy of Illustrator will depend on your system's configuration, your personal preferences in disk organization and structure, and your working habits. This appendix details how my system is set up and configured to give you an idea of how to go about setting up your own.

SYSTEM CONFIGURATION

You do not need an accelerator board, large screen display, or any other special equipment to use Illustrator's full power. However, Illustrator 88 does have substantial color capabilities that we have not discussed much nor used in developing the examples in the text. To use the color capabilities of Illustrator 88 to the fullest extent, you must have a color monitor available. In addition, to create full color output—as opposed to color separations, which can be produced and proofed on a black and white device—a color printer is required.

HARDWARE CONFIGURATION

All the exercises and examples in this book were created and run on a standard Apple Macintosh SE with a hard disk. I used an Apple LaserWriter printer, running PostScript version 38.0. The exercises were also tested on an Apple Macintosh Plus with an additional, external 3.5-inch disk drive. Additionally, many of the exercises were also printed on a QMS PS-800 printer.

SOFTWARE CONFIGURATION

The system software used here was the latest available at the time of writing: Finder 6.0, System 4.2, and LaserWriter and Laser Prep 5.0. I used the Beta versions of Illustrator 88, kindly made available by Adobe Systems. (Although it was the Beta version, it was quite stable and performed, in all respects, as one would hope all application releases would.)

Where appropriate and possible, all the exercises were also tested with Illustrator 1.1, to ensure that you could follow the work if you have that version. As discussed in the Introduction, if you have version 1.1, you should certainly consider upgrading to Illustrator 88, which, as you can see from the examples in this book, has many additional features and capabilities.

For the programming examples in Appendix B, I used the PostScript programming environment provided by LaserTalk. This is a tremendous support system for a PostScript programmer. It provides direct, interactive access to your PostScript printer over an AppleTalk connection, and also provides on-line editing, documentation, and previewing of your PostScript output.

Appendix

B

POSTSCRIPT CONNECTIONS

ILLUSTRATOR AND POSTSCRIPT

PostScript and Illustrator are intimately connected. PostScript is the output mechanism by which Illustrator communicates with the rest of the world. Illustrator is, in a very real sense, a generator of PostScript application code. The code generated is admittedly tailored to a very specific purpose, generation of images, but PostScript itself is oriented toward that end. It is this intrinsic connection and natural relationship that make some knowledge of PostScript so valuable to anyone working seriously with Illustrator output. The power of Illustrator is really just the power of PostScript, packaged and harnessed in a more accessible and useful way.

This is not to say that you need to become a PostScript programmer. On the contrary, Illustrator does such a good job of generating PostScript code that, for many purposes, it is preferable to use it rather than to hand-code some artwork, even if you are a proficient PostScript programmer. Nevertheless, there are functions and features within PostScript that cannot be accessed through Illustrator, such as setting text along an arbitrary path, and there are things that PostScript programs do easily that Illustrator does in a more complex, and therefore sometimes a less satisfactory way, such as generating clipping regions and making circles. In addition, you will be able to understand Illustrator concepts and operations much better when you comprehend the mechanism that is being used to implement them.

You need two types of information to make maximum use of Illustrator. First, you need to have some idea of what PostScript is and how it works. Second, you need to understand how these PostScript concepts have influenced Illustrator operations. Illustrator's job is to translate all the things that you draw on the screen or that you enter into a dialog box into PostScript code that will generate the correct output. Illustrator has adopted some unusual approaches to make sure that this translation process works correctly.

POSTSCRIPT PROGRAM STRUCTURE

It is easiest to become familiar with the PostScript language by doing some work in it. Unfortunately, it is beyond the scope of this book to teach you even basic PostScript. My previous book, *Understanding PostScript Programming* (Sybex, 1987), is an introduction to the language and its use in a variety of applications. It is specifically designed to teach the necessary skills to read and write PostScript. All we can do here is give you a quick overview of those aspects of the PostScript language that are most relevant to the Illustrator user.

PostScript applications generally follow a straightforward, standard structure that provides common ground for sharing graphics, for processing in a complex environment, and allows certain types of document-management programs to work with the application output.

This recommended structure is defined and described in detail in various publications of Adobe Systems, and is also explained in *Understanding PostScript Programming*. These references define global structural conventions, which must be used in any PostScript programs that will exchange information. In particular, the EPSF formats that we discussed in Chapter 6 use these conventions to allow the exchange of the necessary information between Illustrator and other applications.

There are four sections required in a properly structured PostScript program: header, prologue, script, and trailer (in this sequence). The header and trailer segments are primarily devoted to providing certain global information about the program contained between them. The most important point about the header and trailer sections is that, from the viewpoint of the PostScript interpreter, they consist of comments only, and do not contain any executable PostScript code.

The *header* section contains two types of information: *creation data*, which covers who created the document, when it was created, etc., and is primarily required in a network environment for routing and other identification purposes; and information about the fonts used and so on, which is primarily for use by utility programs and by PostScript applications to aid in handling and placement of the graphic within another PostScript program (this is the information required for an EPSF file).

The *prologue* contains procedures and named variables and constants that will be used throughout the rest of the document. The prologue will generally have been written by a programmer and then will be included as the first part of every document (or script) that requires it. This prologue is common to all output from a given application; it is also often called a *prep* file, possibly because Apple calls their prologue Laser Prep. In any case, this prologue must accompany your application or be already resident on the output device. For reasons of speed, many applications send their prologue to the printer with the first document that they print, and then do not resend it with every subsequent document.

The prologue will usually be relatively complex, with a variety of variables and nested procedures defined within it. The prologue from most applications is rather terse and difficult to read. Nevertheless, if you have some knowledge of PostScript, you can usually find your way around a prologue with a little work.

The *script* describes the specific elements to be produced on the output pages in terms of procedures and variables defined in the prologue, along with operand data as required. Each page description is expected to depend only on the prologue and to be independent of all the other pages. The intention here is that it should be possible to produce any page correctly, given only the prologue and the description of that specific page. When the process is done well, each page description within the script will be relatively short and probably quite repetitive, using the same procedures over and over.

Finally, there is a *trailer*, which contains clean-up information. This is also a place for document information that couldn't be easily generated in the header sections. This facility is provided for application programs that are generating PostScript output directly, and would have a problem providing the required document information in the header. For example, one of the required data items in the header is a list of fonts used in the document. This information is particularly important if the document requires nonstandard fonts which need to be downloaded to the printer prior to processing the document. If the PostScript output is being created by an application, however, it may be quite difficult to generate this information with the header, before the document itself has been created. The structural conventions therefore allow that the font information can be deferred to the end of the document and put in the trailer section.

POSTSCRIPT PROGRAMS

In terms of structure, most of the PostScript programming in an application output is done in the prologue, not in the script. This is something to note, since it is a common misconception that application output is, or should be, PostScript code. The script consists of procedure calls and data for those procedures which generate the desired output. The procedures are in the prologue, and the real PostScript program code exists in these procedures.

The procedures that are defined in the prologue have been chosen by the application makers as the ones that will perform the necessary functions that their application will support. Every application will generally have a different set of procedures, or at least of procedure names. For this reason, output from one application will generally not run correctly with another application's prologue. The prologue may itself be divided into sections by grouping the procedures into *proc sets*, each of which serve a single purpose and can be handled, to some degree, as a unit.

Furthermore, the script portion of an application will not run without the matching prologue. This can be a little confusing, since some applications preload the prologue before starting any processing and then send output that is effectively only the script portion of the program. This approach is very efficient in maintaining processing speed, but can be wasteful of the printer memory and resources. Illustrator does not use this approach; instead, each Illustrator output program contains both prologue and script and so is ready to be processed as a single unit.

The PostScript language contains more than 260 primitive operators to perform various functions. Before you begin reading or modifying PostScript code, you need to acquaint yourself with a basic subset of those operators and become familiar with the unusual structure of PostScript itself.

MODIFYING ILLUSTRATOR OUTPUT TO GENERATE SPECIAL EFFECTS

This section of the appendix requires some acquaintance with PostScript because it explains how you can modify the Illustrator PostScript output to do some new and unusual things. Modification of the output requires insertion of new code in the existing code, and you won't understand the new code and where to add it unless you can read the PostScript output, so you will find that a reading knowledge (at least) of PostScript is really essential.

There are several reasons why you might want to modify Illustrator output. To begin with, although Illustrator provides some really powerful and remarkable tools, there are things that you can only do, or do easily, in native PostScript. For example, you cannot create or use a text clipping region in Illustrator, although it is done quite easily in PostScript itself. Or, you might want to incorporate Illustrator output into another PostScript program that you have coded. In addition, working on such an exercise will help you understand what is done to Illustrator output to create the EPSF format. Finally, you might wish to modify text or font handling to control resource usage or page output. Some modest modifications to Illustrator output can allow you to create any of these changes.

WORKING WITH POSTSCRIPT

Illustrator output consists of PostScript code, perhaps combined with a sample graphic bit-map of the image produced by the PostScript program, as described in Chapter 6. In all of its PostScript output, Illustrator follows a very tight and controlled structure that conforms to Adobe's 2.0 Structuring Conventions for PostScript programs and includes some further, subsequent enhancements. This structure makes it easy for you or for an application program like PageMaker to determine where to insert any desired modifications and also allows you to make those modifications in such a manner that you do not conflict with the original graphic output.

Essentially, all modifications to your Illustrator output fall into two classes: those where you change the environment in which the Illustrator program works and those where you modify the program itself. Of course, you might do both things in one program; doing one does not prevent you from doing the other. In both cases, you must add additional PostScript code to the Illustrator output; however, the type of code added and the placement of that code is quite different.

Using Illustrator's Note *Facility*

It may surprise you to learn that modification of the Illustrator output itself is arguably the easiest of these two methods. This is because Illustrator has provided a special facility to aid you in placing added PostScript within your Illustrator program. This is done by using the Note option in the Paint dialog screen, accessed by selecting Paint from the Style menu.

You can use the Note box (in the bottom-right corner of the Paint dialog screen) to enter any text line up to 254 characters. When you have exceeded the size of the box, the text line will run out of the box; you can view the entire line by using the cursor-movement controls to move the text cursor. This line of text is added to the PostScript output generated by Illustrator as a notation line. You can use this line to identify places in the text where you want to insert code.

We'll work through an exercise to show how this feature can be used. In this example, we'll use Illustrator to draw a graphic of a rising sun, modify the PostScript output with code to create a text string (the word *SUN*), paint that text onto the page, and use as a clipping region for the graphic prepared in Illustrator. This example illustrates how a combination of creation techniques is faster and easier than either alone. Although the graphic image is rather simple, it is still much faster to generate in Illustrator than to program directly in PostScript. On the other hand, Illustrator provides no facility whatsoever for adding a text clipping region to its output.

Generating the Illustrator graphic is quite easy using the methods that you have already learned. The finished graphic is shown in Figure B.1.

As you see, the sun itself is a half circle, with a series of rays radiating from it. The half circle was produced by making a circle and ungrouping it, then deleting the bottom half of the circle and connecting the two side points with a straight line, as we did in an earlier exercise. The entire object was painted with Fill of White and Stroke of 100% Black, with a line weight of 1, and then grouped again to make the sun. The rays are all duplicates of the first ray. This was drawn to the

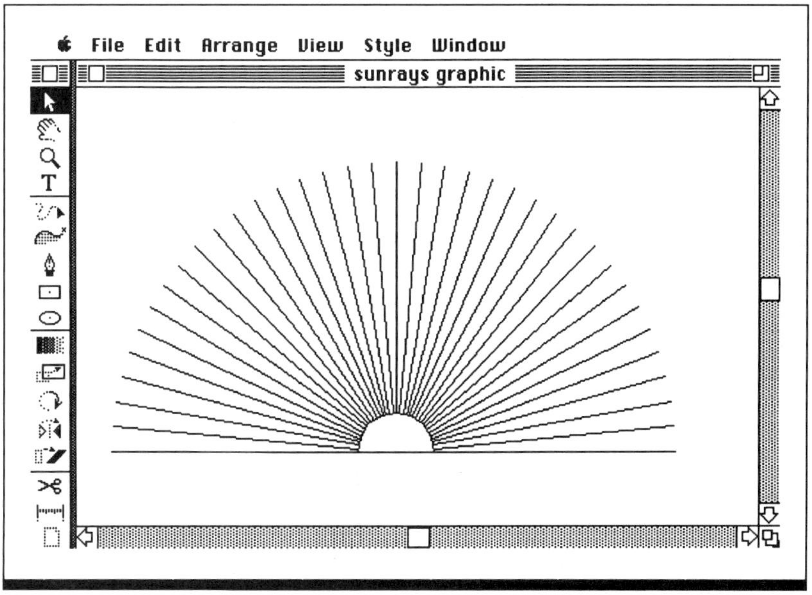

Figure B.1: *Sun rays graphic in Illustrator*

right of the circle, then stroked with 100% Black and a line weight of .5. The ray was then duplicated using the Rotate dialog box, with a rotation angle of 5°. Finally, Transform Again, or ⌘D, was used to create the complete 180° set of rays.

The only difference in the creation of the sun rays graphic was in the selection of the Paint characteristics for the sun (the half circle). This dialog box is shown in Figure B.2. You will notice that the Note box is filled in to provide a text notation in the output file, indicating that this begins the drawing of the sun with rays and that, therefore, this is the point where any clipping should take place. You will remember that the clipping region in a PostScript program must be set as the current path before you paint the image of the object to be clipped. Therefore, you want to create the clipping path and the associated commands before you generate the sun or the rays.

Save the file as PostScript Only and open it with an editor. Then search the file for the string %%*Note:*. The result is shown in Figure B.3.

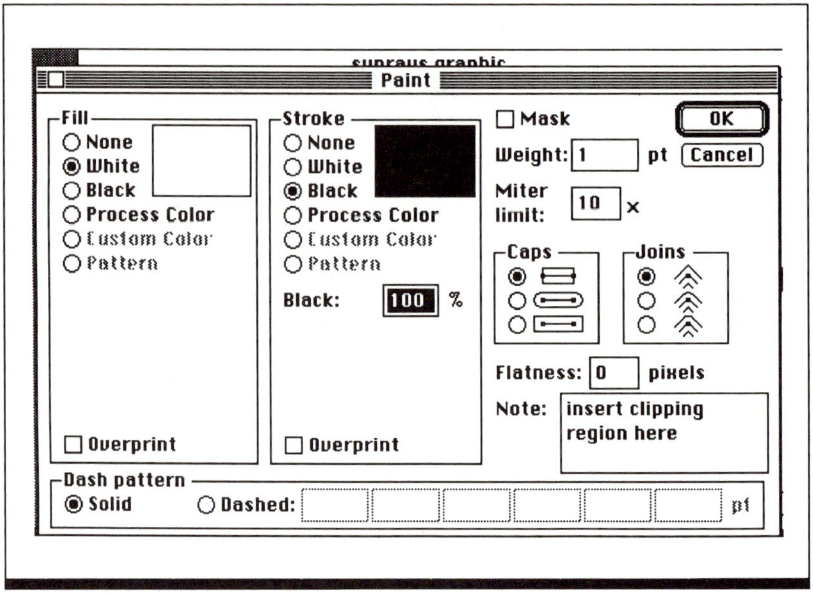

Figure B.2: *Paint dialog box for sun rays graphic*

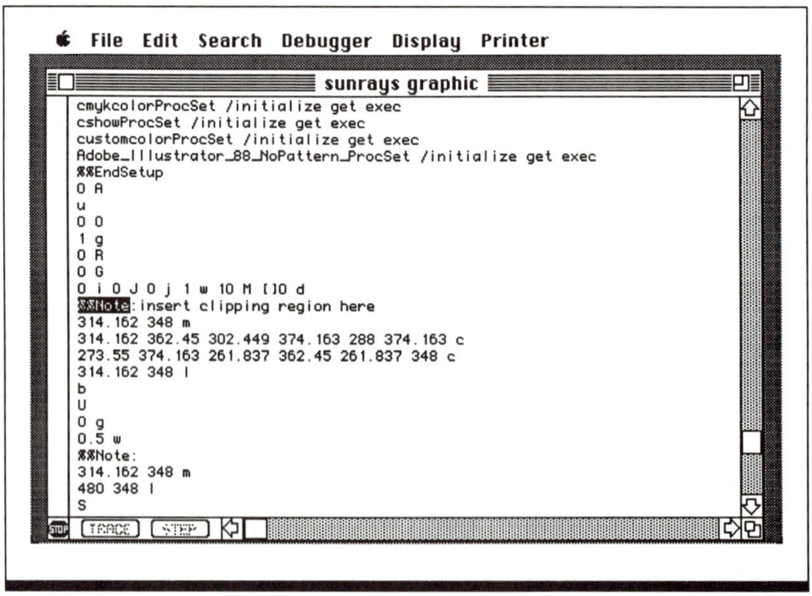

Figure B.3: *% %Note: in Illustrator output*

Like all lines that begin with a %, this line will be ignored by the PostScript interpreter as a comment line. However, the special structure of the line, %%*Note:*, tells you that this is also a comment that is intended for human attention. Every time Illustrator generates a separate call to the Paint dialog screen, it generates a comment of this format in the PostScript output. You will notice, in the code shown in Figure B.4, that the next call to Paint, when you set the revised line weight for the rays, is marked by another %%*Note:* comment. The first instance, however, has the text string that you added to show exactly where you want to insert the clipping code; the second is not relevant to this exercise.

Now you insert the necessary code to generate the string *SUN* and use it as a clipping region. For this exercise, there are two modifications that you want to make. The first is to position the word *SUN* in the appropriate place over the graphic image, and the second is to outline the word (stroke it), and then use it as a clipping region. This is divided into two pieces so that the first piece, the positioning process, could be made a separate procedure. In this way, you can build a library of commonly useful PostScript procedures.

The only note to make here is that the position for the *moveto* command that begins the inserted code was derived from the first lines of the sunrays graphic script, which contains the commands for drawing the center circle. The position was derived by subtracting the final point of the half circle (261.387, 348) from the starting point, (314.162, 348) and adding half the x distance to the starting point. This gives the desired center position for the word *SUN*, which is passed to the procedure centerPoint, which calculates the center point of the given text string and then positions the string.

The code that needs to be added to the original program output consists of one procedure, named centerPoint, and the necessary additional code to insert, print, and set up the text string SUN as a clipping region. These two blocks of code are as follows:

```
procedure:
    /centerPoint
      {  dup
         stringwidth pop 2 div
         4 -1 roll
         exch sub
```

```
        3 -1 roll
        moveto
    }
  def

added script coding:
    /Helvetica-BoldOblique findfont 216 scalefont setfont
    288 348 (SUN) centerPoint
    false charpath
    gsave
      stroke
    grestore
    clip
    newpath
```

The procedure takes three arguments: the x- and y-coordinates for the desired centerpoint and the string to be centered on the given point. The added code sets the font, in this case Helvetica-BoldOblique scaled to 3-inch height (216 points), then centers the desired string, SUN, on the point (288, 348), outlines the string, strokes it (after saving it), and sets it as the clipping region. Since the *clip* operator doesn't clear the current path, it is good practice to follow it with a *newpath* operator, as here, to ensure that you don't cause unintended mischief to the following code.

The procedure can be added anywhere in the prologue; I would suggest after the Illustrator proc set but before the %%*EndProlog* comment. The added code is placed immediately after the %%*Note:insert clipping region here* comment shown in Figure B.3. The final result (without the Illustrator prologue code) is the program shown in Figure B.4, and it will produce the output shown in Figure B.5.

HOUSEKEEPING FOR ILLUSTRATOR FILES

As you read through the code listed in Figure B.4, you will notice that there are some additions that have not been mentioned. These modifications are necessary to change the PostScript output produced by Illustrator into clean, workable, independent PostScript code.

You should understand that Illustrator always produces PostScript code that expects to be included in another program or be output directly by Illustrator itself. In this situation, neither case is accurate; you are not including this code in some other output, and you cannot

```
%!PS-Adobe-2.0 EPSF-1.2
%%Creator: Adobe Illustrator 88(TM) a1
%%For: (David Holzgang) (SYBEX)
%%Title: (sunrays graphic)
%%CreationDate: (4/2/88) (6:03 AM)
%%DocumentProcSets: packedarrayProcSet 0 0
%%DocumentSuppliedProcSets: packedarrayProcSet 0 0
%%DocumentProcSets: cmykcolorProcSet 0 0
%%DocumentSuppliedProcSets: cmykcolorProcSet 0 0
%%DocumentProcSets: cshowProcSet 0 0
%%DocumentSuppliedProcSets: cshowProcSet 0 0
%%DocumentProcSets: customcolorProcSet 0 0
%%DocumentSuppliedProcSets: customcolorProcSet 0 0
%%DocumentProcSets: Adobe_Illustrator_88_NoPattern_ProcSet 0 0
%%DocumentSuppliedProcSets: Adobe_Illustrator_88_NoPattern_ProcSet 0 0
%%ColorUsage: Black&White
%%DocumentProcessColors: Black
%%BoundingBox:92 342 484 544
%%TemplateBox:288 372 288 372
%%TileBox:-552 730 0 1460
%%EndComments
/--save0-- save def
statusdict /jobname (Illustrator Exercises: clipping modifications) put
%%BeginProcSet: packedarrayProcSet 0 0
... Adobe Illustrator prologue proc sets go here
%%EndProcSet
%begin special procedures
/centerPoint
    {
    dup
    stringwidth pop 2 div
    4 -1 roll
    exch sub
    3 -1 roll
    moveto
    }
def

%%EndProlog
%%BeginSetup
cmykcolorProcSet /initialize get exec
cshowProcSet /initialize get exec
customcolorProcSet /initialize get exec
Adobe_Illustrator_88_NoPattern_ProcSet /initialize get exec
%%EndSetup
0 A
u
0 O
1 g
0 R
0 G
0 i 0 J 0 j 1 w 10 M []0 d
%%Note:insert clipping region here
%added procedure to set clipping path
    /Helvetica-BoldOblique findfont 216 scalefont setfont
    288 348 (SUN) centerPoint
    false charpath
```

Figure B.4: *Partial program listing for modified sunrays graphic (continues)*

```
        gsave
            stroke
        grestore
        clip
        newpath
    %end of added procedures
    %   path now set for clipping operation
    314.162 348 m
    314.162 362.45 302.449 374.163 288 374.163 c
    273.55 374.163 261.837 362.45 261.837 348 c
    314.162 348 l
    b
    U
    0 g
    0.5 w
    %%Note:
    314.162 348 m
    480 348 l
    S
    314.063 350.281 m
    479.27 364.735 l
    S
    313.765 352.544 m
    477.085 381.342 l
    S

    ...additional rays will be here
    ...     each rotated to new coordinates.

    261.831 347.999 m
    95.958 347.987 l
    S
    showpage
    %%Trailer
    Adobe_Illustrator_88_NoPattern_ProcSet /terminate get exec
    customcolorProcSet /terminate get exec
    cshowProcSet /terminate get exec
    cmykcolorProcSet /terminate get exec
    statusdict /jobname () put
    --save0-- restore
```

Figure B.4: *Partial program listing for modified sunrays graphic (continued)*

use Illustrator to print it. You may be surprised to find that you cannot take this modified file back into Illustrator. As we have discussed, Illustrator uses the PostScript code to generate its screen images. In this case, you have added PostScript code that the Illustrator screen generator (for want of a better term) does not understand and so cannot render correctly. If you try to open this file with Illustrator, you will see an error screen, such as the one shown in Figure B.6, warning you that the code

Figure B.5: *Page output for modified sunrays graphic*

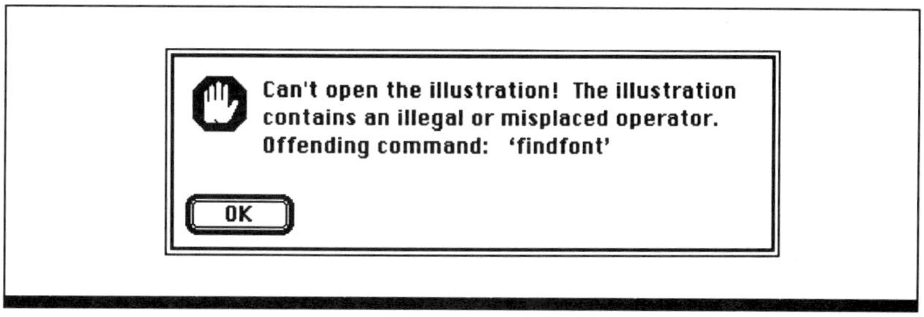

Figure B.6: *Illustrator warning screen*

within the file no longer conforms to Illustrator requirements. In fact, you will see this same error screen if you try to open an Illustrator 88 file with Illustrator 1.1.

Therefore, you need to add some additional code to make the file print and, while you're at it, you should add the code required to make this Illustrator program a "good neighbor" within the PostScript environment by including the necessary housekeeping routines that preserve the printer environment when you run it. Although a detailed discussion of the code necessary to do this is beyond the scope of this book, I will present here in general terms what needs to be done to your Illustrator output.

To begin with, if you want to display output on your printer, you have to insert a *showpage* command in the file. Assuming that the image or images that you have made take up only one page of output, this command would be the last command in the file, either just before or just after the %%*Trailer* statement. If your image extends over more than one page, you will have to do quite a bit of additional work to create the tiling effect that Illustrator provides through its output. Such additional work would really be quite a digression from our point here, so we will assume that all the output involved is one page (or less) only.

There is no *showpage* command in the output prepared by Illustrator. If you call up your file from Illustrator, it places one at the end of the file before sending it to the printer; however, none is saved with the file to allow you to include the file with other PostScript output. If Illustrator automatically placed a *showpage* in the file, you would have to either remove or disable the command before including the graphic on another page because execution of *showpage* from within the Illustrator graphic would cause premature printing of the remainder of the page. So you have to add the command for stand-alone processing, and you can see the *showpage* in Figure B.4, just before the %%*Trailer* comment.

The next housekeeping that you should provide in your Illustrator output is a global *save, restore* to enclose the entire Illustrator file. This matching pair of operators provides a way to manage virtual memory in your printer, and correct use ensures that the maximum memory resources are available at all times for your programs. Let's briefly review the purpose and use of *save* and *restore* so you can see how they are used here.

Every PostScript composite object consumes virtual memory within your printer. This memory is used for storage of all PostScript procedures, fonts, dictionaries, and so on. However, the PostScript interpreter does not automatically recover virtual memory that has been used during a program or a process. It is the user's responsibility to do that by using *save* and *restore* operations. If the user—whether an application like PageMaker or Illustrator, or you as a programmer—does not manage the virtual memory correctly, the processor will run out of memory, and you will have to reboot the printer, with the possible loss of output.

You can avoid that problem by the correct use of *save* and *restore*. When you issue the *save* command, a complete image of the virtual memory is preserved within the interpreter. Then you can go ahead and perform all your processing and output functions. When you are finally done, you can issue the matching *restore*, which returns the virtual memory to the exact state it was in when the *save* was issued. In this way, all the virtual memory that your program consumed is returned to the interpreter for use by the next program.

The *save* command can be placed anywhere before the first executable line of PostScript code in the program. Applications generally put it ahead of all statements in the program, for obvious reasons, but I prefer putting it after the header comments (which are, of course, not executable code) and before the first line of the prologue, just after the *%%EndComments* line that ends the header material. It is placed there in Figure B.4, just before the *jobname* setting that we will discuss next. The matching *restore* is the last line of code in the program, as you can also see in Figure B.4.

That completes the truly essential housekeeping for your programs. This is no different, as you can see, than the housekeeping that you would do for your own PostScript code. In general, all this has not been done by Illustrator because insertion of these commands into a file could cause disastrous results when that file was combined with other code.

There is, however, one more thing that you might want to add to your program for convenience and clarity. That is to set the *jobname* in the *statusdict*. This is certainly not essential. Your PostScript program will function quite well without it. On the other hand, it is a great convenience to be able to query the printer and have it return the correct status of a job, including the name. Indeed, when running various applications, particularly if you normally use an AppleTalk network, you have probably seen messages regarding the status of the laser printer that gave the name of the job being run. Setting this variable is how you control the name that is reported over the network.

The *jobname* parameter is stored in a special PostScript dictionary, called *statusdict*, which contains a variety of status and device-specific information and is itself a part of the *systemdict*. You can set the *jobname* most easily by placing the the name that you want explictly into the *statusdict*, as shown in Figure B.4. You might choose to set the *jobname* either before or after the *save*. Whatever order you do it in, you should use the reverse order at the end of the program. It is probably best to set it after you do the *save* and remove it before you do the *restore*, as shown in the example. In this way, you can be sure that it is explicitly set, and removed after your job is finished.

COMBINING ILLUSTRATOR OUTPUT INTO YOUR PROGRAMS

You can adapt your Illustrator output to place it into your own PostScript programs. Illustrator is, unsurprisingly, perfectly suited to such adaptation because it is designed from the beginning for exactly such a fate. This was, for example, the reason that you had to add a *showpage* to the output file in order to get a printed result. However, before you place your Illustrator file into another program, you will want to position and, possibly, to scale the Illustrator graphic for the new program. This is exactly the kind of thing that an application like PageMaker does when it places the Illustrator image on a page. Moreover, you use the same kind of mechanisms to make the transition.

An Illustrator file is included into a page generated by another PostScript program as a unit. That means that you will take the entire PostScript output from Illustrator and include it with your other PostScript code. In order to do that successfully, you need to define several things: where on the page you want to place the Illustrator graphic, what coordinates it uses, and what size you want it to be. The first two issues must always be addressed; you only need to take care of the third one if you don't want to use your graphic at the same size as you created it.

All these issues can be taken care of by two PostScript operators. The first is *translate*, which can be used to both position the graphic on the new output page and adjust the coordinates, if required. The second is a *scale* operator that will set the size of the graphic on the new page. In all cases, there also needs to be some housekeeping done to ensure that the Illustrator file does not interfere with your work in the process of generating the output to be included on the page generated by your code; this is done by using the *save, restore* operators that we just discussed.

The first change that you have to make is to correct for the default Illustrator coordinates. You will remember that Illustrator has defined its origin as the bottom-left corner of the output page. If this output is included directly onto an ordinary PostScript page, you will get an entire page as output, instead of just the graphic that you created.

Futhermore, you cannot be sure that the Illustrator file uses the default page origin. As you saw earlier, it is quite easy and possible for the origin of an Illustrator page to be moved to any arbitrary location. Because you can move the origin of an Illustrator page anywhere, you need to have an adjustment mechanism that allows you to readjust the coordinates independently of the default settings.

The necessary adjustment can be easily made by using the information provided by the *%%BoundingBox:* comment. This comment is followed by four numbers. These represent the lower-left and upper-right corners, respectively, of the graphic that will actually be created by the Illustrator file, and in the coordinates that the file was created in. In particular, the x- and y-coordinates of each of these corners provides the necessary information for positioning and adjusting the coordinate system on the output page. Figure B.7 illustrates the effect of the PostScript operations on the Illustrator output.

As you can see, the first requirement is to move the lower-left corner of the Illustrator graphic to the new origin. This can be done most easily, conceptually, by issuing a *translate* that first moves the origin of the graphic to (0, 0) in the normal PostScript coordinates, and then *translate* again to the new position that you want.

The first move is done by the following PostScript command:

```
llx neg lly neg translate
```

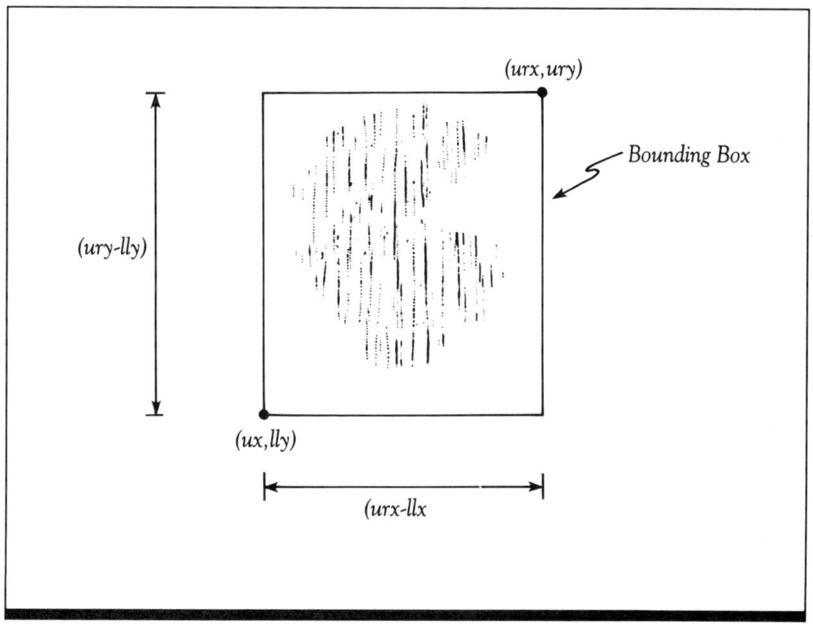

Figure B.7: *%%BoundingBox coordinates*

This readjusts the coordinates for the output to a position that is −llx and −lly because the *neg* operator just reverses the sign of the given number. That will mean that the Illustrator graphic will begin at the point (llx − llx) and (lly − lly), or (0, 0), because subtracting something from itself will always result in zero. After the origin of the graphic is translated to (0, 0), the coordinates on the Illustrator page will map correctly into those of the output page.

After you have positioned the Illustrator output at (0, 0) on the new output page, it is quite straightforward to move it to any desired location on that page by issuing another *translate*. As is always the case in PostScript, you will reposition the lower-left corner of the image by repositioning the origin. If you want to move the output graphic so that its lower-left corner is at the new position (nx, ny), you would follow the command above with the command:

```
nx ny translate
```

which moves the graphic to the point you wanted. Although the order in which you issue the commands is irrelevant to the PostScript interpreter, I would strongly recommend that you do them in some consistent and logical order; for me, that means doing the translation to (0, 0) first and then moving to (nx, ny), rather than the other way around.

The one other change that you may want to make to your Illustrator output is to scale it to fit on a defined space in the new page output. This also can be done with the help of the *%%BoundingBox:* information. In this case, what you want to do is adjust the height and width of the existing output to fit into some new space. Referring to Figure B.7 again, you can see how this can be done.

Suppose that the new space to be filled has a width of *w* and a height of *h*. Then scaling the Illustrator graphic to this window means simply that the width of the graphic must be scaled to *w* and the height, in similar fashion, scaled to *h*. For example, if the window that you wanted to fit were 1 unit by 1 unit, and the graphic was 2 by 4, you would have to scale the graphic by 1 divided by 2 in width and 1 divided by 4 in height. This is the general approach for scaling a graphic: the new dimension divided by the old dimension is the scale factor for that coordinate. As you see in Figure B.7, the width of the graphic is determined by subtracting the two x-coordinates from one another, and the height by subtracting the two y-coordinates. Therefore, the scale factor for width will be *w / (urx - llx)* and for height it will be *h / (ury - lly)*. Obviously, you can use the same method to compute the width and height of the new window: subtract the x- and y-coordinates of the lower-left and upper-right corners. Using this technique with a new window whose coordinates for the lower-left corner is given by (nlx, nly) and whose coordinates for the upper-right corner are (nux, nuy), the PostScript commands for the scaling operation are as follows:

```
nux nlx sub   %calculate the width of new window
urx llx sub   %calculate width of graphic
div           %use two results on stack for ratio
              %and leave result on stack
nuy nly sub   %calculate the height of the new window
ury lly sub   %calculate height of graphic
div           %use two results on stack for ratio
              %now both x and y scale are on stack
scale         %so issue scale command
```

This can be compressed into one or two lines of PostScript code, but it is expanded to several lines here to help you see all the operations and the stack results more clearly.

This concludes our look at PostScript and Illustrator. You have seen how to modify your Illustrator code to generate special PostScript effects and how to modify Illustrator output so that you can include it in your own PostScript programs. These two basic techniques allow you to experiment with Illustrator as a PostScript program generator and to use Illustrator as an independent source of PostScript graphics. In addition, you should review the Illustrator prologue, which provides examples of PostScript coding techniques and procedures to accomplish many useful and common tasks.

Index

Note: A page number followed by an *n* (e.g., 134n) refers to a margin note on the page.

A

B

C

D

E

N

O

P

Q

R

S

Selections from The SYBEX Library

APPLE/MACINTOSH

Mastering ProDOS
Timothy Rice/Karen Rice
260pp. Ref. 315-5
An in-depth look at the inner workings of ProDOS, for advanced users and programmers – with discussion of system programming techniques, sample programs in BASIC and assembler, and scores of ready-made ProDOS utility routines.

Programming the Apple II in Assembly Language
Rodnay Zaks
519pp. Ref. 290-6
This tutorial on 6502 programming is for newcomers to assembly language, as well as programmers interested in an Apple IIc/IIe-specific presentation. Topics include the 65C02, the Apple mouse, the ProDOS interface, graphics and animation.

Understanding HyperCard
Greg Harvey
550pp. Ref. 506-9
The enormous potential of this major software development is clarified and explained in this extensive hands-on tutorial which covers all aspects of the HyperCard and HyperText world, using step-by-step discussions, examples, and insights. The best way to construct, fill, and use stacks efficiently is covered in detail.

Mastering AppleWorks (Second Edition)
Elna Tymes
479pp. Ref. 398-8
New chapters on business applications, data sharing DIF and Applesoft BASIC make this practical, in-depth tutorial even better. Full details on AppleWorks desktop, word processing, spreadsheet and database functions.

AppleWorks Tips and Techniques (Second Edition)
Robert Ericson
462pp. Ref. 480-1
An indispensible collection of timesaving techniques, practical solutions, and tips on undocumented problems for every AppleWorks user. This expanded new edition covers all versions through 2.0, and includes in-depth treatment of macros.

Inside the Apple IIGS
Gary Bond
449pp. Ref. 365-1
An inside look at the hardware and system organization, with numerous programming examples showing how to access the system's ROM calls, soft switches, and tool calls using 65816 assembly language. Includes sound and graphics programming. The author, Gary Bond, was a member of the Apple IIGS development team.

Mastering Excel on the Macintosh (Second Edition)
Carl Townsend
607pp. Ref. 439-9
A new edition of our popular hands-on guide to using Excel's extensive worksheet, database, and graphics capabilities. With in-depth coverage of special features and techniques, sample applications, and detailed treatment of macros.

Advanced Excel Solutions
David K. Simerly
253pp. Ref. 389-9
High-level business applications using linked spreadsheets serve to demonstrate Excel's most advanced database, report, chart, table, and macro capabilities. Also: data interchange, optimizing disk storage, and the Switcher.

Programming the Macintosh in Assembly Language

Steve Williams

779pp. Ref. 263-9

A comprehensive tutorial and reference covering assembly-language basics, the 68000 architecture and instruction set, the Macintosh Toolbox, linking with high-level languages and more; plus an extensive macro library and sample programs.

Programming the Macintosh in C

Bryan J. Cummings/Lawrence J. Pollack

294pp. Ref. 328-7

A comprehensive introduction to C programming, especially for Macintosh users. Covers the design philosophy and special advantages of C, as well as every feature of the language. With extensive reference material.

DOS

ABC's of MS-DOS (Second Edition)

Alan R. Miller

233pp. Ref. 493-3

This handy guide to MS-DOS is all many PC users need to manage their computer files, organize floppy and hard disks, use EDLIN, and keep their computers organized. Additional information is given about utilities like Sidekick, and there is a DOS command and program summary. The second edition is fully updated for Version 3.3.

Mastering DOS

Judd Robbins

572pp. Ref. 400-3

"The most useful DOS book." This four-part, in-depth tutorial addresses the needs of users at all levels. Topics range from running applications, to managing files and directories, configuring the system, batch file programming, and techniques for system developers. A major book.

MS-DOS Handbook (Third Edition)

Richard Allen King

362pp. Ref. 492-5

This classic has been fully expanded and revised to include the latest features of MS-DOS Version 3.3. Two reference books in one, this title has separate sections for programmer and user. Multi-DOS partitons, 3 1/2disk format, batch file call and return feature, and comprehensive coverage of MS-DOS commands are included.

MS-DOS Power User's Guide, Volume I (Second Edition)

Jonathan Kamin

482pp. Ref. 473-9

A fully revised, expanded edition of our best-selling guide to high-performance DOS techniques and utilities – with details on Version 3.3. Configuration, I/O, directory structures, hard disks, RAM disks, batch file programming, the ANSI.SYS device driver, more.

MS-DOS Power User's Guide, Volume II

Martin Waterhouse/Jonathan Kamin

350pp, Ref. 411-9

A second volume of high-performance techniques and utilities, with expanded coverage of DOS 3.3, and new material on video modes, Token-Ring and PC Network support, micro-mainframe links, extended and expanded memory, multitasking systems, and more.

Performance Programming Under MS-DOS

Michael J. Young

436pp. Ref. 420-8

Practical techniques for maximizing performance in MS-DOS software by making best use of system resources. Topics include functions, interrupts, devices, multitasking, memory residency and more, with examples in C and assembler.

SYBEX Computer Books are different.

Here is why . . .

At SYBEX, each book is designed with you in mind. Every manuscript is carefully selected and supervised by our editors, who are themselves computer experts. We publish the best authors, whose technical expertise is matched by an ability to write clearly and to communicate effectively. Programs are thoroughly tested for accuracy by our technical staff. Our computerized production department goes to great lengths to make sure that each book is well-designed.

In the pursuit of timeliness, SYBEX has achieved many publishing firsts. SYBEX was among the first to integrate personal computers used by authors and staff into the publishing process. SYBEX was the first to publish books on the CP/M operating system, microprocessor interfacing techniques, word processing, and many more topics.

Expertise in computers and dedication to the highest quality product have made SYBEX a world leader in computer book publishing. Translated into fourteen languages, SYBEX books have helped millions of people around the world to get the most from their computers. We hope we have helped you, too.

For a complete catalog of our publications:

File

New... ⌘N
Open... ⌘O
Place...

Close
Save ⌘S
Save As...

Page Setup...
Print... ⌘P

Quit ⌘Q

Edit

Undo Copy ⌘Z

Cut ⌘X
Copy ⌘C
Paste ⌘V
Clear
Select All ⌘A

Paste In Front ⌘F
Paste In Back ⌘B

Bring To Front ⌘=
Send To Back ⌘-

Preferences... ⌘K

Arrange

Transform Again ⌘D

Group ⌘G
Ungroup ⌘U

Join... ⌘J
Average... ⌘L

Lock ⌘1
Unlock All ⌘2
Hide ⌘3
Show All ⌘4